CREATIVE WATERCOLOR

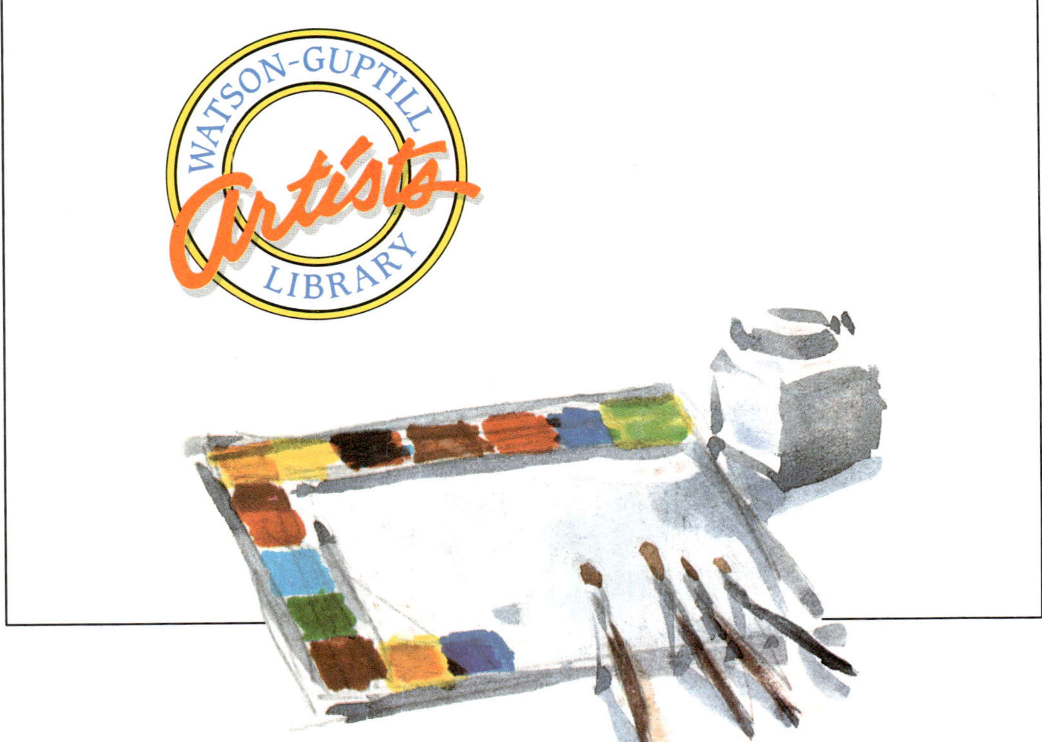

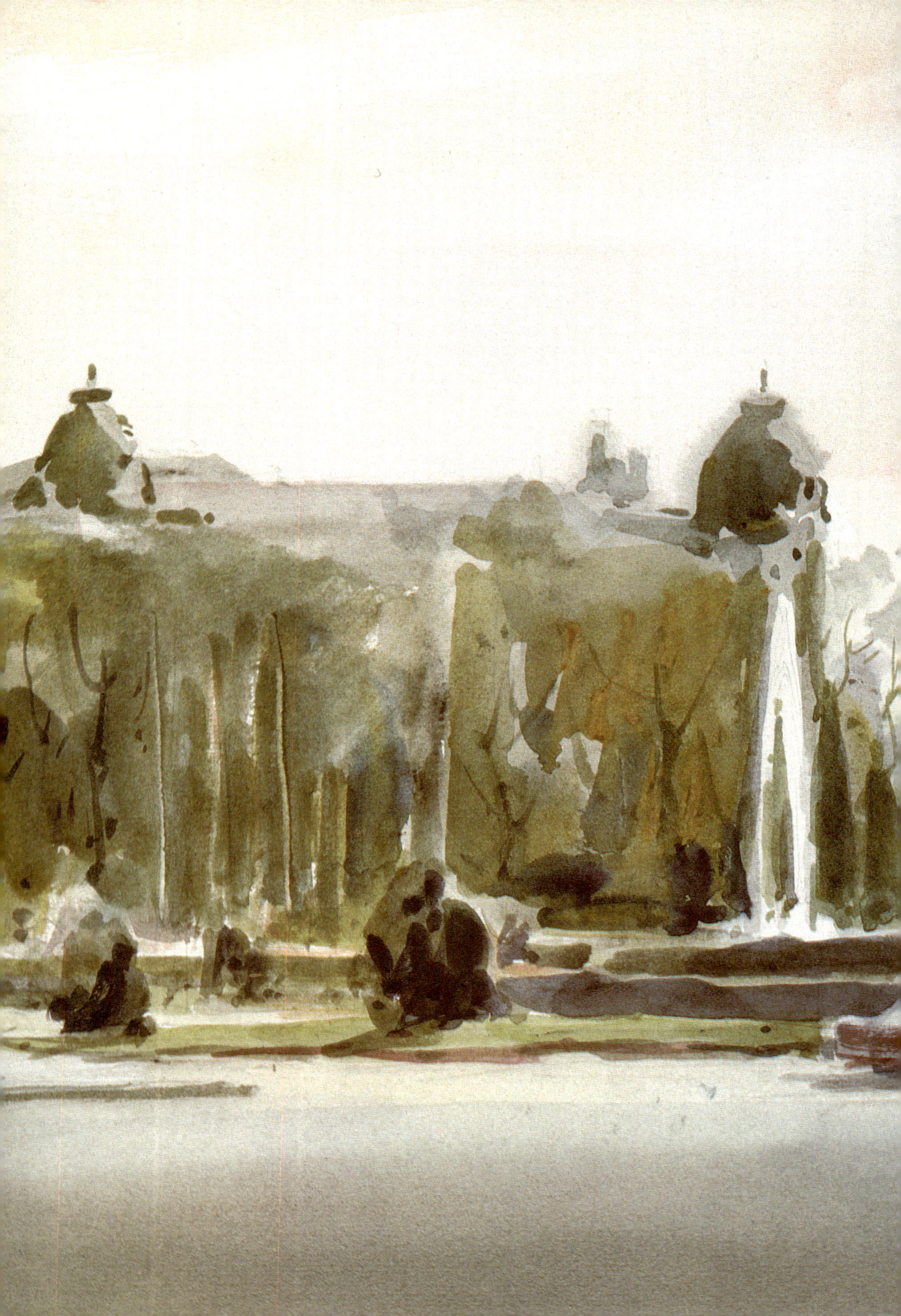

CREATIVE WATERCOLOR

José M. Parramón

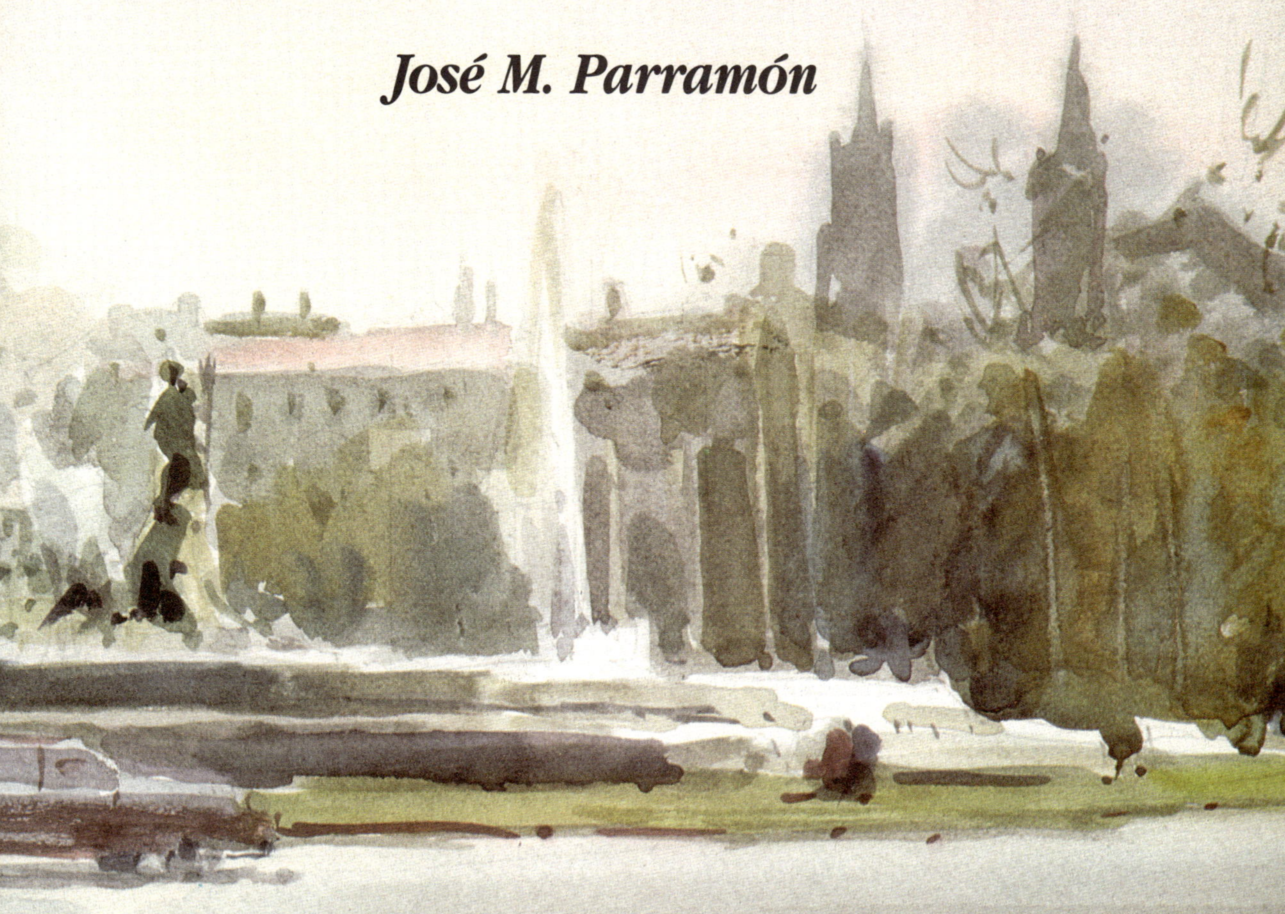

Watson-Guptill Publications/New York

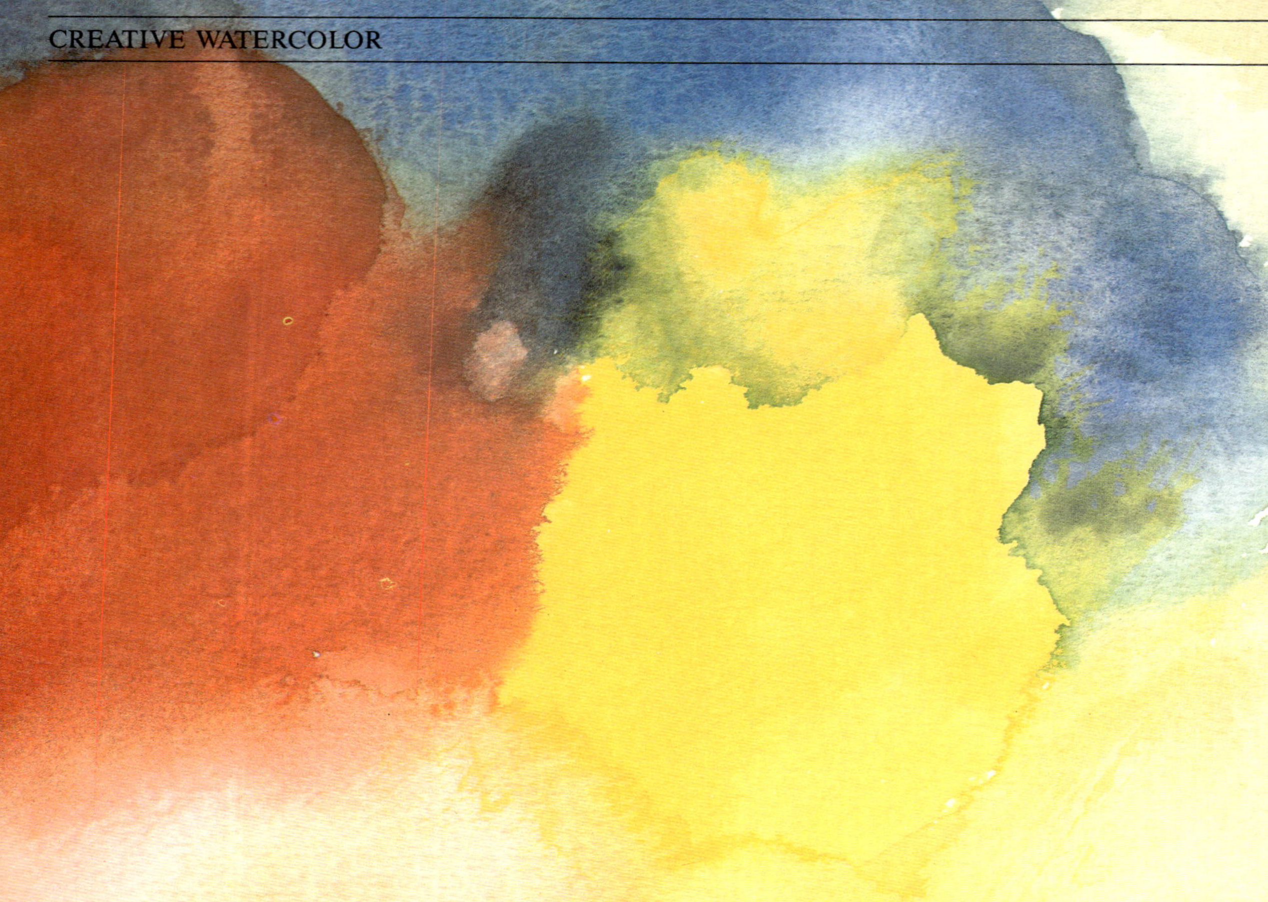

Director of the book: José M. Parramón Vilasaló
Text: Ana Roca-Sastre and David Sanmiguel
Editor: Ángela Berenguer Gran
Dummy: Josep Guasch Cabanas
Color Separation: Cromoherma, S.A.
Typesetting: Lettergraf, S.A.
Photography: Nos & Soto

Published in 1992 in Spain by Parramón Ediciones, S.A., Barcelona.

First published in 1993 in the United States by Watson-Guptill Publications, a division of BPI Communications, Inc., 1515 Broadway, New York, NY 10036.

Library of Congress Cataloging-in-Publication Data

Acuarela creativa. English
Creative watercolor / edited by José M. Parramón.
p. cm.—(Watson-Guptill artists library)
ISBN: 0-8230-5683-X
1. Watercolor painting—Technique. 2. Visual perception.
I. Parramón, José María. II. Title. III. Series.
ND2420. A2813 1993
751.42'2—dc20 92-34437
CIP

Manufactured in Spain

2 3 4 5 6 7 8 9 / 97

Contents

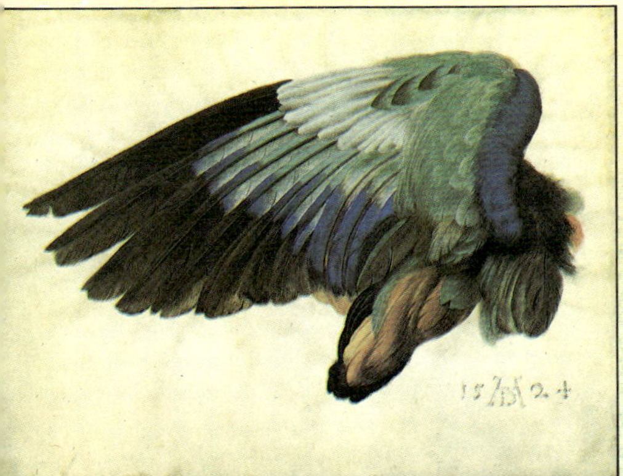

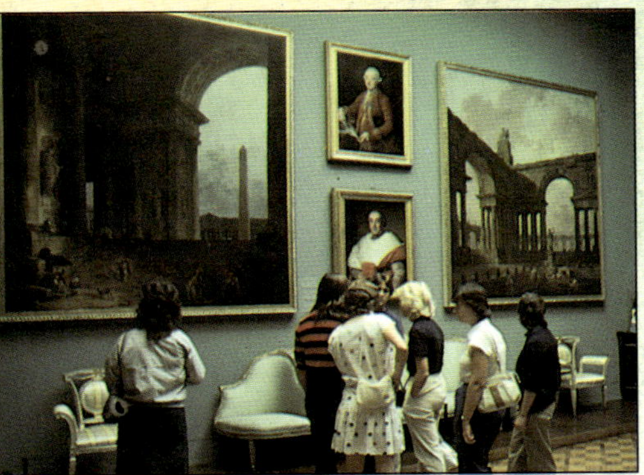

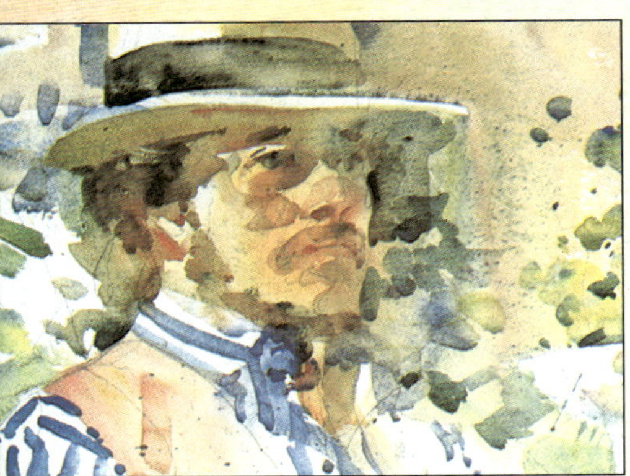

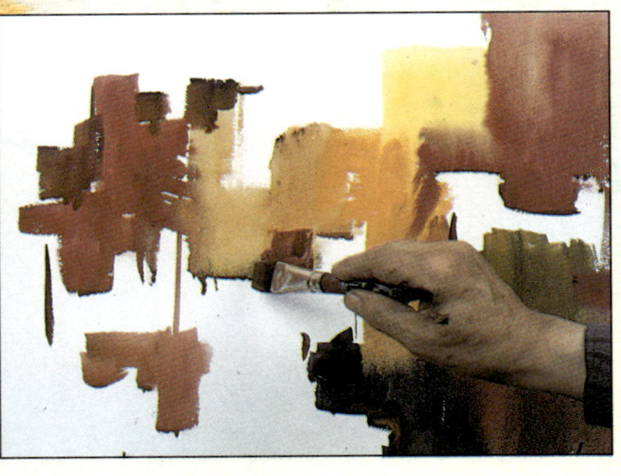

1

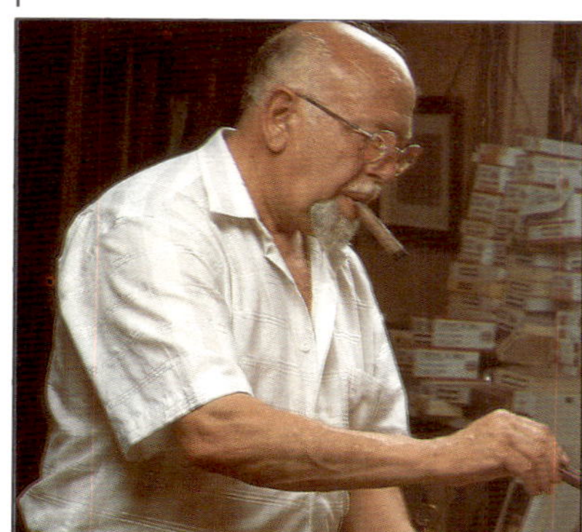

2

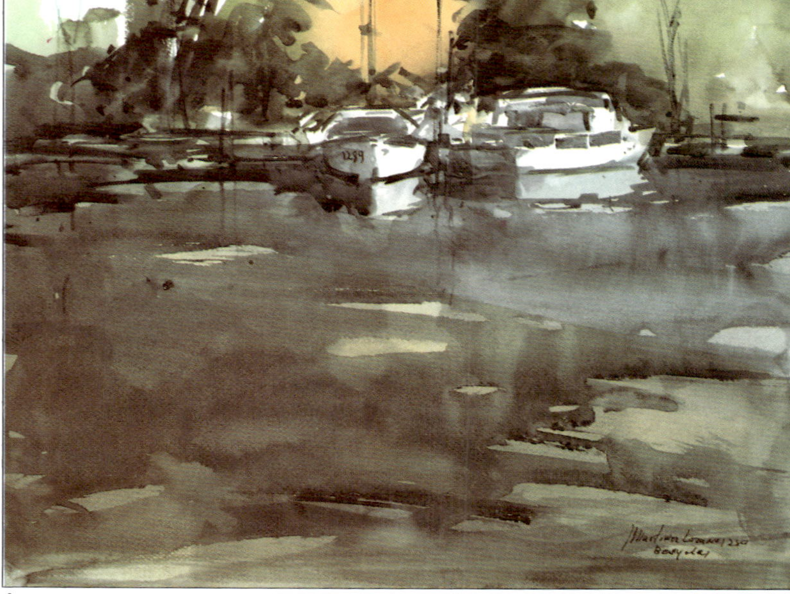

4

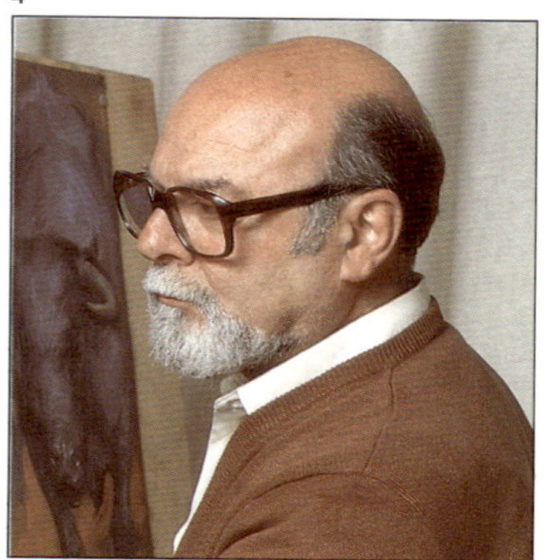

Figs. 1 and 2. Josep Martínez (1923-), *Banyoles*. Private collection. Although Martínez paints as much in oils as he does in watercolor, it is in the latter that his mastery of technique is revealed with such clarity.

Figs. 3 and 4. Vicenç Ballestar (1929-), *Human Figure from Behind*. Private collection, Barcelona. Ballestar's work embraces all pictorial procedures and all kinds of themes. As a watercolorist, Ballestar reveals a sharp sense of form and an admirable and carefree technical realization.

3

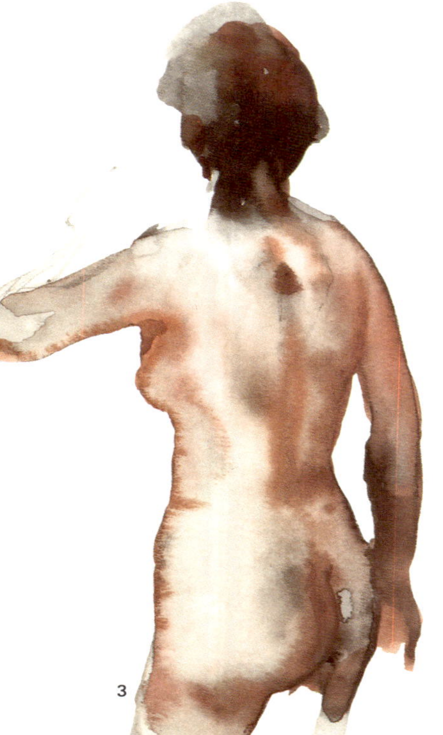

5

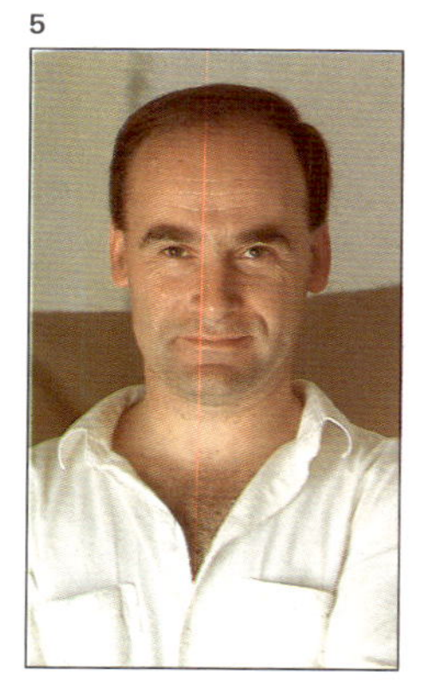

Figs. 5 and 6. Manel Plana Sicilia (1949-), *El Forcall*. Private collection. Manel Plana has developed a truly personal pictorial style: a lively drawing with brilliant color. The freedom with which he interprets the theme never fails to surprise the viewer.

6

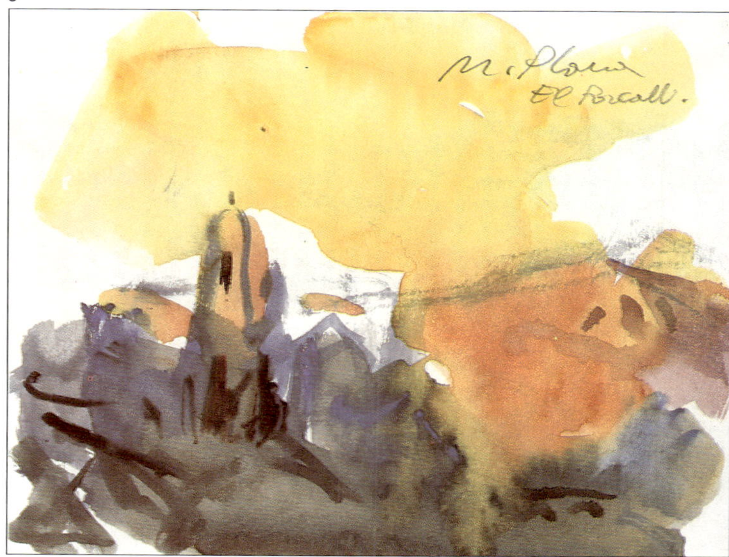

Introduction

The concept of creativity is very much in fashion. All professions require creativity, and we speak of creative artists. But what is creativity? In response to this question the Russian artist Marc Chagall replied: "We see nature as an everyday thing; the artist has to see it as something wonderful and fantastic." That's all very well, but what must one do to be creative?

I would say that the creative artist has to be able to *see and paint with a new attitude, based on a desire for change.* In his book *Art and Coexistence* Fischer analyzes creative fantasy and reaches the conclusion that creativity depends on the *capacity for representation and the capacity for combination*; that is, on the one hand, the ability to remember other images, and on the other, the ability to combine them with the theme one is seeing, in order to study new possibilities. This is where the contents of this book come in handy. This book will help you to paint creatively—first, because the selection of great watercolor masters is a guide in itself to creative watercolor; and second, because you will learn the basics for developing creativity in your own work. We will go over the fundamentals of artistic composition, the choice of theme, the point of view, expression, blocking in, and contrast. We will explain the value of sketches and using washes to develop your technique and creativity. All of this is put into practice in the form of exercises that have been specially prepared for this book by our guest artists Vicenç Ballestar, Manel Plana, and Josep Martínez Lozano.

It is a real privilege to work with these three recognized and creative watercolor artists, not only because they are great friends of mine whose work I highly respect, but also because they offer a unique opportunity for you to learn about the principles and practice of creativity. As a practical demonstration of the colorist and value styles of watercolor, Vicenç Ballestar paints one work in each style. He also shows you how to apply a whole range of technical resources to landscape painting. The theoretical fundamentals of composition are put into practice by Manel Plana in two pictures of the same theme from different points of view. Martínez Lozano proves that terms such as "interpretation" and "formal creativity" are not simply intellectual concepts but also have their place in a practical approach to watercolor painting.

The last chapter of this book, entitled "Creative watercolor in practice," provides an in-depth study of the creative processes of our guest painters. Three step-by-step practical demonstrations, accompanied by abundant illustrations and informative captions, give you the chance to see and understand in detail the distinct personality of each of these artists and how they work out a painting in their own original and creative way.

It has often been said that creativity cannot be taught. However, a study of the works and techniques of talented artists arouses such interest in the reader that he or she feels inspired to emulate them; and creativity undoubtedly begins with emulation. The aim of this book is to stir the reader's creative spirit and artistic ambition, and I have reason to believe we will achieve this.

José M. Parramón

7

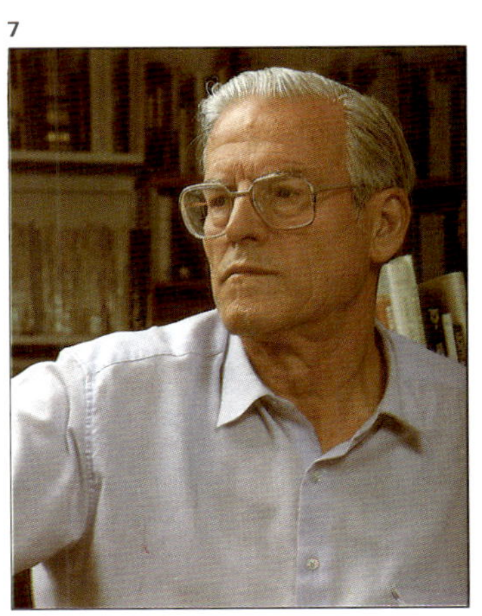

Fig. 7. José M. Parramón is a painter and art teacher, as well as writer and editor of books and treatises on artistic technique. His works have been translated into more than nine languages.

For many years watercolor was unjustly considered to be a secondary technique, a medium halfway between painting and drawing, and its use was limited to making studies and sketches. However, painters such as Dürer and Rembrandt exploited the qualities of this medium in order to express their pictorial creativity and vision.

In the eighteenth century, English painters found watercolor to be an ideal procedure for poetically expressing their vision of landscapes. From then on, a great number of painters have provided this medium with the technical innovations that have made it a universal art form. You will see for yourself in the pages of this chapter.

8

Great masters of creative watercolor

Albrecht Dürer

9

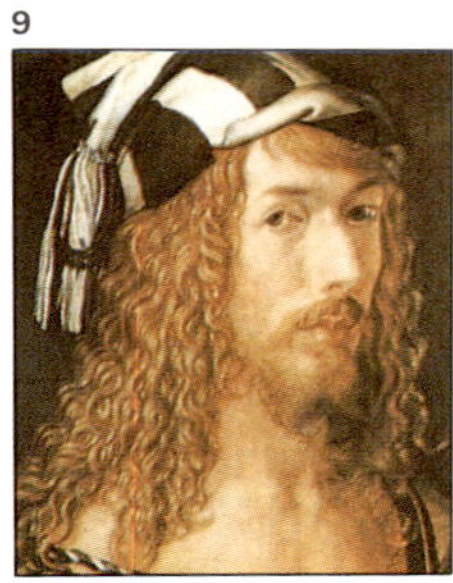

The apprenticeship of the German painter Albrecht Dürer (1471-1528) was deeply affected by the traditional arts of Nüremberg, his native city. The young Dürer became very skilled in etching and woodcut, for which he was internationally recognized as an unrivalled master. His zeal for new ideas took him to many countries in Europe, including Italy. There he spent long periods of time with Italian artists who introduced him to the fundamentals of the Renaissance. On returning to Germany, Dürer became one of the principal promoters of this movement in northern Europe. He demonstrated his skill in producing works of art in the creative fields of painting, drawing, and etching, in a profoundly personal and original way, which combined fantasy and Nordic expressionism within the context of the Renaissance.

The bulk of Dürer's work comprises etchings, drawings, and paintings, of which eighty-six are watercolors. What is most extraordinary is how Dürer used this technique at a time when watercolor was not very common. He did not limit himself to sketches and studies of nature in this medium, but also painted extremely delicate landscapes from nature, which Dürer himself considered to be finished paintings. He used the medium's trans-

10

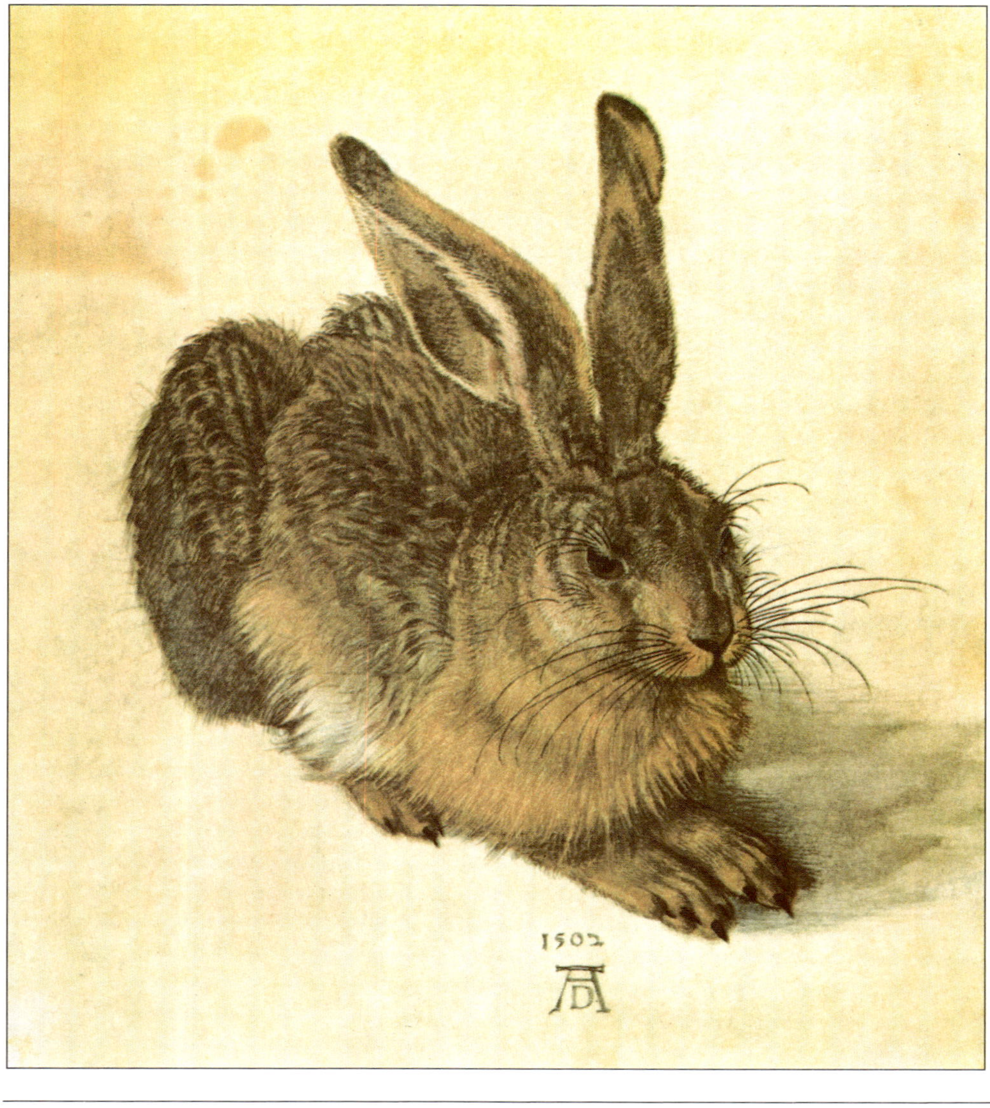

Fig. 8 (preceding spread). J.M.W. Turner (1775-1851), *Venice: Looking East Toward the Campanile of St. Mark's: Sunrise*. Clore Gallery Turner Collection, London.

Fig. 9. Albrecht Dürer, *Self-Portrait with Gloves* (detail). Prado Museum, Madrid. When Dürer painted this self-portrait in oil, he was only a young artist but he was already famous, especially for his etchings of the Apocalypse.

Fig. 10. Albrecht Dürer, *The Hare*. Albertina, Vienna. Dürer painted his watercolors of animals, landscapes, and plants directly from nature. The end result is a spontaneous and extraordinarily fresh creation. The delicate realism of the hare's fur in this picture was achieved by painting with an extremely meticulous brushstroke.

parency and fineness with extraordinary sensitivity to paint landscape themes he had encountered on his travels around Europe. In addition to their technical quality, these landscape paintings were unique in themselves as a thematic subject, since during the years of the sixteenth century, the landscape did not exist as an independent pictorial genre. Dürer revealed himself to be an admirable landscape painter. His sketches and studies of animals and plants reveal an artist of analytical facets; Dürer's love for detail and precision in representing forms greatly contrast with the freer and more direct style of his landscapes. Dürer's sensitivity in these subjects make these watercolors authentic works of art.

11

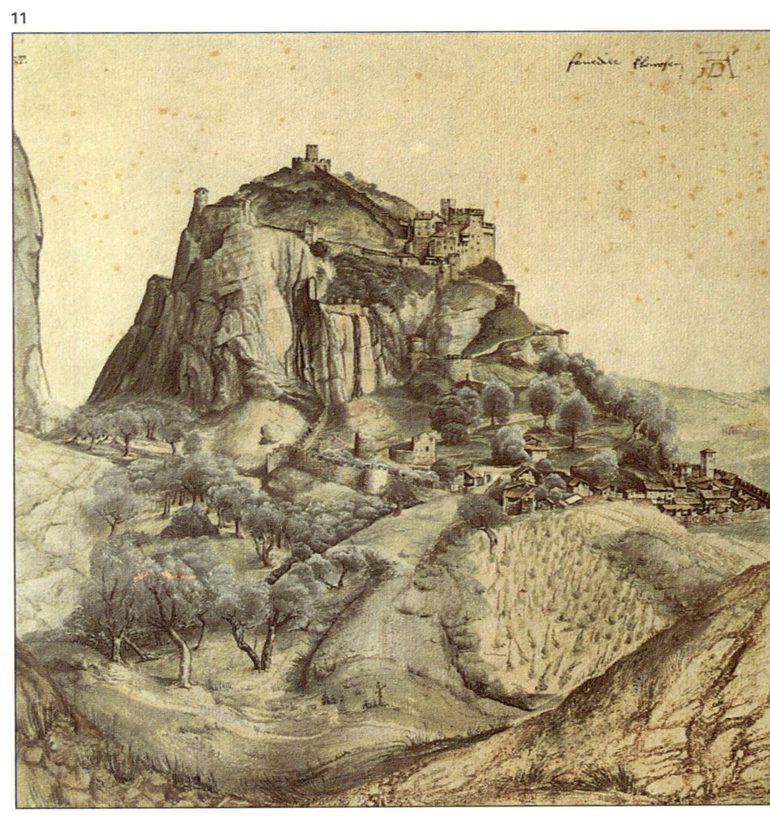

12

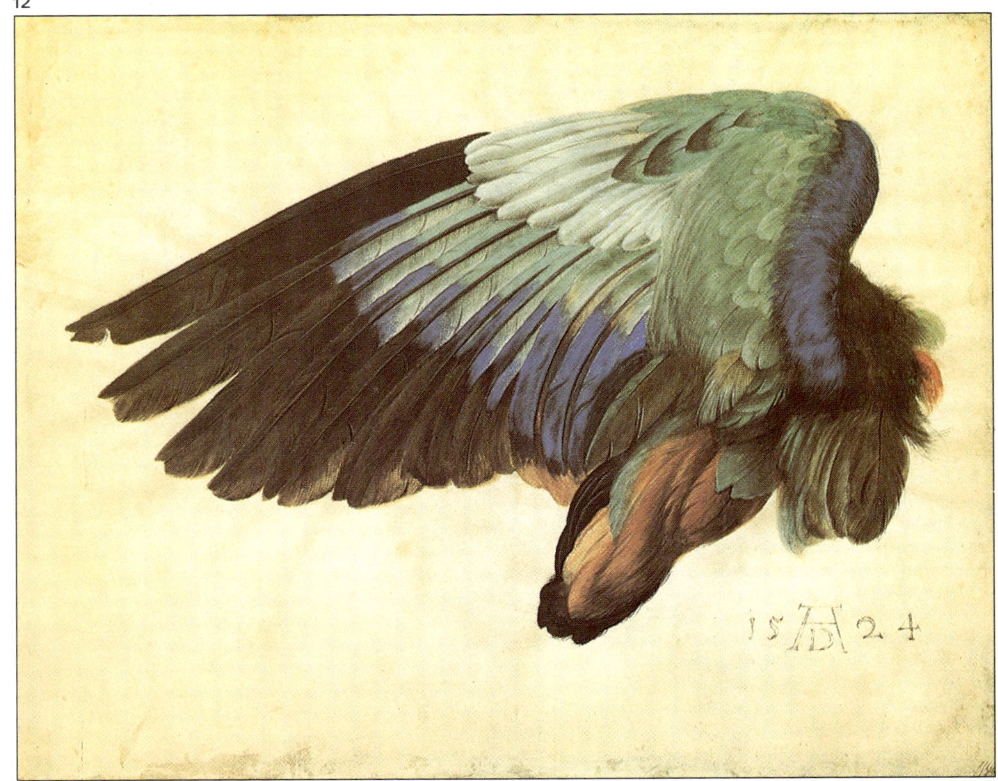

Fig. 11. Albrecht Dürer, *View from Val Dàrco*. Louvre, Paris. Dürer's watercolor landscapes are a marvelous example of the painter's sense of color and composition. The transparent color (still intact today), the graceful composition, and the rhythm of the forms make these small works authentic masterpieces in the history of watercolor.

Fig. 12. Albrecht Dürer, *Wing of a Small Blue Bird*. Albertina, Vienna. This is without doubt a magnificent work, continuing along the same analytical and naturalist lines as his other watercolors, such as *The Hare*. The meticulous execution of this type of work does not prevent Dürer from maintaining the spontaneity and richness of color that is so characteristic of his style.

Rembrandt

Dürer had reached an extraordinary level of technique, but above all had managed to acquire a level of prestige that was almost on a par with that of a great oil painter. Many years after Dürer's death, watercolor was once more relegated to a secondary medium because it was used only for painting studies and sketches. In fact, watercolor possesses certain special characteristics that make it ideal for painting them rapidly. This is the reason why we find a fantastic synthesis of stroke, composition, light, and color in these small works. Such is the case of Rembrandt (1606-1669), a great Dutch painter in whose enormous collection of works there is not one watercolor to be found, although there are many works done in ink wash.

13

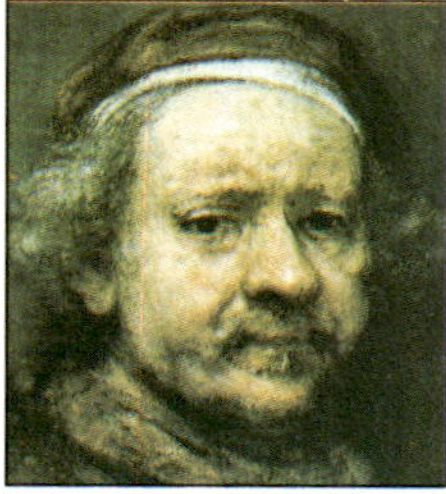

14

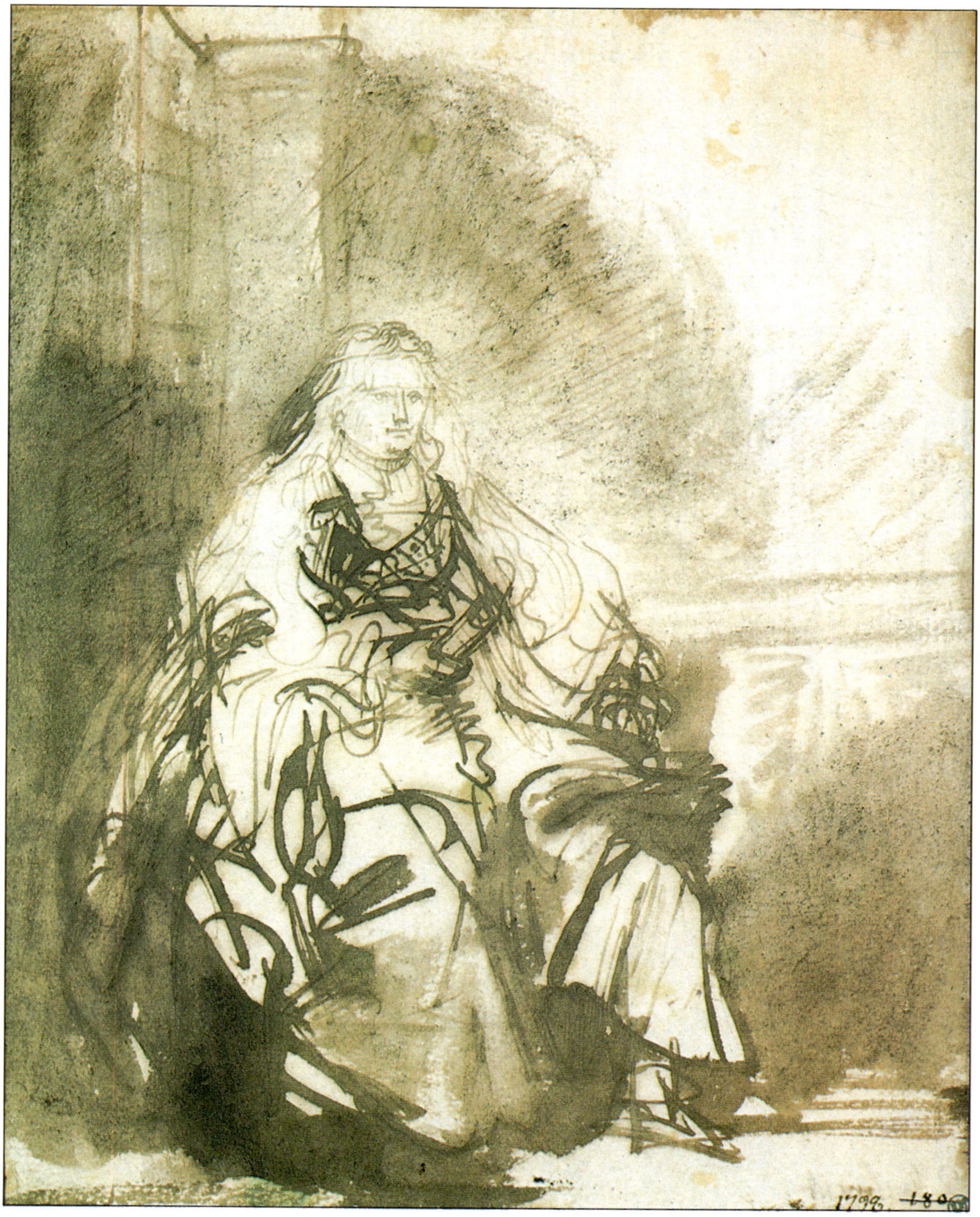

Fig. 13. Rembrandt van Rijn (1606-1669), *Self-Portrait at the Age of Sixty-Three*. National Gallery, London. Rembrandt painted himself on numerous occasions throughout his life, and he did it using all the mediums he mastered (oils, engravings, wash, and so on). Some of the self-portraits painted toward the end of his life, such as this one, are said to be among his best for their extraordinary expressive power and for their extremely high technical level.

Fig. 14. Rembrandt van Rijn, *Figure Study*. Stockholm National Museum. Rembrandt's washes provide us with an excellent example of how the painter combines the lights and shadows, thus creating a rich atmosphere that produces such psychological depth in his personages.

Fig. 15. Rembrandt van Rijn, *Woman and Hairdresser*. Albertina, Vienna. Rembrandt possesses a great capacity for representing, in a subtle and delicate manner, his many everyday scenes painted in wash. In this one, the painter makes the chiaroscuro stand out by way of the great stains of ink, thus achieving a very powerful lighting technique.

Wash permitted Rembrandt to paint sharp, direct pictures, which at times appeared to be guided by fulminating inspiration, revealing the painter to be a master of the technique. Rembrandt endowed his works with a perfect synthesis of composition, expression, and atmosphere with his precise and dynamic strokes. His themes are intimate, everyday scenes, captured with sensitivity and delicateness, or biblical scenes expressed with a special tenderness that constantly reminds us of his many great oil paintings. One of the most relevant characteristics of Rembrandt's wash pictures is the way he treats the combination of lights and shadows, suggesting all the richness of an entire spectrum of color . . . with only one hue. The expressive possibilities of wash were also explored by other artists, such as Claude Lorrain and Nicolas Poussin, who applied it with great delicateness above all in landscape painting. The love of landscapes was precisely the beginning of the rediscovery of watercolors by eighteenth-century English artists.

Fig. 16. Rembrandt van Rijn, *Figure Study*. Rijsprentenkabinet, Amsterdam. Rembrandt produced an immense body of work that included the drawing, engraving, woodcut, and wash. This study of a figure manifests the artist's characteristic graphic and gestural power.

15

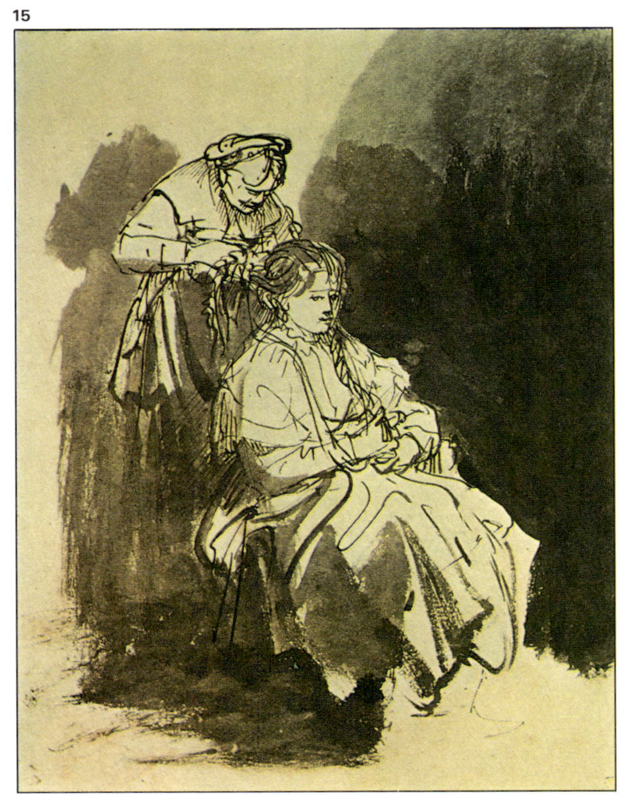

16

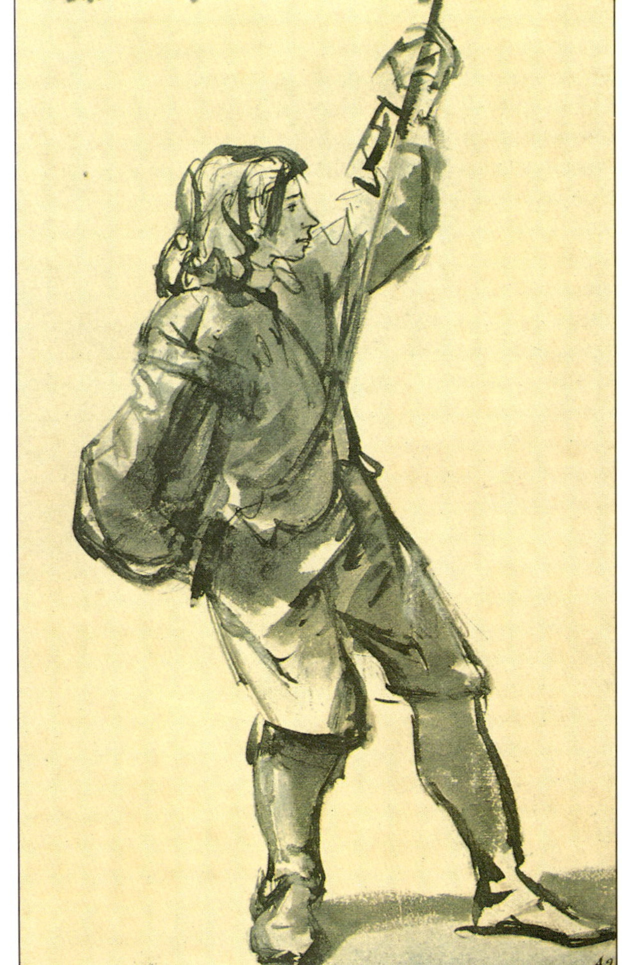

William Blake

William Blake (1757-1827) was born and lived in England. He worked as an etcher, although he dedicated much of his time to writing poetry. Years later, Blake published his poems in several volumes that he edited and illustrated himself with his etchings, which were hand-finished with watercolors. It is precisely here in these illustrations that we discover this artist and poet's imaginative potential. Inspired by biblical and mythological themes, Blake's pictures are fantastic visions of a supernatural world, replete with allegorical personages and oneiric scenes. With a flexible but firm stroke, the artist drew the strange mythological characters and landscapes that made up his personal universe. Blake would add color in a totally subjective manner, increasing the unreal sensation of his drawings even more. Blake introduced a new theme into watercolor: imaginary figures, which until then only a few artists (such as Fuseli and Palmer) had touched on. It was a subject of great potential and imagination. Throughout his life, Blake received only contempt and incomprehension from his contemporaries, despite the fact that his work paved the way for the exploration of a magical and supernatural world that years later would be associated with the surrealist movement of the twentieth century.

17

18

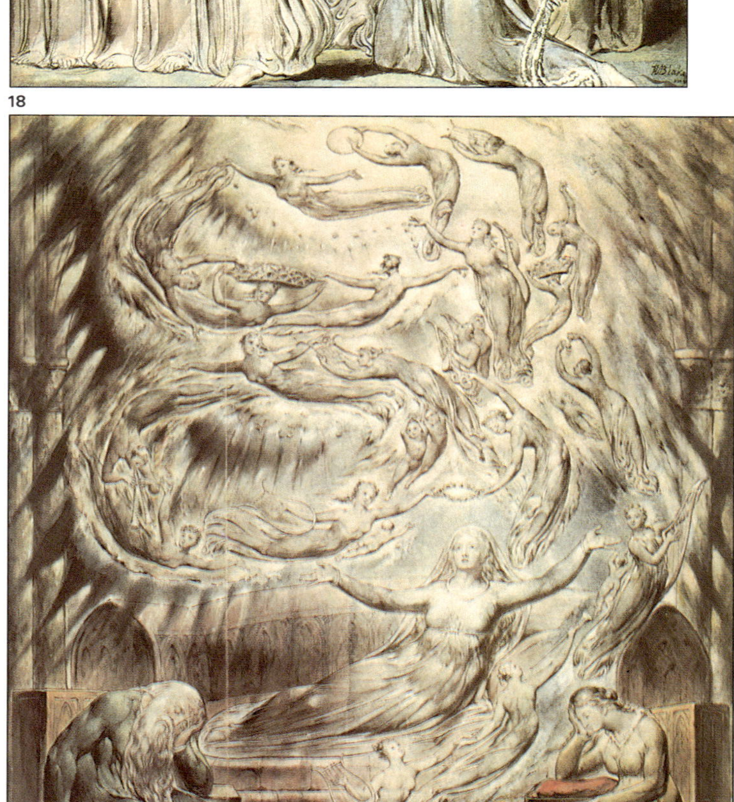

Fig. 17. William Blake (1757-1827), *Wise and Foolish Virgins*. Fitzwilliam Museum, Cambridge. Blake's style is characterized by his ability to incorporate very diverse influences into his work: from imaginary medieval images to a conception of the human figure according to the classic canons that dictated an almost sculptural build.

Fig. 18. William Blake, *Queen Catalina's Dream*. National Gallery of Art, Washington. Blake is considered to be one of the greatest forerunners of surrealism because of the presence of magic and oneiric scenes in his works. The appearance of gigantic, unreal creatures make this work acquire a unique and special character within the artistic context of the time.

John Sell Cotman

Toward the end of the eighteenth century, the prosperous English bourgeoisie created the tradition of the "Grand Tour," a journey that took in several European countries and inevitably ended in Rome, which was visited with great fervor because of its huge ancient and classical monuments. Etchings conceived as travel souvenirs came into vogue. At about the same time topographers, painters whose name derives from their characteristic minuteness and detail, appeared on the scene. They specialized in drawing landscapes that were filled in with watercolors. Interest in the watercolor landscape continued to grow until it was finally considered the English national art.

John Sell Cotman (1782-1842) painted in a very personal style and was one of the artists who took part in the first watercolor exposition in London in 1804. He specialized in painting landscapes, a genre in which he produced works of beautiful fineness thanks to his innate sense of color harmony and composition.

19

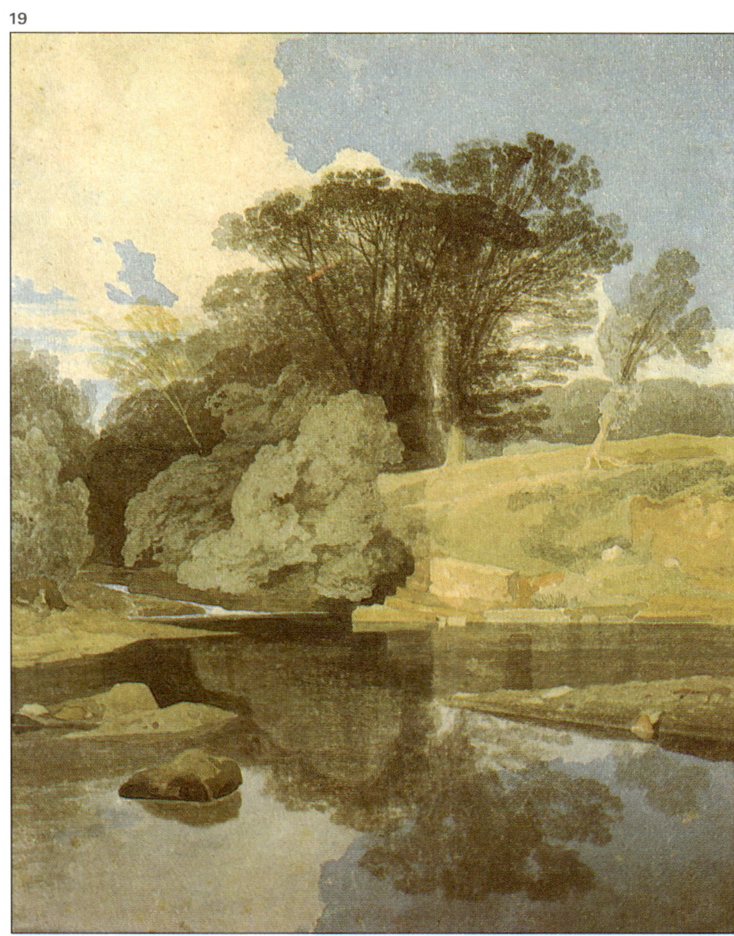

20

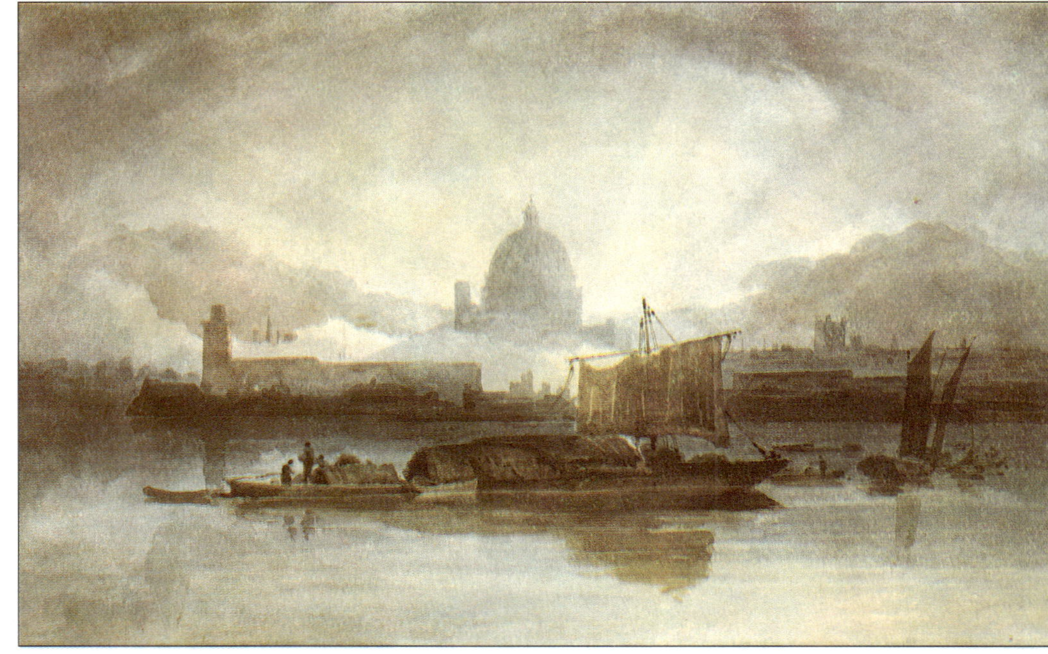

Fig. 19. John Sell Cotman (1782-1842), *Shady Pool*. National Galleries of Scotland, Edinburgh. In Cotman we find an artist who captures the colors and harmony of nature with delicate sensitivity. His own special way of composing his works using planes of color can be admired in this painting.

Fig. 20. John Sell Cotman, *St. Paul's Cathedral*. British Museum, London. Cotman was considered one of the best landscape watercolorists of his time. The English artists' love for nature is well represented in Cotman's magnificent works.

J.M.W. Turner

21

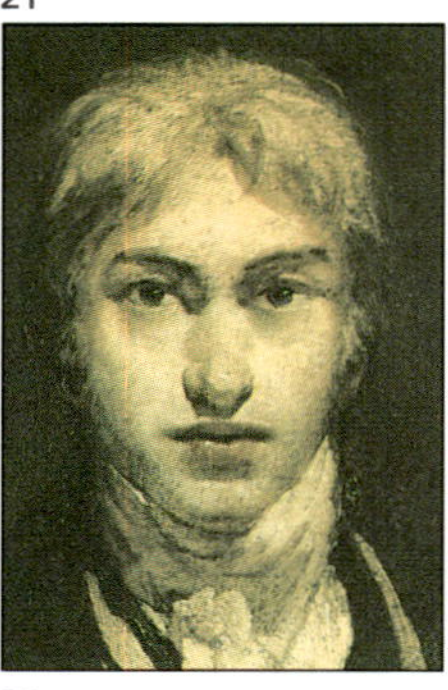

Joseph Mallord William Turner (1775-1851) was already a recognized painter when he began to frequent the Academy of Dr. Monro. Despite his youth, Turner was able to prove his skills by painting in oils along the classical lines of Claude Lorrain, the French painter for whom he felt a great devotion. When Monro, a London doctor and great watercolor enthusiast, opened up his house as a watercolor studio for young painters, Turner was there among a group of painters who all shared one thing in common: their passion for this medium. This group, comprising Girtin, Cozens, De Wint, Varley, and so on, found a friend and sponsor in Dr. Monro. He urged them to study and practice the technique, and encouraged them to develop their own pictorial language. Dr. Monro's advice was highly valued by his students, who were later to become known as the best English watercolorists of the nineteenth century.

Turner started working with Thomas Girtin, a promising young watercolorist for whom Turner felt great admiration, but he died at an early age, cutting short what would have been a brilliant career. Turner had been very much influenced by Girtin, who had introduced great technical innovations into the watercolor medium—gradually distancing himself from the topographical genre and acquiring a new and modern form of expression. Turner learned Girtin's lesson well, and this helped him to open the door of his own stylistic evolution.

Watercolor was the ideal medium for directly expressing the romantic feeling of

22

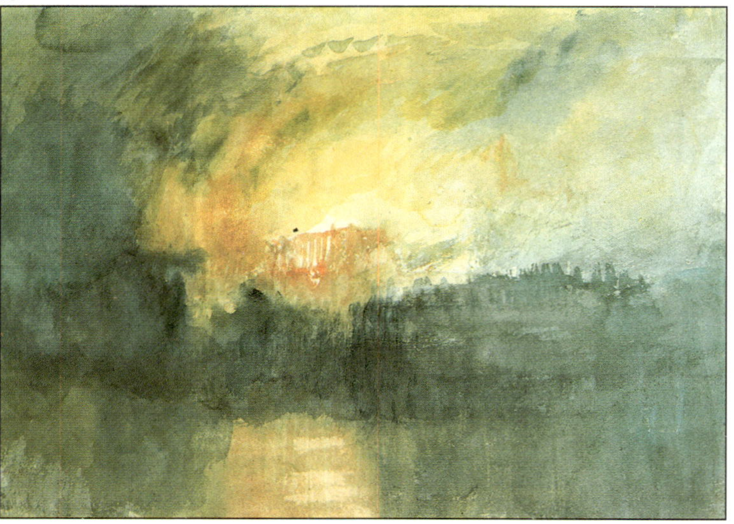

23

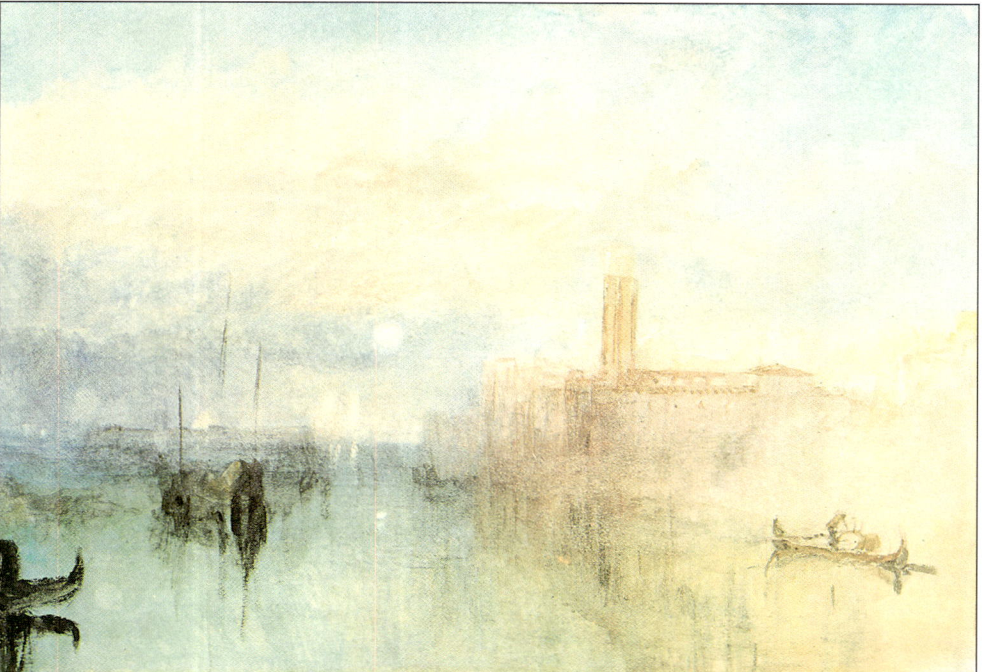

Fig. 21. J.M.W. Turner (1775-1851), *Self-Portrait*. Tate Gallery, London. Turner is the main representative of English romanticism. His work anticipated the stylistic revolution of impressionism.

Fig. 22. J.M.W. Turner, *The Burning of the Houses of Parliament on the Night of October 16, 1834*. British Museum, London. Turner's outstanding technique and mastery of all the medium's resources enabled him to tackle very difficult subjects.

Fig. 23. J.M.W. Turner, *Venice: Moon-rise*. Tate Gallery, London. Venice's spectacular light was one of the themes that Turner painted frequently.

a landscape. A constant evolution can be observed in Turner's work: The forms gradually disperse to make way for a much more poetic evocation of light and atmosphere, the most characteristic aspects of his paintings. The delicacy of watercolors, the combination of glazes and humid color fusions express in an extraordinary way the magnificence of nature. Turner discovered themes that were particularly appropriate for his style. They enabled him to exploit his incredible talent of combining the effects of light and atmosphere, such as his views of Venice or those of London and the Thames, in which the reflection of light on the water expresses a phantasmagoric and mysterious reality. Although there is no proof of a direct connection between Turner's painting and the advent of impressionism in France, it is indisputable that this great painter's art foreshadowed the new aesthetic of atmospheric effects, expression of light by way of pure color combinations and freestyle painting and sketching of forms, which would also become characteristic of impressionist painting.

Fig. 24. J.M.W. Turner, *Venice: View from the Giudecca*. British Museum, London. Turner was often inspired by sunrise and sunset. Such motifs gave his colorist intuition total freedom.

24

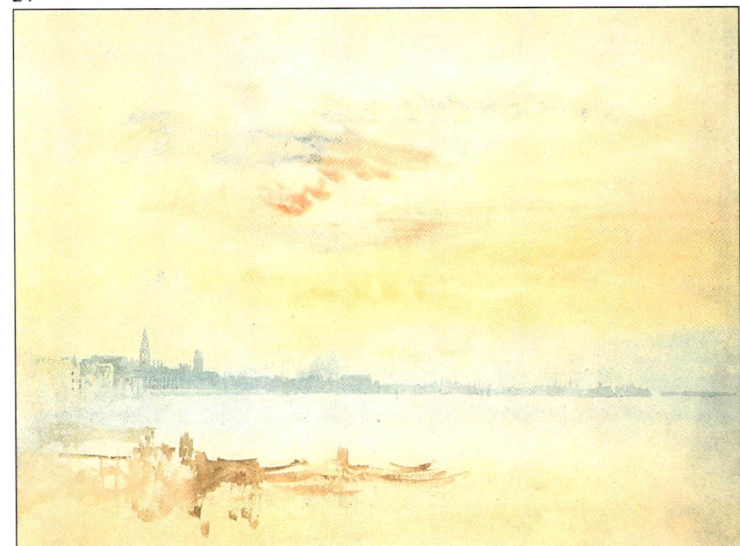

25

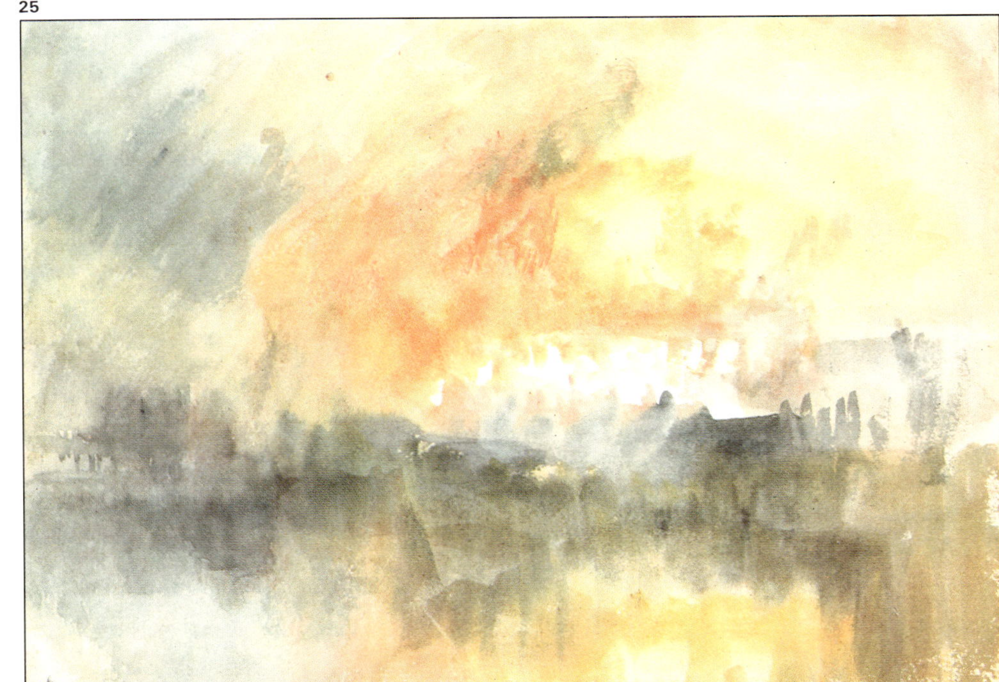

Fig. 25. J.M.W. Turner. *The Burning of the Houses of Parliament, 1834*. British Museum, London. This theme was painted on various occasions; Turner always interpreted the event in an almost abstract dramatisim.

De Wint, Varley, Cozens, Girtin

Watercolor was so popular in England during the second half of the eighteenth century that in 1804 a foundation was set up known as the "Old Water-Colour Society." To a certain extent this was an attempt on the part of the watercolorists to be treated with the same respect as oil painters. The momentum toward this goal was inexorable. Many young painters were soon attracted to watercolors, and their experimentation in this medium brought about new and interesting innovations, technical as well as formal. With time, new painters joined the ranks of the innovators, thus enriching the watercolorist tradition.

It is necessary to remember the important work carried out by Dr. Monro, whose teachings and whose attitude toward art helped to shape a key generation of watercolorists. John Robert Cozens (1752-1797) was of the generation prior to Dr. Monro's students, and his works influenced them greatly. Cozens possessed a poetic sense of landscape that he transmitted through his delicate

26

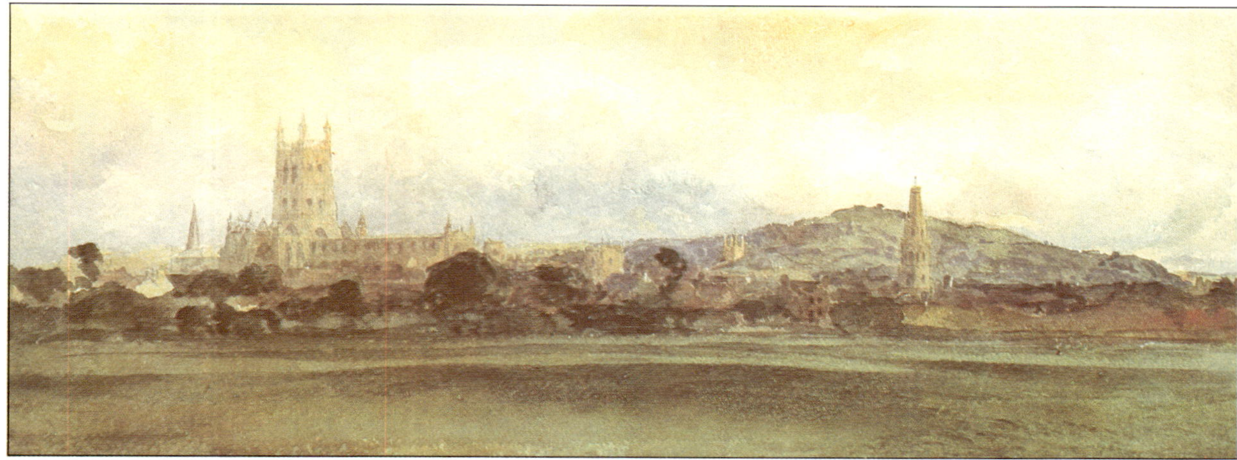

27

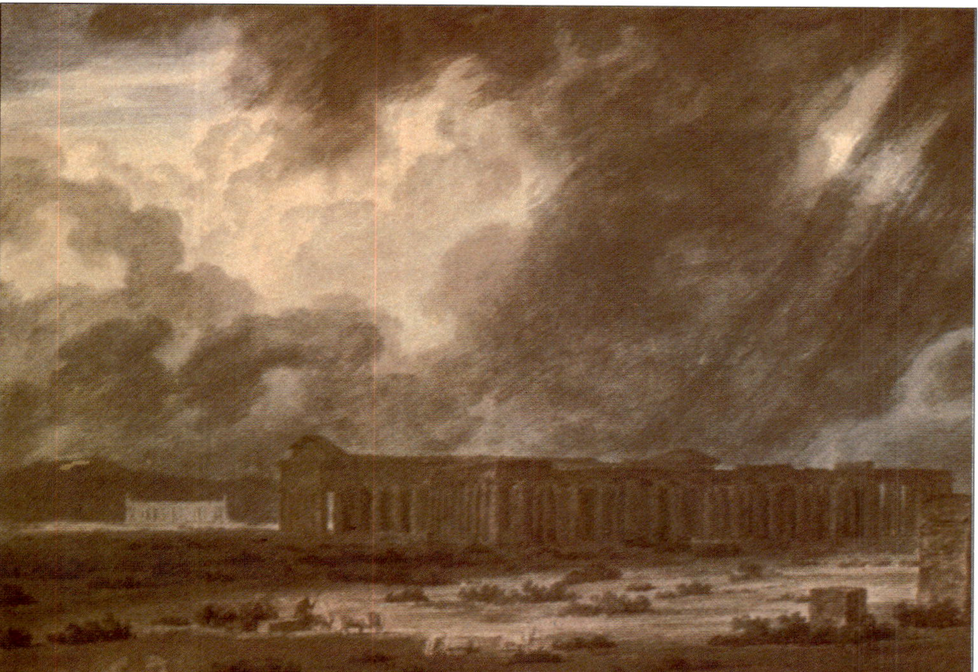

Fig. 26. Peter de Wint (1784-1849), *Gloucester*. British Museum, London. De Wint's watercolors unite realist observation with a special sensitivity toward atmospheric effects.

Fig. 27. John Robert Cozens (1752-1797), *The Paestum Ruins, Near Salerno*. Oldham Art Gallery, Oldham. The numerous possibilities that watercolor has to offer are displayed in this picture's dramatic light effects and atmospheric transparency.

ranges of blues and grays. His work was very much influenced by the painters whom he met on his travels in Italy and Switzerland.

The landscape paintings of John Varley (1778-1842) and Peter de Wint (1784-1849) display the artists' preoccupation with expressing an atmospheric sensation through a refined sense of color. Thomas Girtin (1775-1802), whom we have already mentioned, rediscovered local color: he shaded with full color, not with grays, gradations, or browns. This led the artist to a new conception of colorism: atmospheric landscape painting, which paved the way to modern landscape painting.

28

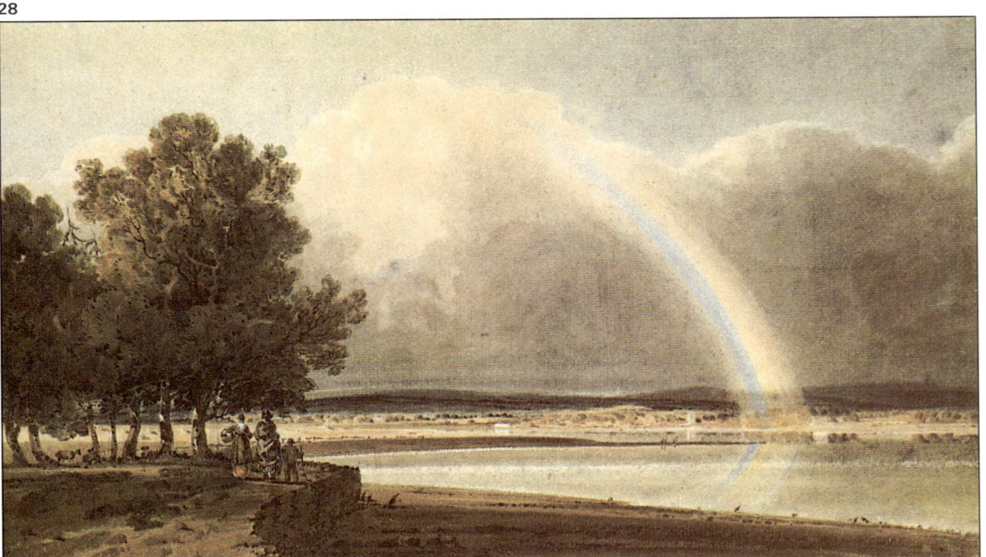

Fig. 28. Thomas Girtin (1775-1802), *Rainbow over the Exe*. Henry E. Huntington Library and Art Gallery, San Marino, California. The influence of the Dutch landscape, very common in English landscape paintings of the eighteenth century, can be seen in this splendid watercolor.

Fig. 29. John Varley (1778-1842), *York*. British Museum, London. The clarity of color gradation exaggerates the distances of the landscape. The artist achieves a high level of subtlety when realizing such effects.

29

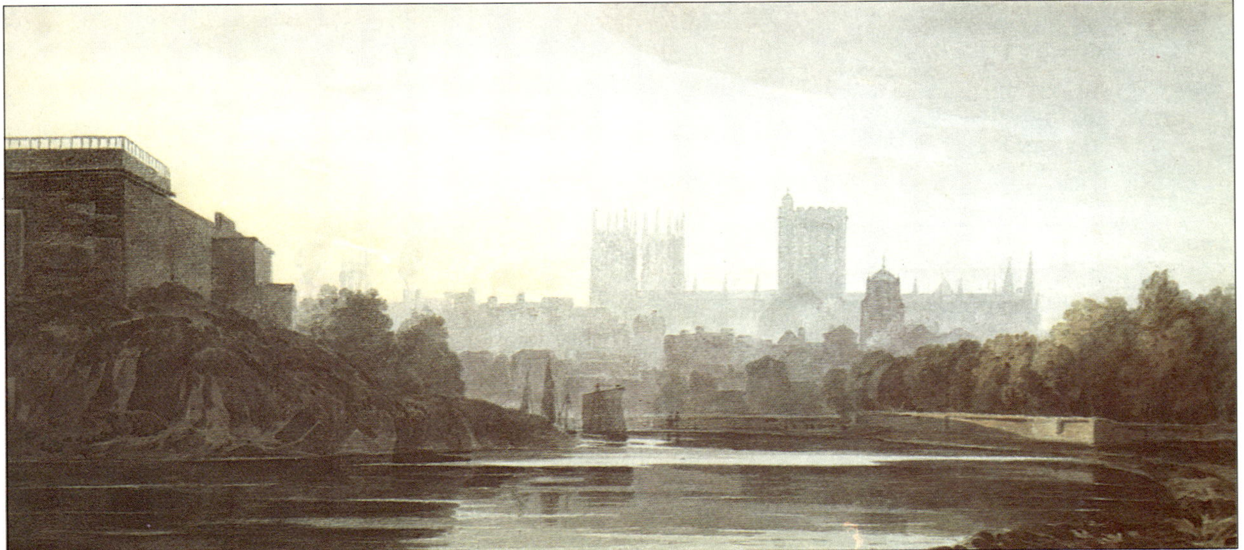

Paul Cézanne

30

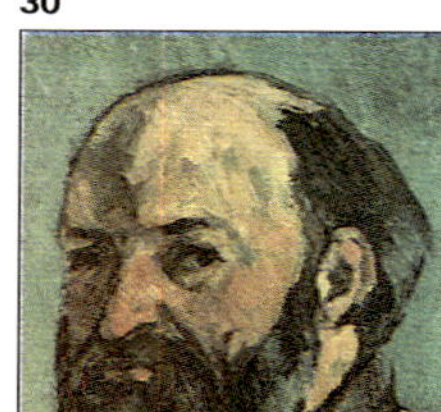

Fig. 30. Paul Cézanne (1839-1906), *Self-Portrait*, Orsay Museum, Paris.

Fig. 31. Paul Cézanne, *Apples, Bottle and the Back of a Chair*. Courtauld Institute Galleries, London.

The artistic world of the French painter Paul Cézanne (1839-1906) in Paris during the second half of the nineteenth century was at the height of a revolution of artistic ideas. The cause of this was the audacity with which the so-called impressionists had parted company with the official painting movement, which for years had been bogged down in thematic and stylistic conventionalism. The impressionists categorically rejected this by painting pictures stressing light and color in themes as simple and banal as a landscape or a scene of everyday life, which caused great confusion among the Parisian public.

Cézanne participated in the expositions by impressionists painters, but he was totally disillusioned by the criticism and so decided to retire to Aix, his native city, to paint in complete solitude.

From then on the painter dedicated his whole life to obtaining recognition for impressionism as a valid art form. For many years, and until the end of life (such was his obsession that he once swore: "I will die painting"), Cézanne was searching for a way of conciliating the methods of impressionism with a sense of order in the composition, using form and color in a way superior to what many of his contemporaries achieved.

31

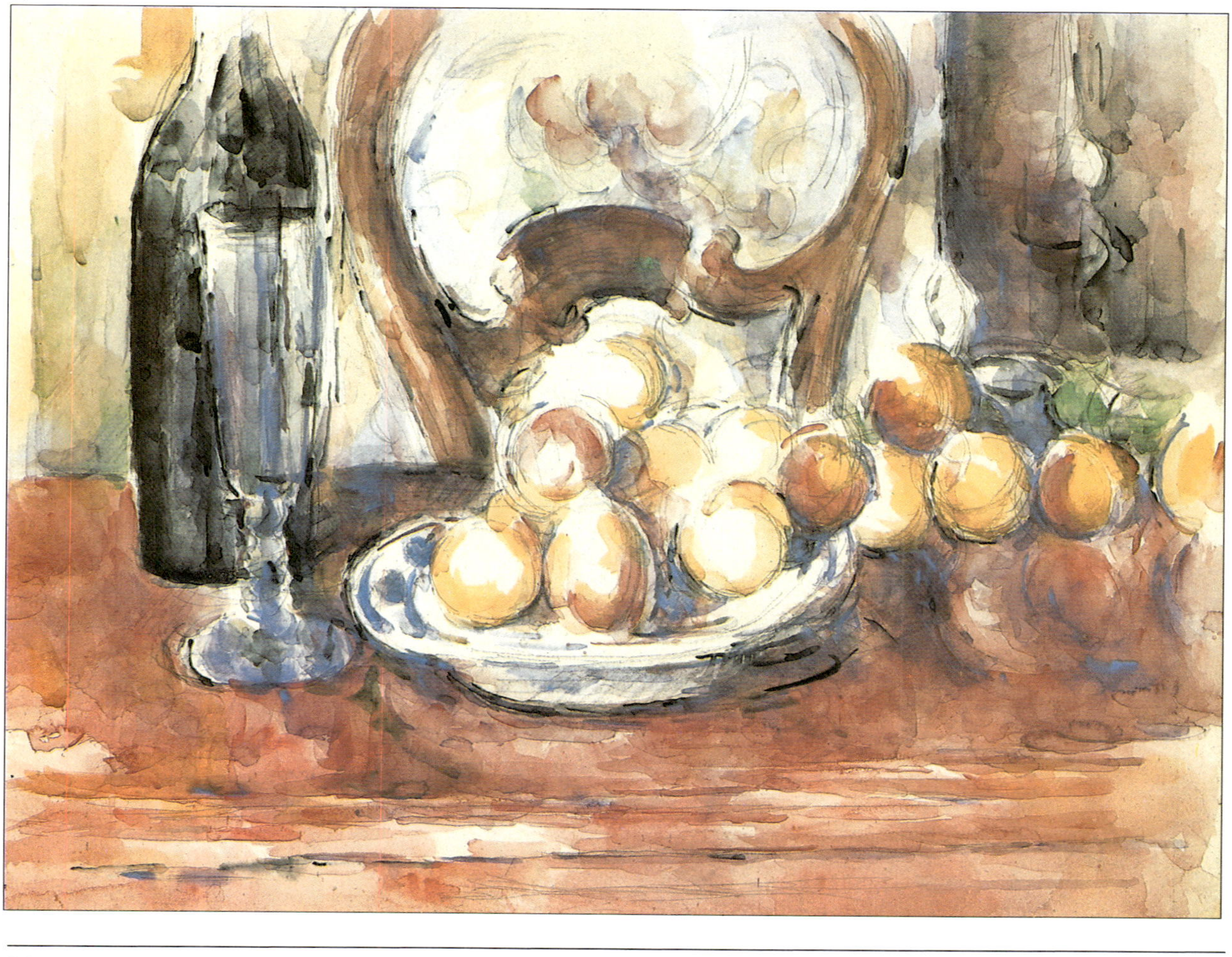

Fig. 32. Paul Cézanne, *Young Man with a Red Jacket*. Marianne Feilchenfeldt Collection, Zurich. Cézanne's impressionist watercolor is characterized by his free brushstroke and his sincerity of vision and fresh realization, without idealizations or corrections.

Fig. 33. Paul Cézanne, *The Forest of the Black Chateau*. The Newark Museum, New Jersey. Cézanne's technique consists of applying a multitude of small brushstrokes which, little by little, construct the natural forms.

In general, watercolor was not widely used by the impressionists, but Cézanne found it to be an ideal technique for obtaining expressive freedom. Cézanne used watercolor only for his sketches and studies; the medium was merely a work tool. However, the truth is that many of his works in this medium are considered among the most sensitive and delicate he ever painted.

In Cézanne's watercolors, the transparency of the colors helps to express the picture's forms by way of the subtle brushstrokes of color. Cézanne used colors to convey volume, and he did not hesitate to arrange the composition to his own liking if that would help the painting as a whole to reflect a solid and harmonious construction. Cézanne's watercolors also reveal, with exceptional clarity, his particular way of composing.

Cézanne would go over the shallow sketch lines with small brushstrokes of varying tones until he achieved a clear and firm linear structure. In the empty areas, or "holes" left by the lines, Cézanne allowed his colorist instinct to take over and construct the volume of the forms. The artist worked with glazes as well as with solid, covering color, accentuating the profiles and areas in shadow. This is why his watercolors possess such intense brightness, which nevertheless allow the drawing and the body of the objects to appear with total clarity and precision.

32

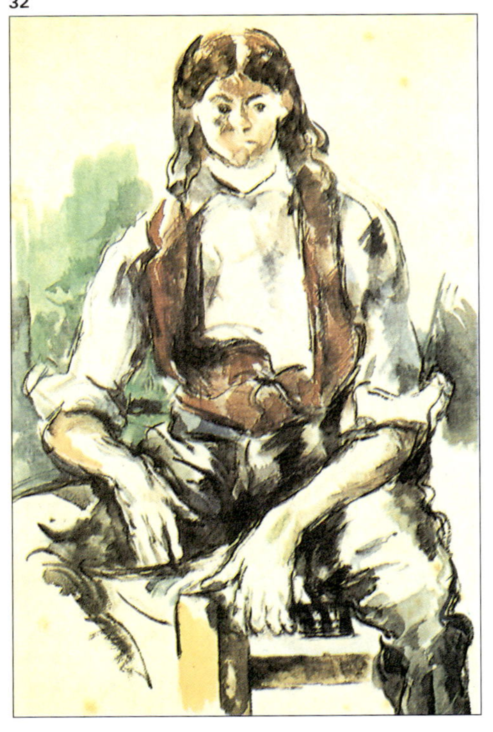

33

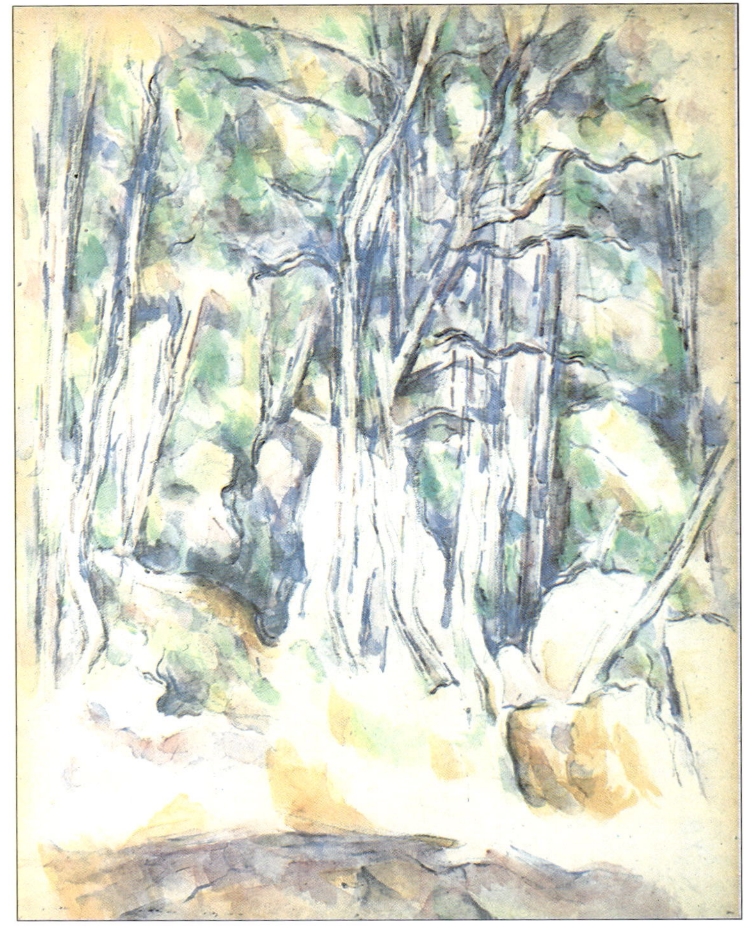

John Singer Sargent

Fig. 34. John Singer Sargent (1856-1925), *Cafe on the Riva degli Schiavoni, Venice*. Collection of the Ormond family. The predominating range of neutral grayish colors provides the scene with a subtle and very attractive atmosphere.

Unlike Cézanne, who experimented with his creative themes in total isolation, his contemporary John Singer Sargent (1856-1925) personified the extrovert artist who lived actively and expressed the pulse of the period through his very characteristic style.

John Singer Sargent was North American, although he spent most of his life in England, with a few stays in France and Italy. Throughout his life he moved in the circles of high society, a frequent theme in many of his paintings. Sargent's style is extroverted, lively, and brilliant, and it reflected his innate talent for painting. His many works done in watercolor proved his extraordinary abilities as a brilliant and vigorous draftsman, as well as his great sense of color, rhythm, and light. During his youth, Sargent studied in the studio of the French portrait painter Carolus-Duran, an artist who was highly respected in Parisian high society. Without doubt, Sargent owes much of his mature style to Carolus-Duran's painting, but also to the French impressionists, or more specifically, to Claude Monet, whose short brushstrokes and free use of color were adopted by Sargent.

34

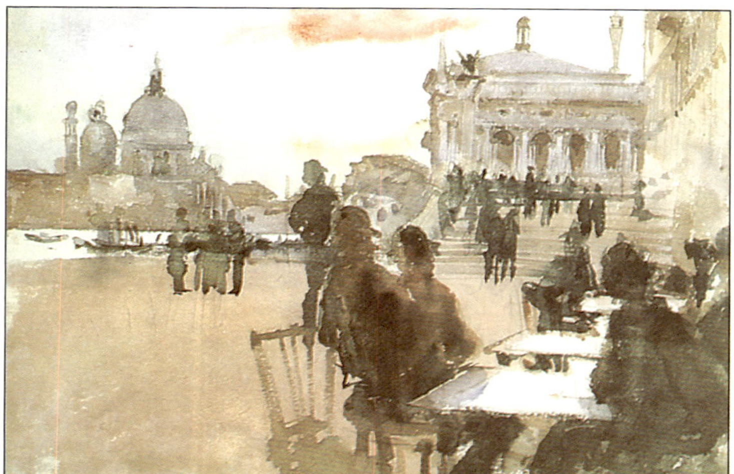

35

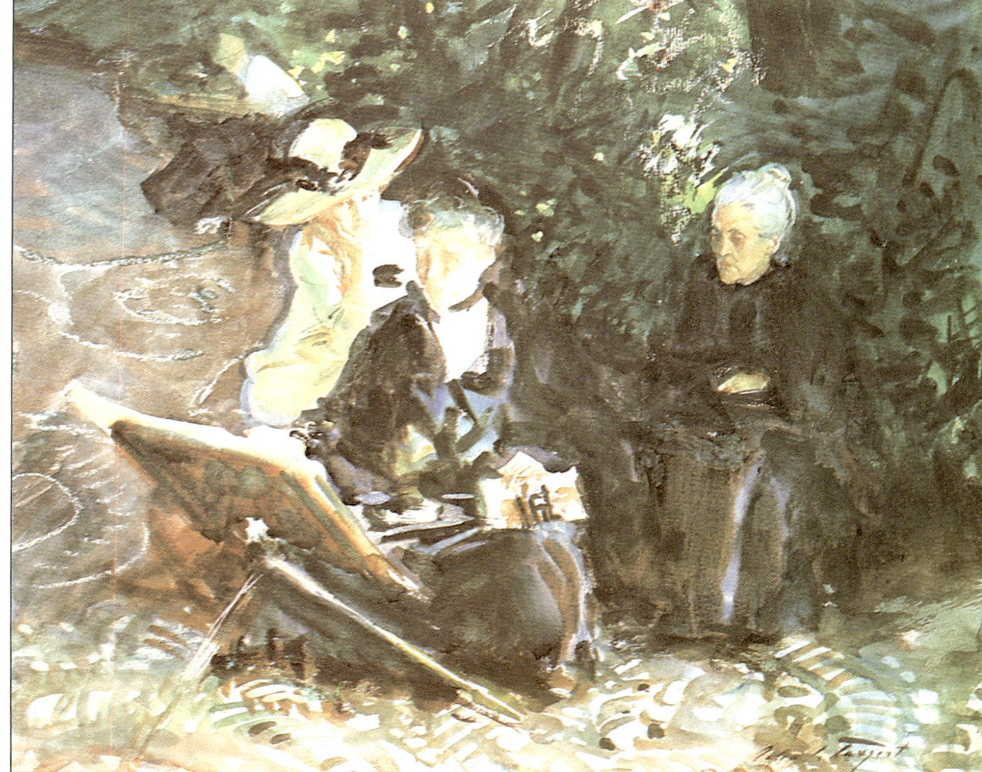

Fig. 35. John Singer Sargent, *In the Generalife*. Metropolitan Museum, New York. Sargent was a faithful documenter of the customs of the time. The ease with which he captures the attitude of the subjects of his paintings is obvious in this work.

The themes of Sargent's watercolors are, almost exclusively, scenes painted directly from nature that suggest a sensation of direct light and movement. They possess a kind of spontaneity, which is sometimes lost in his oil paintings. The painter's watercolors are a lesson in how to employ the technique for directly expressing real life in perfect compositional synthesis of form and color. Sargent always worked from color stains, captured on first sight. He hardly drew forms since the stains already contained the drawing within them, so as to speak. His scenes were constructed through contrast and opposition to the stains. This method, derived from the impressionist technique, was to become one of the most influential and imitated in twentieth-century watercolor technique.

Fig. 36. John Singer Sargent, *Mountain of Fire*. Brooklyn Museum, New York. The landscape's color and instant light are captured with an absolute mastery in this work.

36

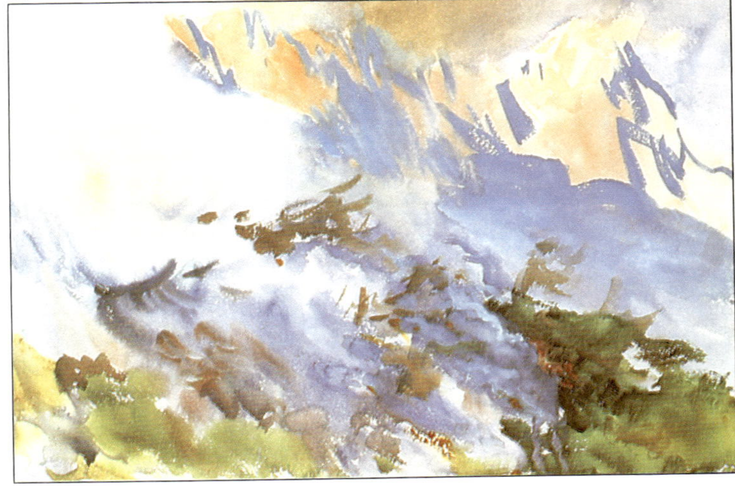

Fig. 37. John Singer Sargent, *Guideca*. Brooklyn Museum, New York. The importance of this watercolor lies in the free use of color and the loose brushstroke; the result is a work of great realism.

37

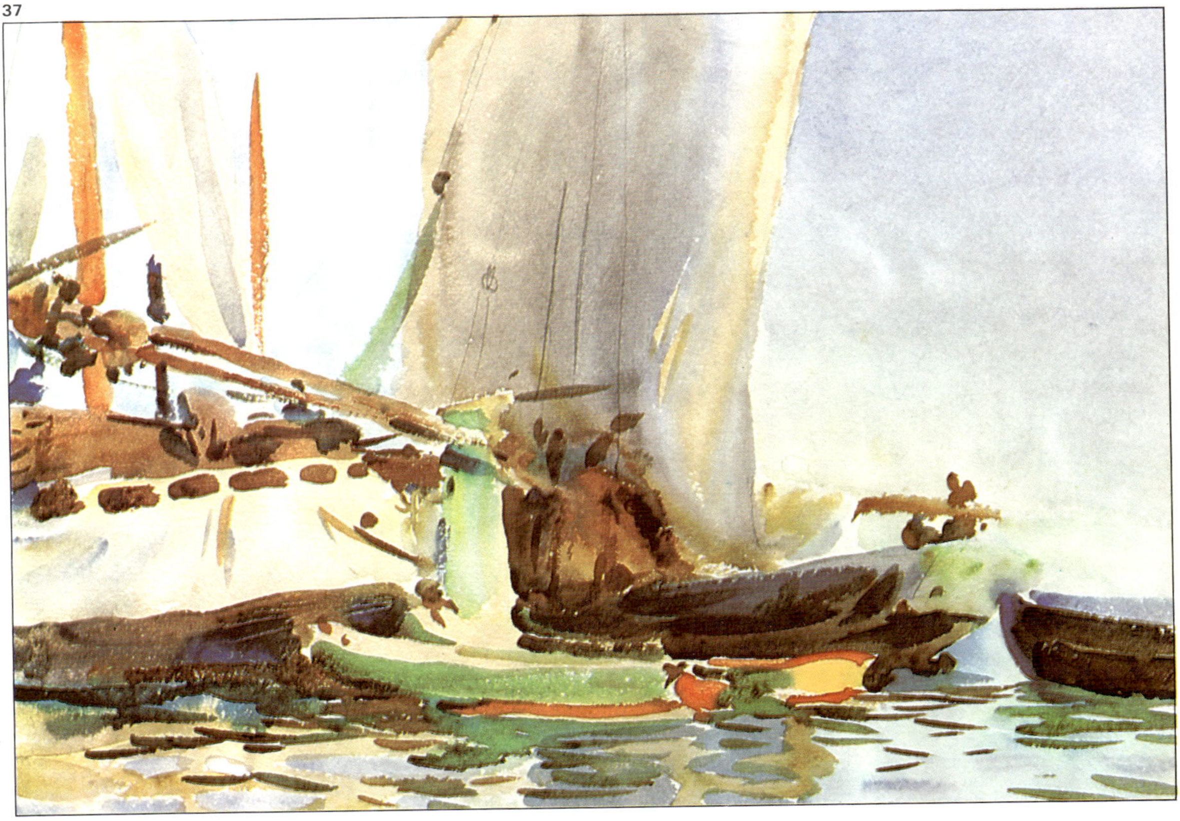

Contemporary impressionist watercolor

The thematic and technical innovations introduced by the impressionist school—everyday scenes and objects, urban landscapes, capturing fresh light and atmosphere, and so on—were naturally adapted to the characteristics of watercolor painting. Many of the great watercolorists, especially the English ones, have survived the spirit of impressionist art, and in them we can find the same pictorial attitude as in the great masters of this school. Revolutionary in its time, impressionism is now adopted by both professional and amateur watercolorists. Watercolorists like Seago, Wesson, Yardley, Chamberlain, and countless others have certain things in common: the freshness of their touch, freestyle brushstrokes, and in general a spontaneous execution.

In the works reproduced on these pages, it is easy to appreciate these artists' fidelity to the quality of light and atmosphere of the time and place. They have found a way to suggest a realist image that perfectly harmonizes with the subtleties of color and glaze so characteristic of the watercolor medium.

38

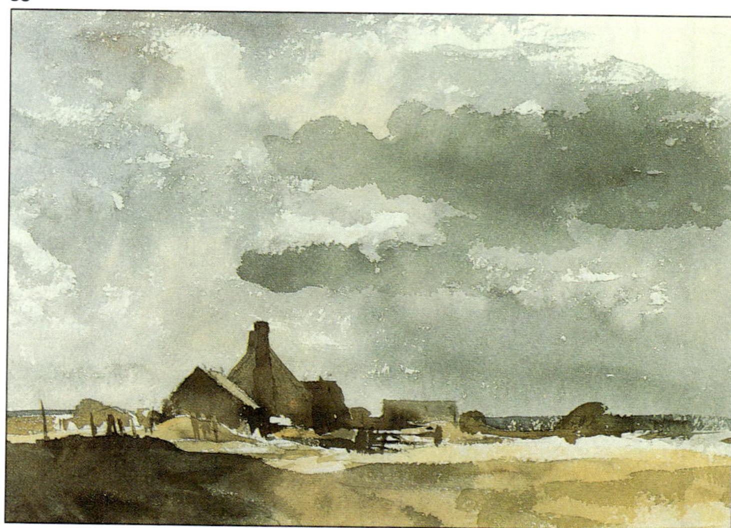

39

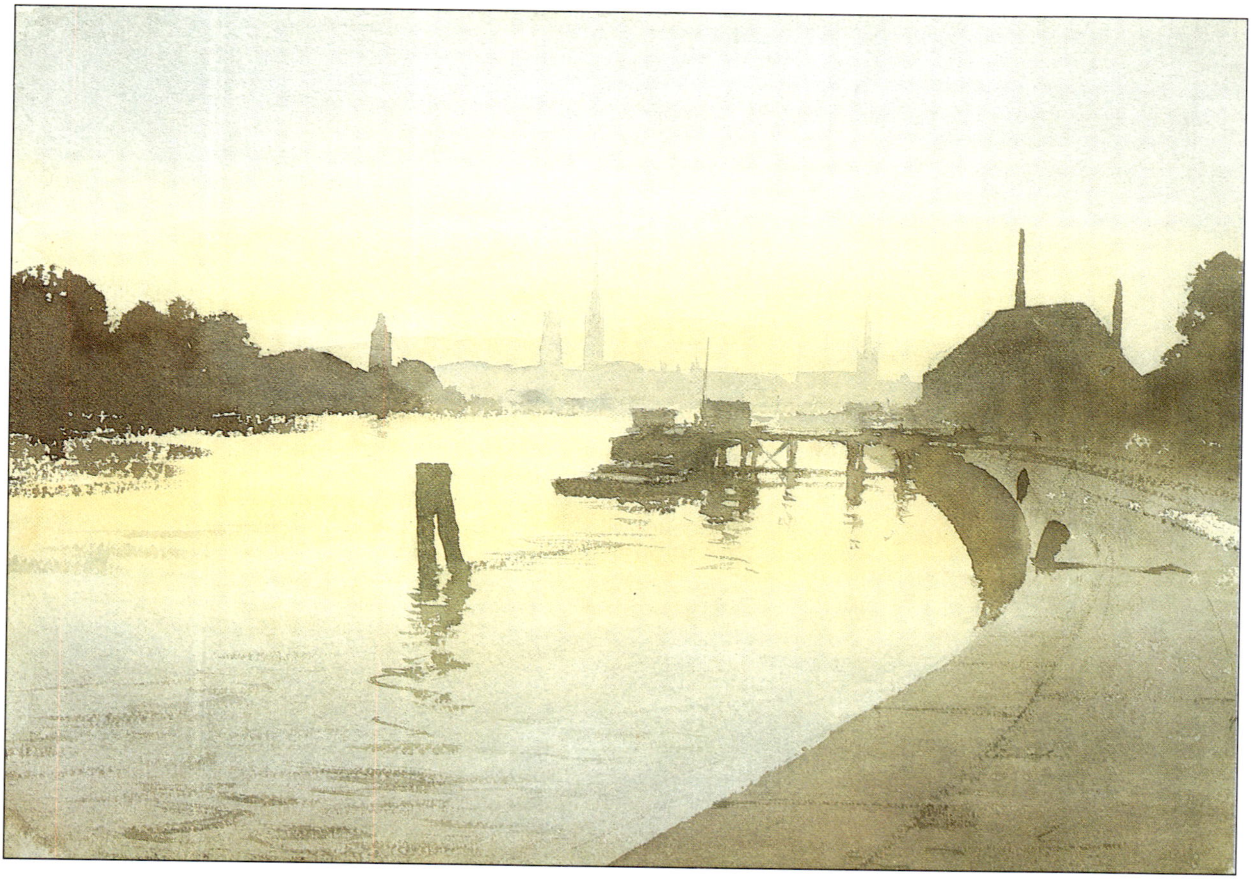

40

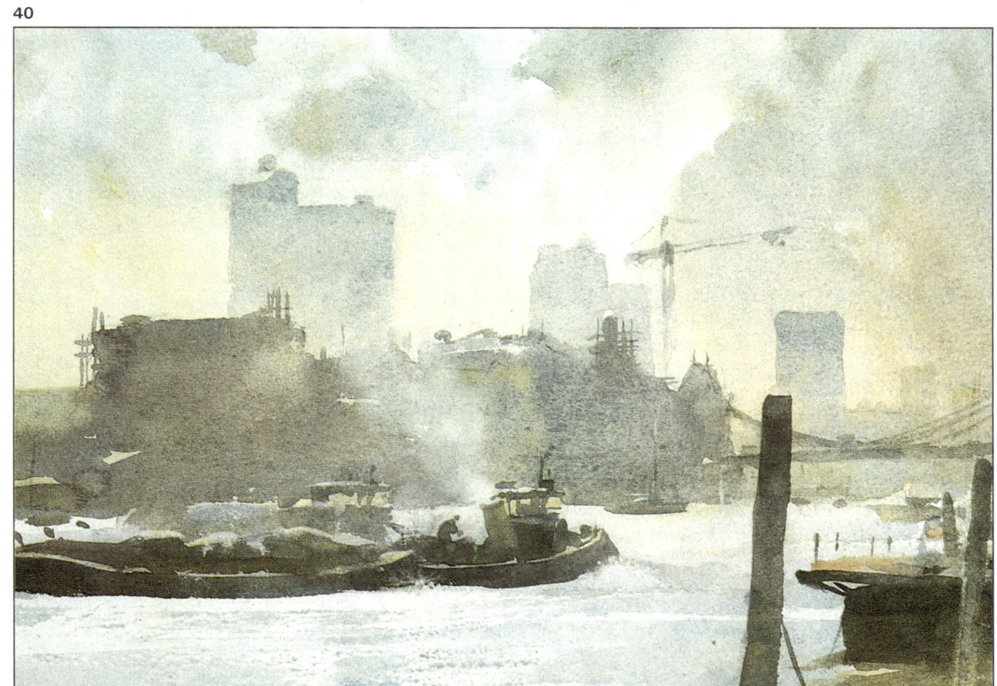

41

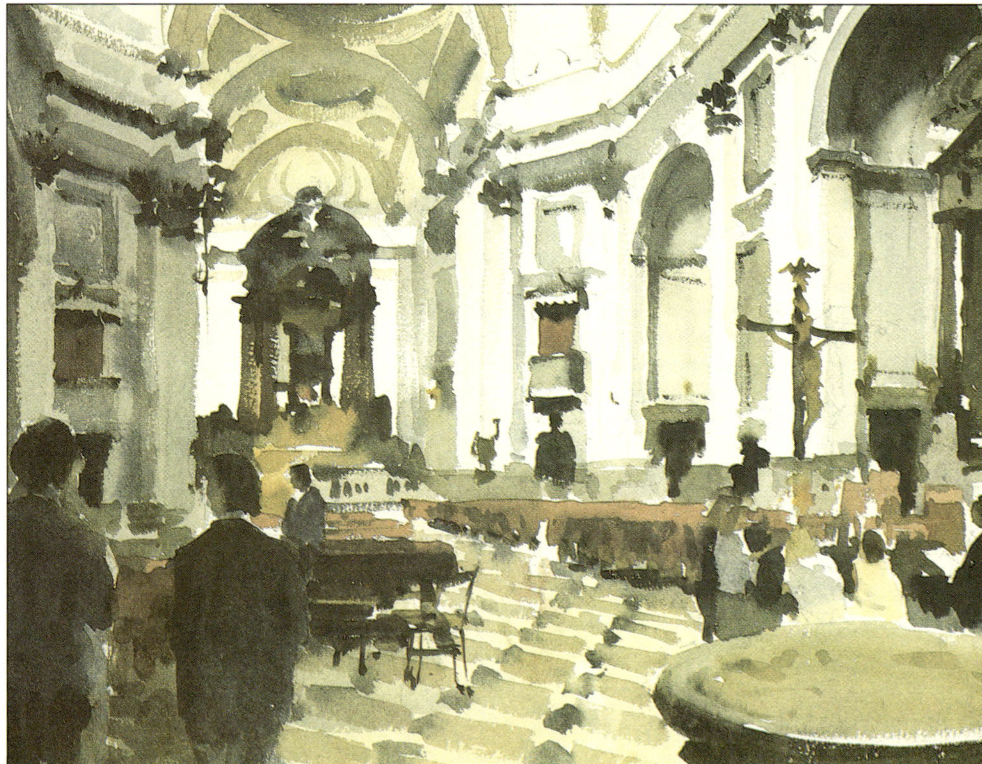

Fig. 38. Edward Seago (1910-1974), *Green's Farm*. Bankside Gallery, London. Courtesy of David & Charles Publishers. Seago was one of the most representative twentieth-century impressionist watercolor painters. His work is very rich in subtle color gradations and intense contrasts.

Fig. 39. Edward Seago, *Evening Light, Rouen*. Private collection, London. Courtesy of David & Charles Publishers. This watercolor was painted with a very limited range of colors, but the painter exploited them to the fullest.

Fig. 40. Trevor Chamberlain (1930-), *Off Wapping*. Private collection, London. This watercolor magnificently captures the combination of fog, clouds, water, and vapor. The characterization of atmosphere has been superbly resolved.

Fig. 41. John Yardley (1933-), *Jesuit Church*. Private collection, London. This is a fine display of observation and technical virtuosity. Both the forms and choice of tones demonstrate the hands of a master at work.

Creativity in watercolor painting today

A still life, an urban landscape, everyday scenes of life on the street—in fact, any theme is a stimulus for the modern watercolorist. From the rural landscape, whose theme was limited to the picturesque for such a long time (remember the beginnings of the Old Water-Colour Society) to the freedom that today's watercolorists enjoy, there have been many renovations, innovations, and all manner of new styles. Today's painters can find pictorial possibilities practically everywhere, and many great contemporary watercolor works have been inspired by the most unlikely subjects. Such circumstances dictate that the watercolor medium is alive and well; the countless technical solutions and stylistic possibilities at its disposal favor a creative vitality for those who wish to take up the challenge.

42

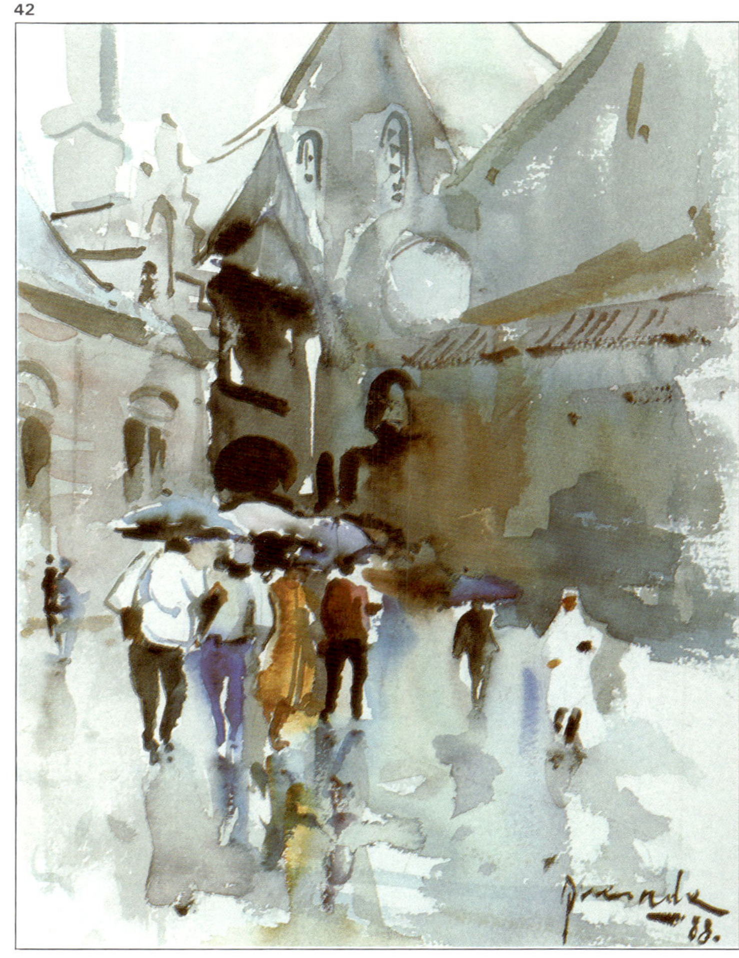

43

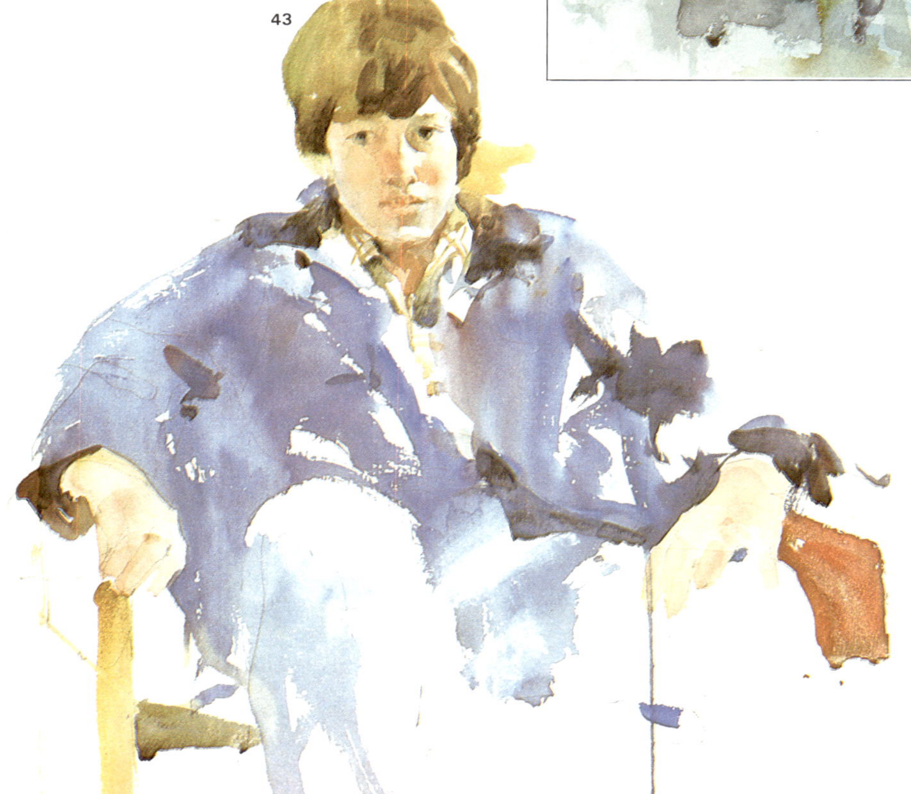

Fig. 42. Julio Quesada (1926-), *Rainy Day*. Private collection, Madrid. The rain, the wet streets, the gray atmosphere—such factors are always appealing to the watercolorist. This relevance of this work lies in the contrast between the warm tones of the people and the walls and the general gray of the picture.

Fig. 43. Charles Reid (1942-), *Peter, May 14*. Collection of Judith Reid. In this work, this great North American watercolorist combines precision of form with a loose stroke and staining.

Fig. 44. Josep Gaspar Romero (1920-), *Yacht Club*. This is a composition essentially based on the contrast of vertical and horizontal lines. The cool tendency of the colors is compensated for by some small warm and dark touches to the boats.

Fig. 45. Philip Jamison (1928-), *Foggy Day*. Private collection, London. Despite its title, this is a very bright painting and full of color. The sharp contrast between the flat color zones and the numerous details given to the flowers is noteworthy.

44

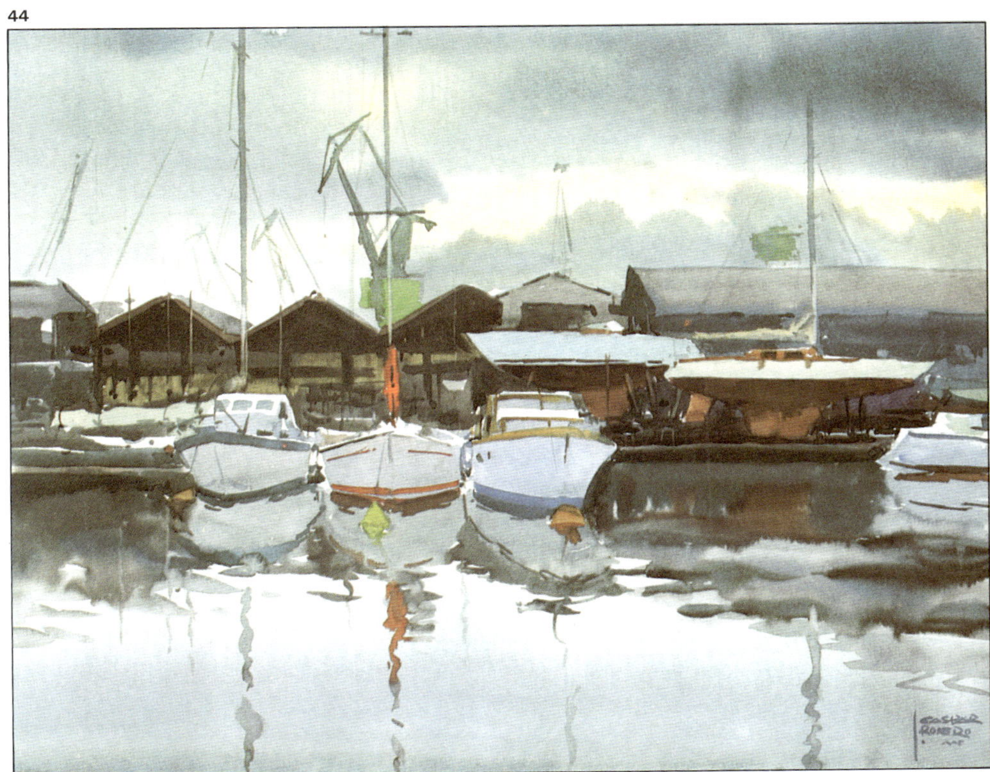

45

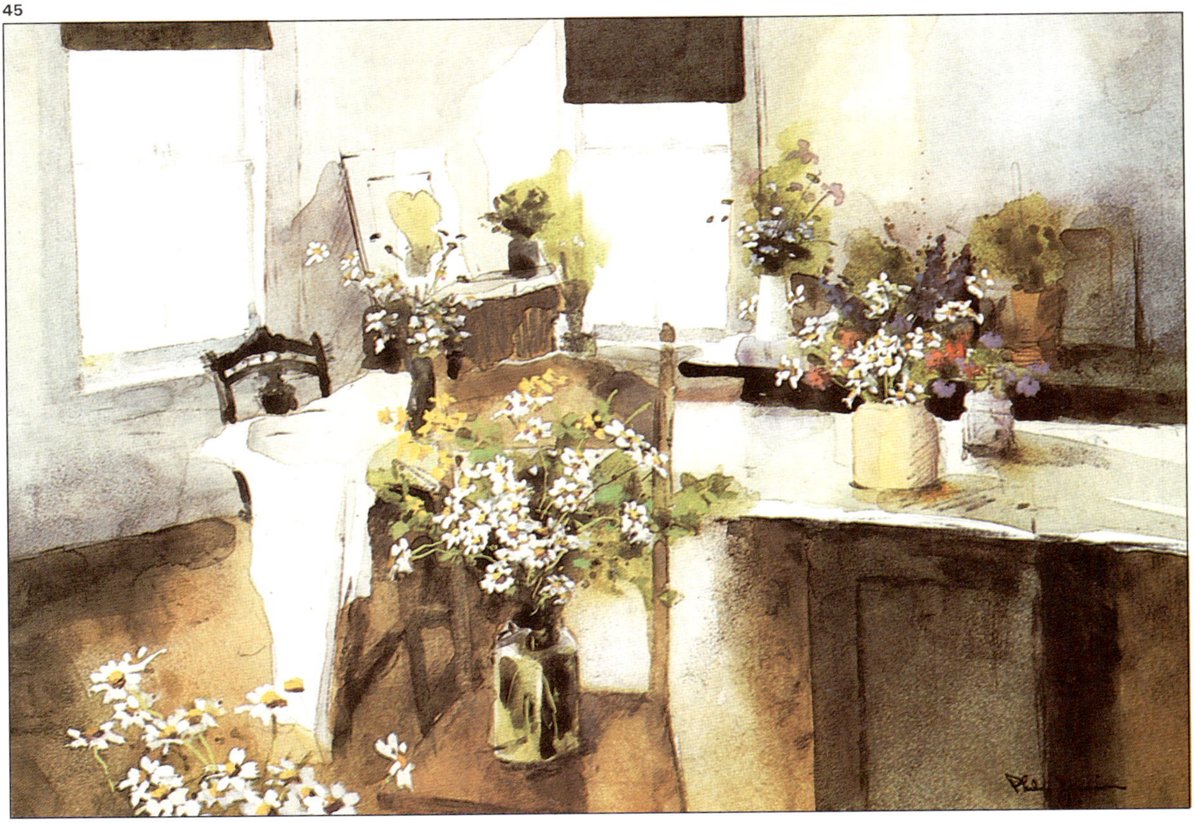

Ballestar, Martínez Lozano, and Plana Sicilia: contemporary watercolorists

Among the numerous and extremely varied tendencies that comprise contemporary watercolor, the pictorial styles of our three guest painters occupy a central position. Vicenç Ballestar, Josep Martínez Lozano, and Manel Plana Sicilia will illustrate their works in this book, and with their help you will be able to carry out the practical exercises. Although these painters are from different generations, they all share the same passion for watercolor.

Vicenç Ballestar's work has been exhibited in many different countries. His extraordinary mastery of drawing, combined with his great pictorial sensibility, is reflected in watercolors of a refined linear sense and color. Ballestar has developed a cultured and restless personality, always in search of new themes that he can adapt to his pictorial universe. The artist paints as much in oil and pastel as he does in watercolor. But his mastery of the watercolor medium has enabled him to treat all themes in an equal manner. To his high standing as a painter we can add his personal charisma as a teacher in the Society of Watercolorists of Catalonia.

Josep Martínez Lozano is a prestigious artist. He has received more than forty awards and has exhibited his work in many countries. He possesses an extraordinary creative capacity. Martínez Lozano works mainly with oils and watercolor, and in both mediums he has developed his own characteristic style, a vigorous and daring brushstroke, which he combines with his special technique, based on transparent areas and washes of incredible expressive potential. He is an innovative and creative painter par excellence who places technique at the service of his acute color sense and freedom of expression.

The works of Manel Plana Sicilia reflect his particular interpretation of themes that can be denominated as traditional (still life, urban landscape, and so on) which in his hands acquire a new and personal meaning. Plana's work is a testimony to the artist's constant search for new formulas, innovations, and renovations. Plana interprets reality with daring compositions and points of view, using a direct technique. The artist has been awarded countless prizes, among them the 1980 National Watercolor Prize, and his work has been exhibited in many European cities.

Fig. 46. Vicenç Ballestar (1929-), *Horses in the River*. Private collection. This is an outstanding work for its richness in details and color shading. These factors, however, do not in any way reduce the impact of the forms' profile and volume.

46

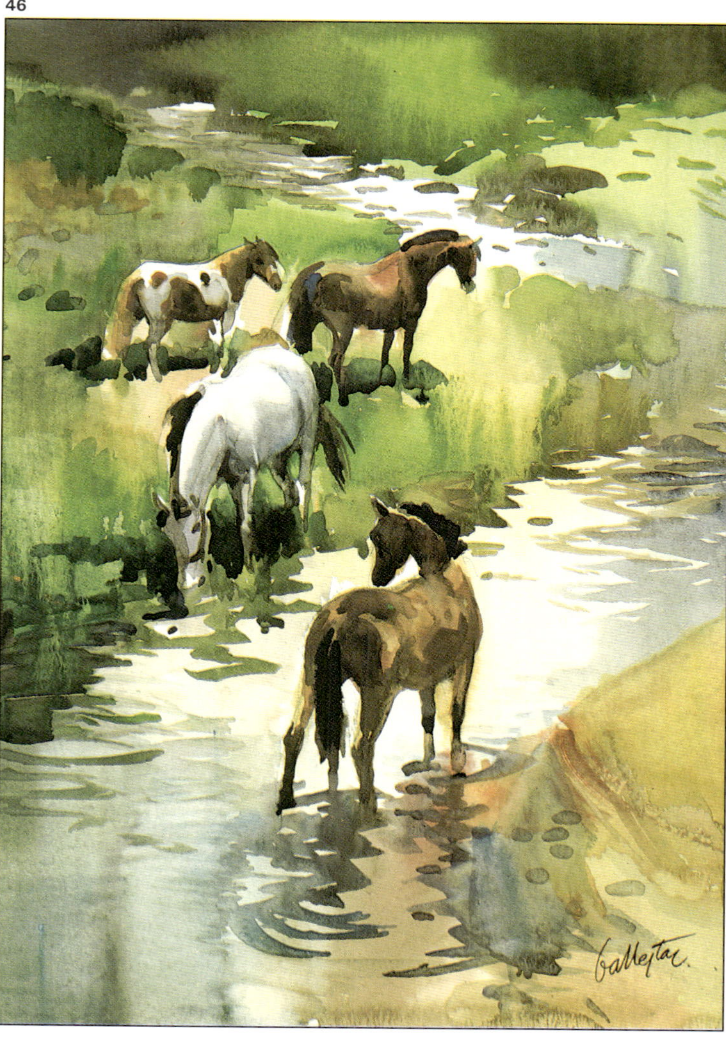

47

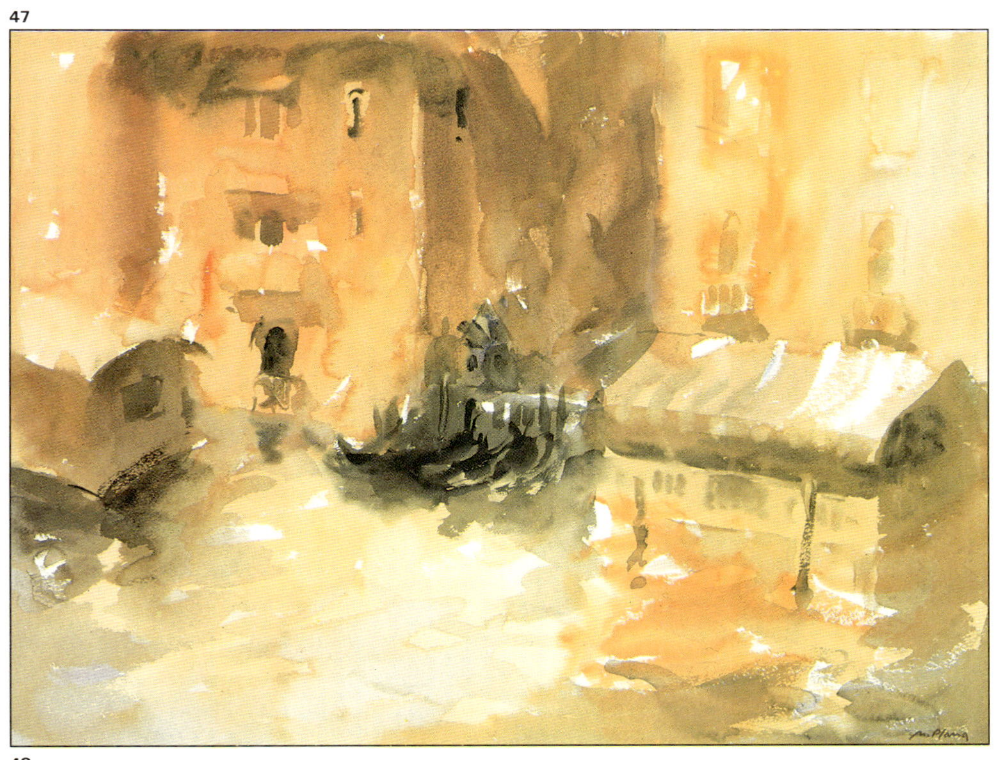

48

Fig. 47. Manel Plana (1949-), *Venetian Canal*. Private collection. The atmosphere, the free brushstrokes, and the bright colors evident here are omnipresent in all of Plana's works.

Fig. 48. Josep Martínez Lozano (1923-), *Fishing Harbor*. Private collection. Lozano's creativity is especially noteworthy in his inventiveness with form and color.

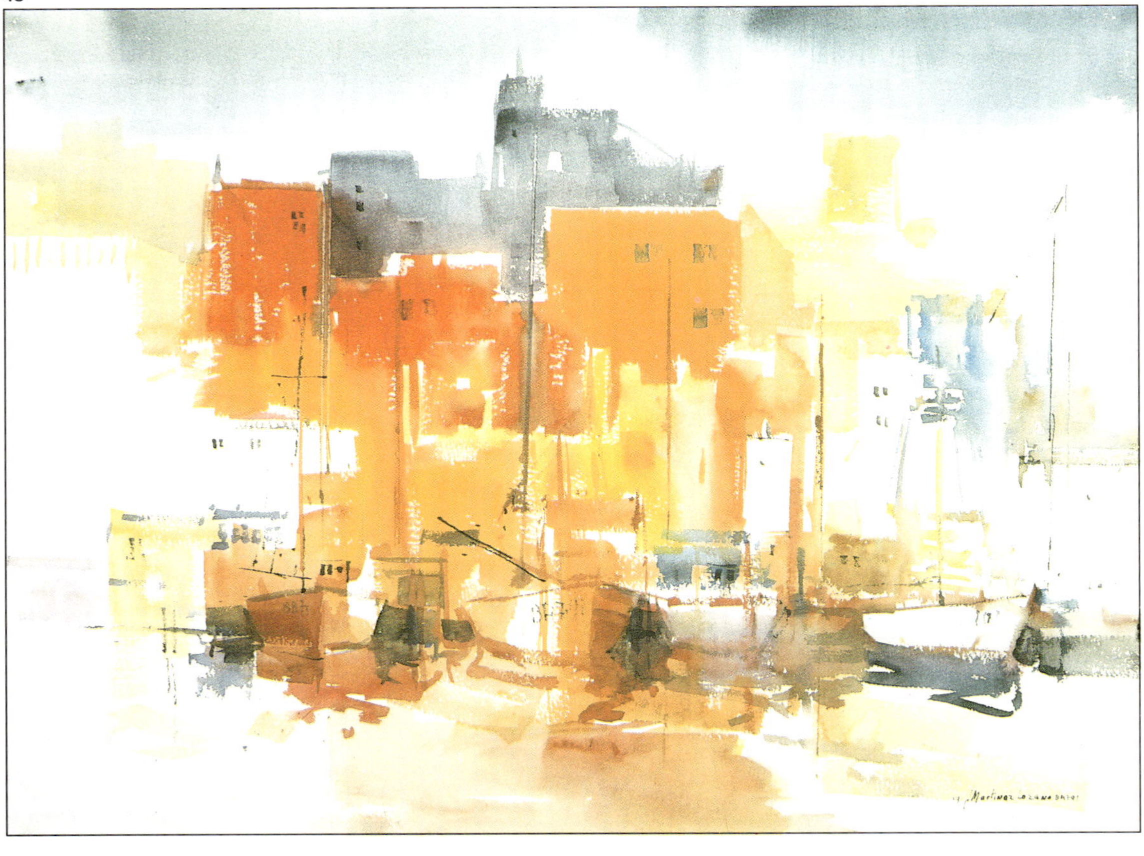

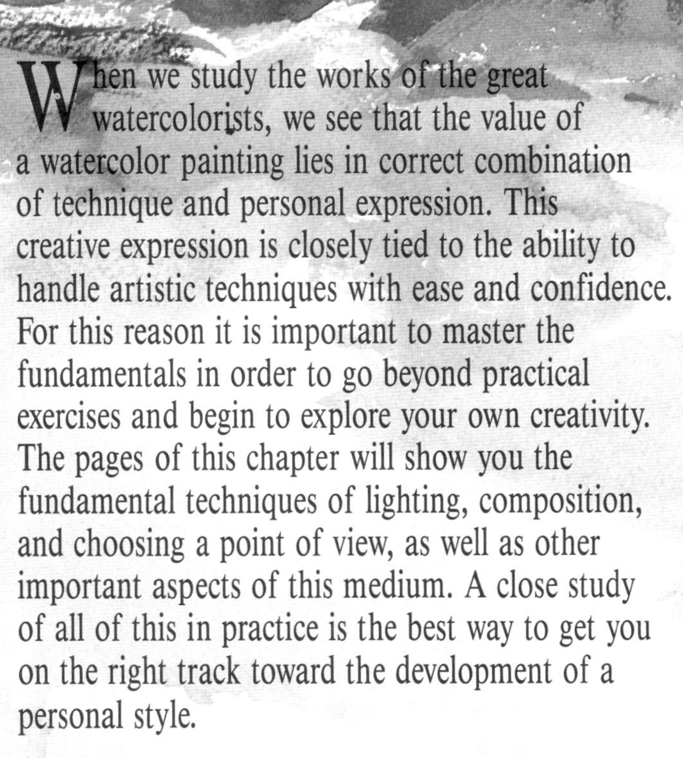

When we study the works of the great watercolorists, we see that the value of a watercolor painting lies in correct combination of technique and personal expression. This creative expression is closely tied to the ability to handle artistic techniques with ease and confidence. For this reason it is important to master the fundamentals in order to go beyond practical exercises and begin to explore your own creativity. The pages of this chapter will show you the fundamental techniques of lighting, composition, and choosing a point of view, as well as other important aspects of this medium. A close study of all of this in practice is the best way to get you on the right track toward the development of a personal style.

How to develop creativity

Visit museums

See actual works of art by great masters. Visit art galleries as often as you can, and generally take advantage of occasions that allow you to see painting. This is the best way of learning how to see and understand all the factors entailed in a composition, such as form and color. Furthermore, we don't look at all pictures with the same pictorial interest: sometimes we are more concerned with the composition and on other occasions the peculiarity of the forms or the color may attract attention, so there is always a possibility of discovering new and interesting elements in a painting. Again, I must stress the importance of seeing the paintings themselves since there is no better way of seeing and appreciating the quality of a brushstroke, glaze, and texture, such details that can only be seen from close up. The technical and creative aspects acquired from these visits can only help to enhance our work—and other people's work is always a source of inspiration to help us work with greater enthusiasm.

Fig. 49 (preceding spread). Manel Plana (1949-), *Two Boats (Fuenterrabia)*. Private collection, Barcelona.

50

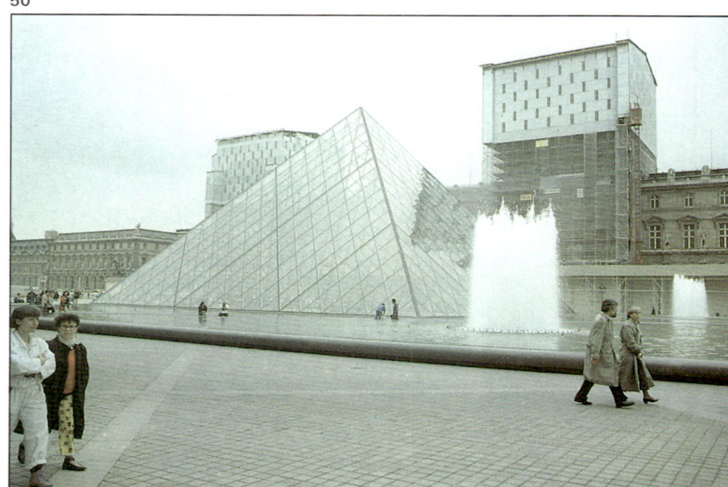

51

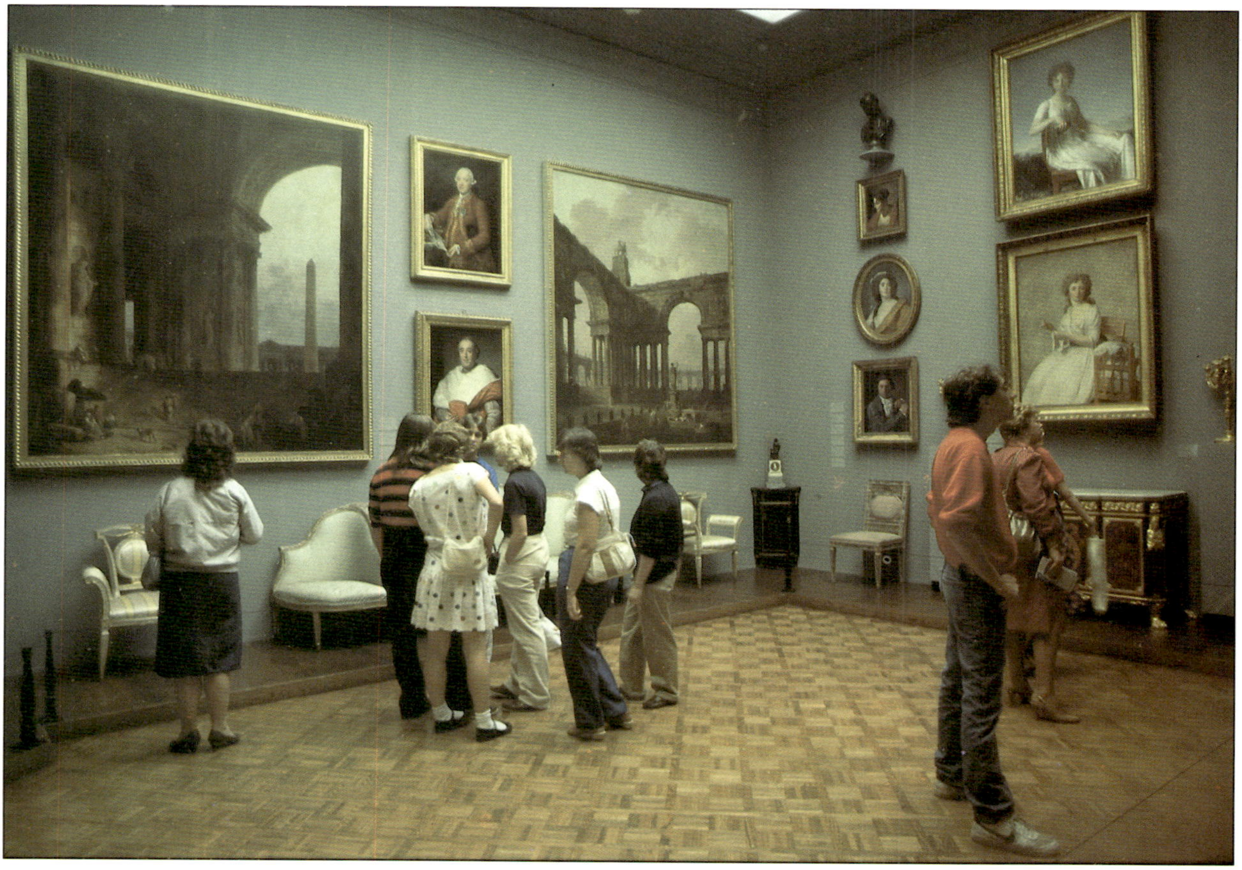

Look at books and reproductions

Fig. 50. Exterior view of the Louvre Museum. The biggest museums house masterpieces of all styles. A visit to these museums is always a help and stimulus.

Fig. 51. View of one of the exhibition halls in the Chicago Art Institute. (Photo: A.G.E. Fotostok.)

Fig. 52. We recommended that you get a good set of illustrated art books, as well as a series of postcards or individual reproductions, which can be bought in all museums. They will enable you to study and better understand how artists from past to present have realized their works.

Not everyone can visit museums and expositions so easily, especially those who live far from big cities. But everyone has the possibility of acquiring books with quality reproductions of paintings. Try to obtain books of a large format (such as 8½×11″, or 22×28 cm) whose reproductions are big enough so that you can see and study the works reproduced. You may find these books to be somewhat expensive, but they will be extremely valuable work tools, so consider them an investment. Also, think about buying a good universal history of art, which will help you to study all the themes, techniques, mediums, textures, and styles of the great masters, from classical to contemporary artists. Such a book will help you see and analyze all the genres: landscape, human figure, still life, and so on. Also consider acquiring books about your favorite painters (van Gogh, Cézanne, Matisse, Vlaminck, or whoever) so that you can analyze their style, use of color, and color harmony in an attempt to apply such factors to your own paintings.

Clearly, it is never the same to study a photographic reproduction as it is to stand before the original: Something of the original is always lost, especially the notion of the exact size of the real work. But there are many advantages to having books. The works are always available for study, and many of the works in books are difficult for the general public to gain access to because they are in private collections or in museums very far off the beaten track.

A good collection of art books can be complemented by high-quality prints. Besides providing a much more detailed reproduction, prints are invaluable for carrying out copying exercises or pictorial interpretation—something highly recommended for all those who really want to learn from the great masters.

All important museums sell posters that reproduce all or most of the paintings on display, and many of the paintings reproduced in such posters are rarely illustrated in art books. It is always advisable to buy one or two whenever you visit a museum; they are not very expensive and the reproduction quality is often very high.

52

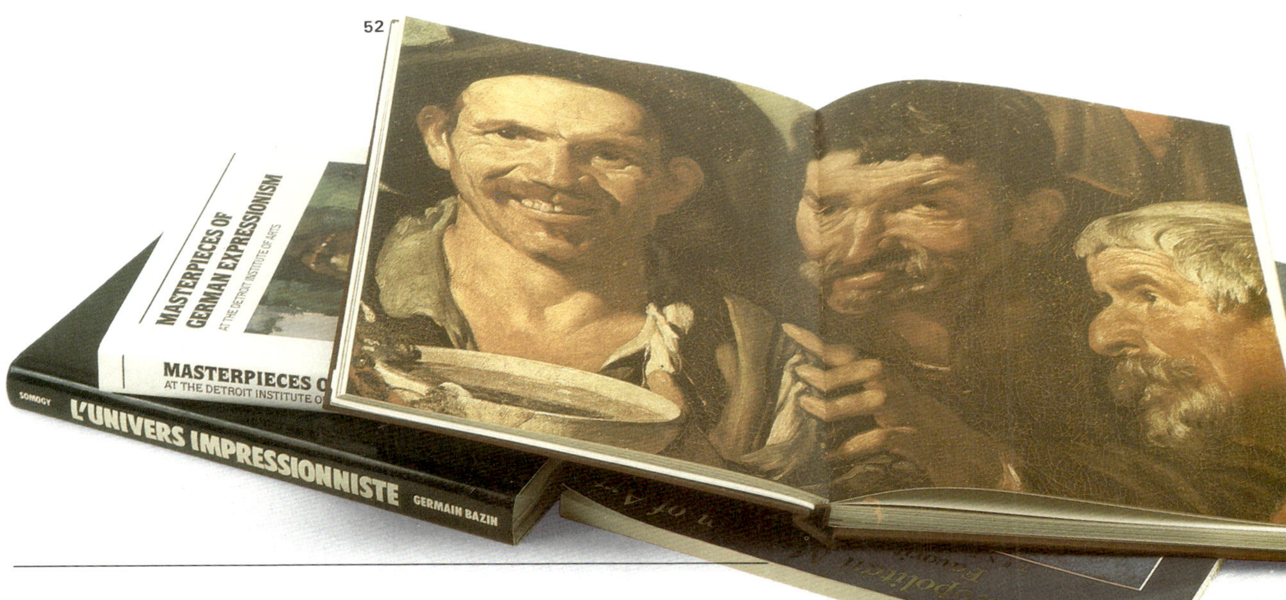

Study and draw

Creativity does not depend so much on *what* to paint as on *how* to paint it. Pictorial themes and motifs have been repeated over and over again throughout history, with differences and preferences according to the moment. But what really characterizes a painter's artistic quality is his or her personal vision and capacity to develop this vision in a picture. This is precisely the moment where creativity comes into play. Having said this, we have to face up to one important fact: The only way to acquire a personal vision is by studying and practicing the medium. As Degas said: "The drawing is not a form, but our way of seeing the form." We could also express the principle of creativity thus: The drawing allows the form to be understood; such is its importance.

The practice of drawing is essential in the education of the artist. In academies of art, students are taught to draw the model from nature. This is an extremely satisfying experience and a useful exercise in understanding how to sketch in the forms of the subject, calculate their dimensions and proportions, and evaluate the light and shadow. All this carried out in the classroom in front of the live model. Of course, a model is not indispensable; any real form or object possesses infinite possibilities of interpretation. At home, on the street, in the country—in fact, everywhere we can find motifs to express our vision of form, our temperament and creativity.

Fig. 53. One of most important exercises in art schools is drawing the live model. The study of the human figure enables you to develop the basics of drawing (judging distances and values accurately, and so on) and is fun to do.

53

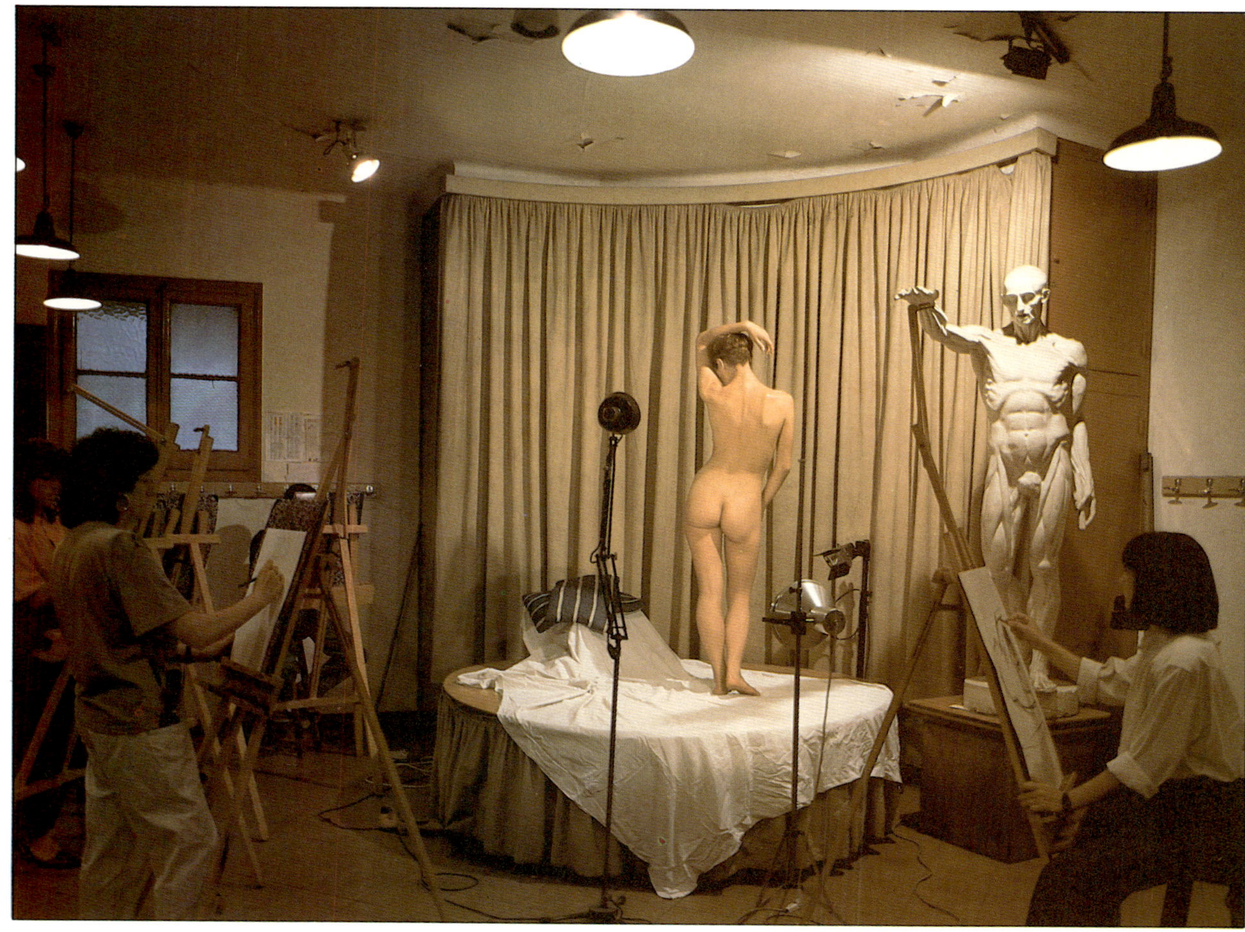

Study and copy paintings, reproductions, and prints

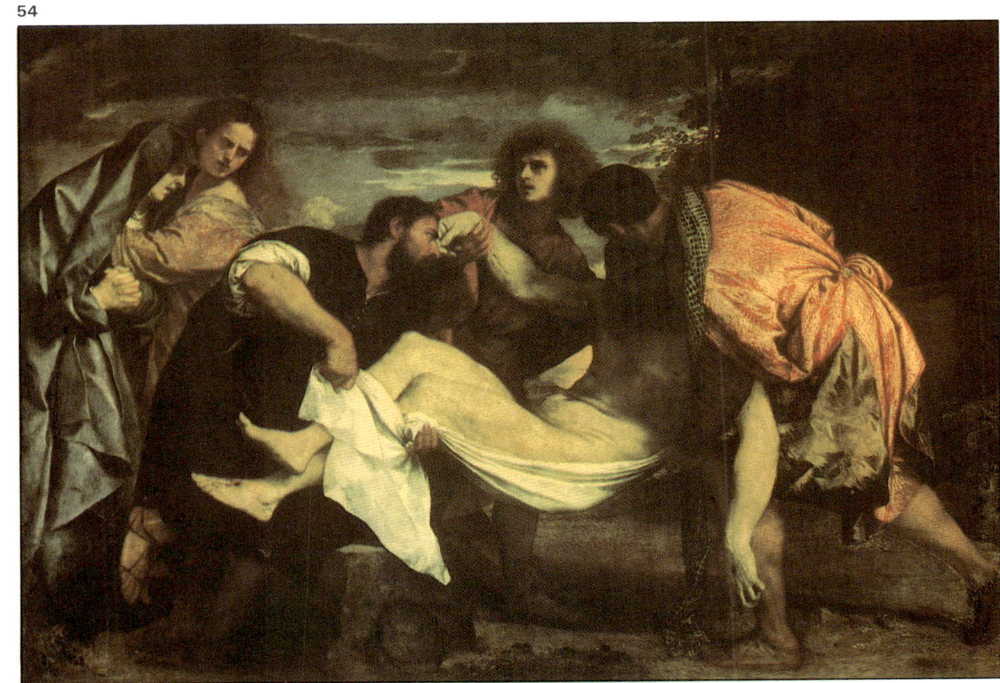

Fig. 54. Titian (ca. 1488-1576), *The Entombment*. Louvre, Paris. Copying the works of the great masters is an enriching exercise that all great painters have done at one time or another.

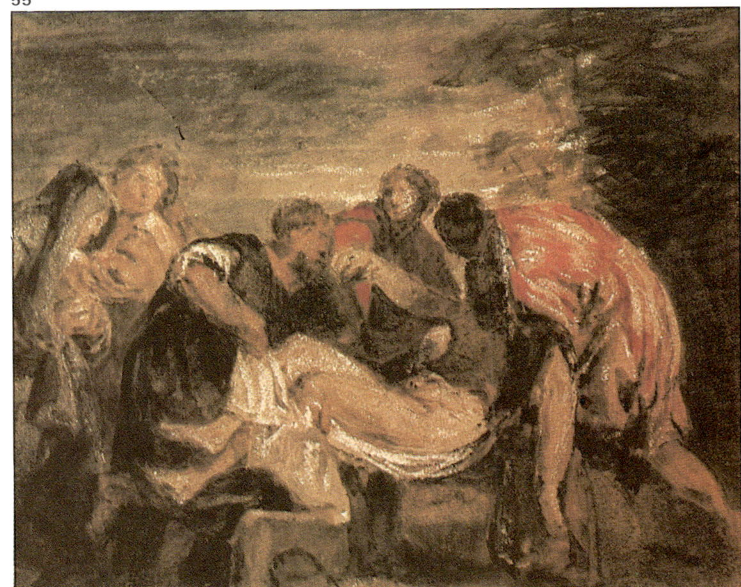

Fig. 55. J.M.W. Turner (1775-1851), *Copy of Titian's "The Entombment."* Clore Gallery, Turner Collection, London. The young Turner copied Titian's magnificent work in watercolors. Copying the works of the great masters is very helpful for improving your knowledge of composition, color, and the tonal evaluation of great works.

It is extremely important to study works by the great masters for their educational value. One good way to do this is to sketch paintings. This can be done at home, from reproductions, or at a museum or exposition. All you need is a drawing pad to capture them based on an analysis of composition, chiaroscuro, color range, and so on. If you want to go one step further and copy the work, it is possible to do so at the museum, having obtained prior permission, which is not so difficult to acquire. Of course, you could also paint a copy at home from a quality reproduction.

Remember that, during their youth and even later on in life, all these great masters have painted copies of other people's works as study exercises. The impressionists often reverted to copying paintings in museums to enhance their knowledge from the great masters of the past. Manet went to Madrid to copy Velázquez's paintings; Cézanne was a habitual visitor to the Louvre; van Gogh copied works by Millet and Delacroix, as well as collecting and studing prints and etchings of other artists. Copying the works of other artists does not necessarily mean renouncing you own style; on the contrary, it is a stimulus, a lesson, and a source of personal enrichment.

Plato's rule

56

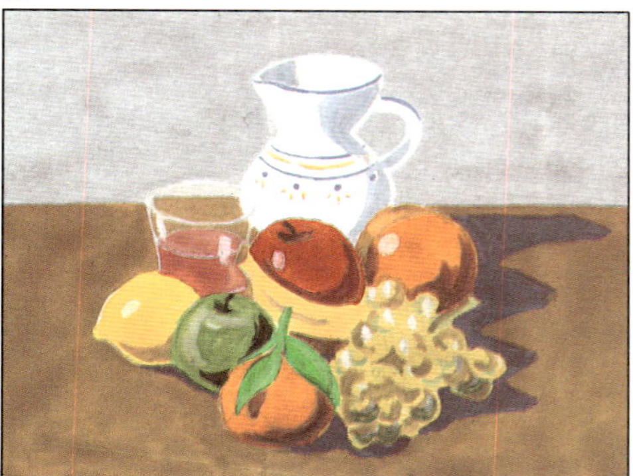

57

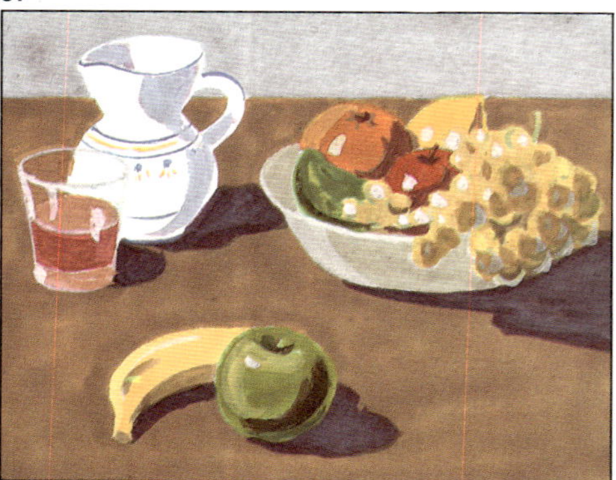

58

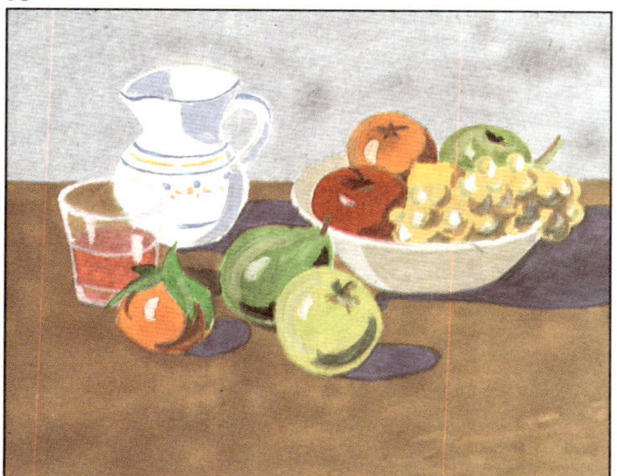

Certain rules of balance and beauty can be used to organize a composition. A faithful reproduction of the motif is not enough for a successful picture; there must also be an agreeable arrangement of the painting's elements. How can we work out a composition so that it appears neither fractured nor monotonous? The great Greek philosopher Plato explained the secret of composition to one of his disciples in a few simple words:

> "You have to find unity within variety and variety within unity."

When confronted with the task of composing a painting from a natural motif, beware of the undefined number of forms, colors, and hues, which need to be arranged to obtain an attractive work. Any excess in order will lead to monotony; too little order will result in fatigue when contemplating an unorganized array of elements. So, *unity within variety* has to be taken into account.

There is also another basic rule of composition, whose graphic explanation can be seen at the foot of this page. The problem is this: Where should the main elements of the work be placed on the pictorial surface?

Figs. 56 to 58. Here are three examples that clearly illustrate Plato's rule. According to the Greek philosopher, for an area divided into unequal sections to be agreeable and aesthetic, there should be unity within variety. Too much unity (fig. 56) creates monotony that bores the viewer. Exaggerated diversity (fig. 57) is distracting and makes a chaotic composition. Figure 58 shows a composition that respects Plato's rule.

59

Fig. 59. The places where the lines meet on the adjoining diagram show the golden points, those locations where the most important elements of a composition should be placed. When you want to find the golden section for your composition, multiply each side cf your canvas by 0.618 and then draw the lines to find the golden points.

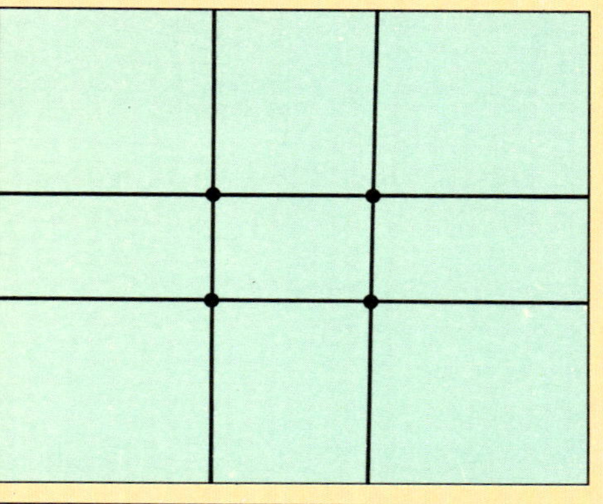

The solution is very old and is found in a geometrical and arithmetical formula, first in Pythagoras (sixth century B.C.) and later in Euclid (fourth century B.C.). We are talking about the golden section or golden mean. The great writer of architectural treatises, Vitruvius (first century B.C.), expressed the section solution thus:

> ''For an area divided into unequal sections to be agreeable and aesthetic, there should be the same relationship between the larger section and the whole as between the smaller and larger sections.''

Throughout time, pictorial works have obeyed the golden section in the distribution of the composition, whether consciously or by the artistic instinct of the painter.

60

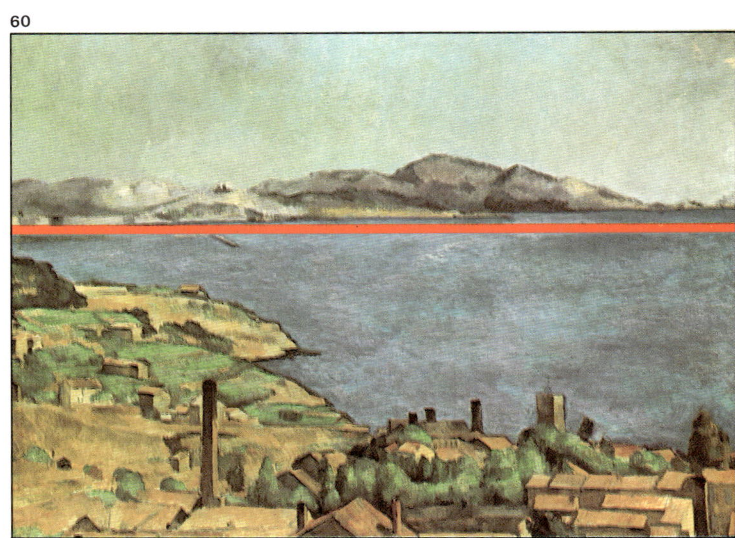

61

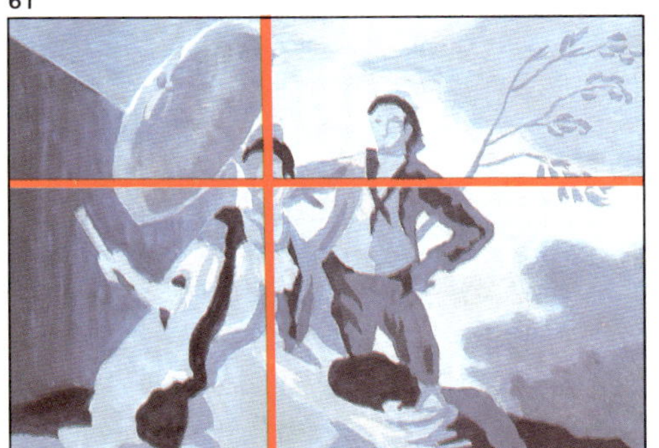

Fig. 60. Paul Cézanne (1839-1906), *The Gulf of Marseille*. Metropolitan Museum, New York. The horizon line of this landscape is positioned exactly on the golden section of the canvas. The artist probably did this by intuition, not by previously calculating it.

62

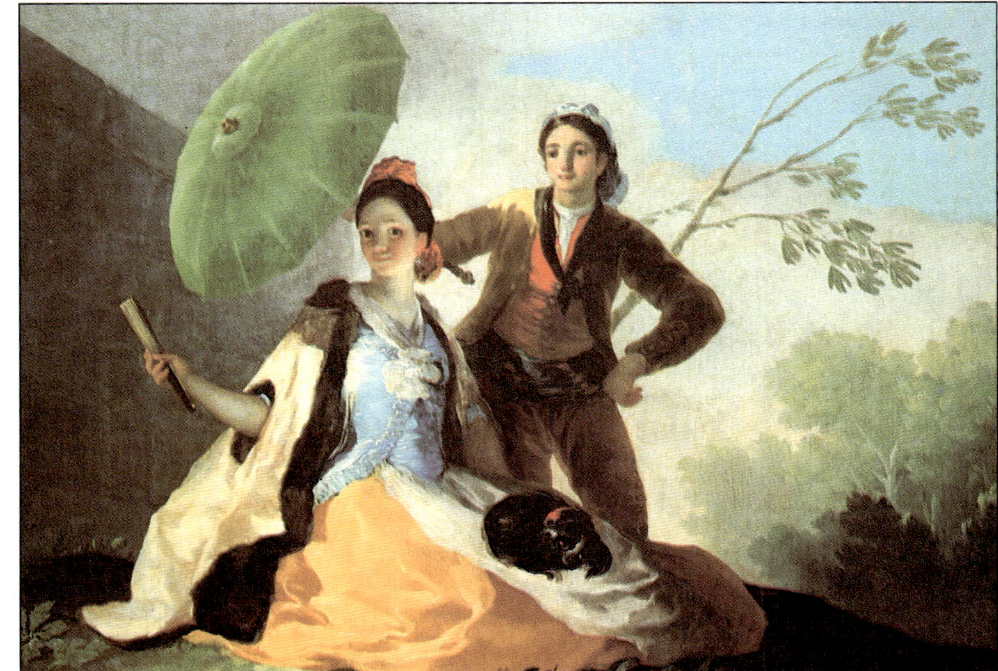

Fig. 61. This value sketch (from fig. 62) clearly demonstrates how Goya situated the female figure, and especially her head, where they will recieve the most attention from the viewer. The woman's head is at a golden point, corresponding to the intersection where two of the golden sections meet.

Fig. 62. Francisco de Goya (1746-1828), *The Parasol*. Prado Museum, Madrid.

Composing by geometric forms

Figs. 63 and 63A. Vicenç Ballestar (1929-), *The Medas Islands*. Private collection, Barcelona. The compositional scheme of this watercolor is defined by the horizon.

Figs. 64 and 64A. Manel Plana (1949-), *Beached Boats*. Private collection, Fuenterrabia. This simple theme gains special interest thanks to its diagonal composition.

The principle of the golden section, which we have just studied, is not the only link between painting and geometric forms. On the contrary, there is an intimate relationship between pictorial representation and geometric regularity. This is especially evident when confronting the problems of composition. It has been proven through experiments that a geometric form appears more attractive than an irregular one.
What the artist must have in mind is that it is necessary to find the geometry in the guise of the elements and apply it to the painting. The straight lines, the angles, the arcs, and so on are all *there*. You must simply konw to find them and, as is graphically demonstrated in the watercolor painting on this page, organize your work by using them.

63

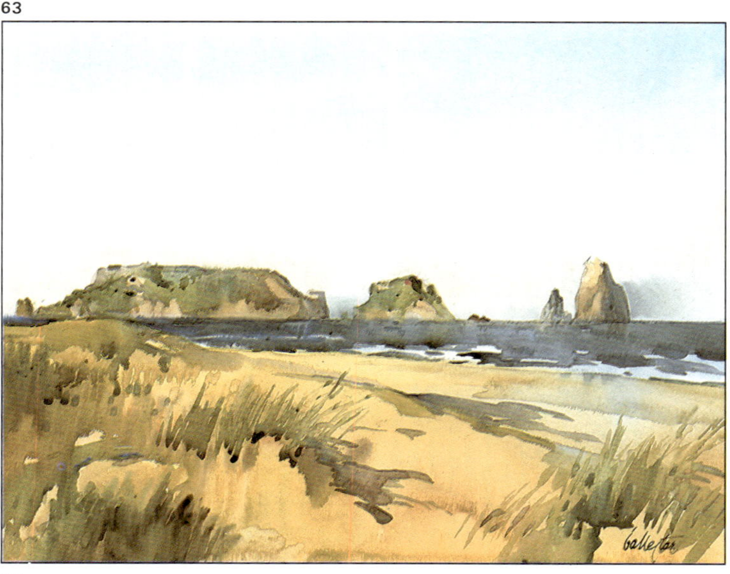

63A

64A

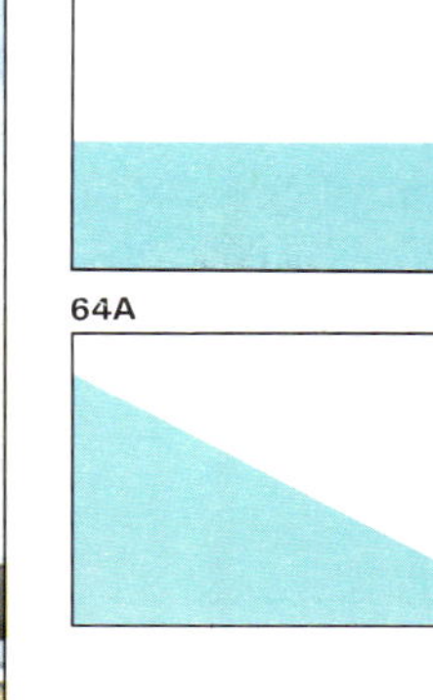

65A

Figs. 65 and 65A. Vicenç Ballestar, *Landscape after the Rainfall*. Private collection, Barcelona. This compositional scheme exaggerates the perspective, and the forms are ordered according to the lines of the bend in the road.

64

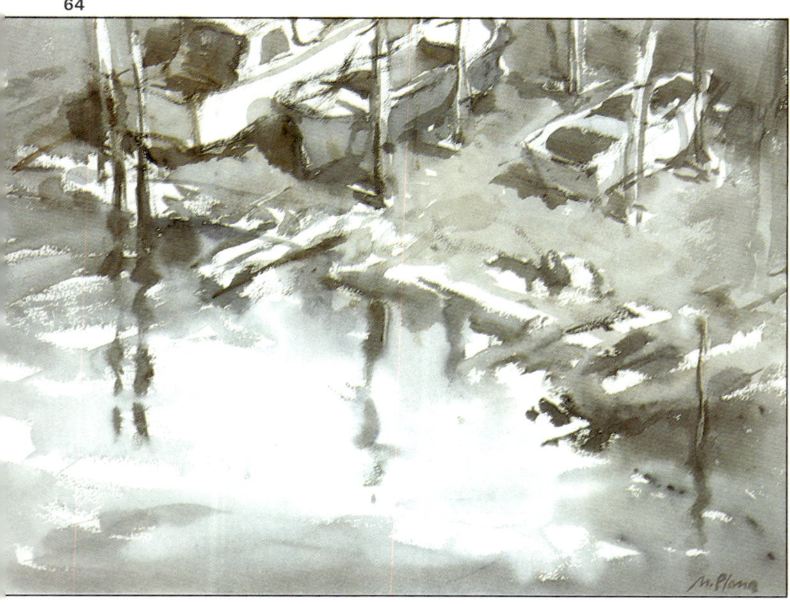

65

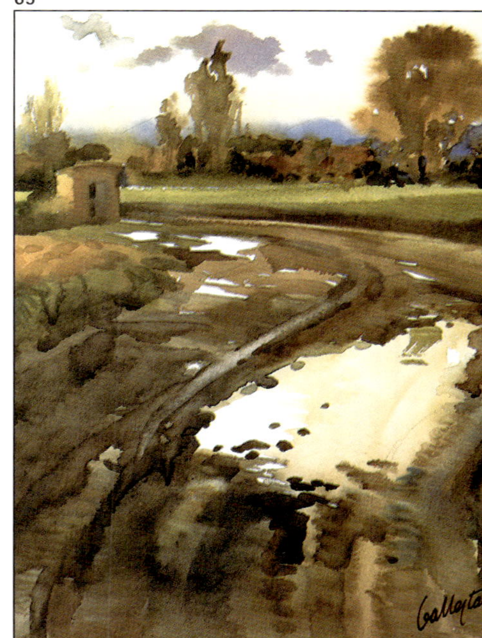

... and by masses

When we speak of masses, we are referring to the zones of light and shade that are seen in general, creating an abstraction of the details, that make up the picture's whole. You yourself can check it out by observing a painting while squinting your eyes: Having lost the definition of the forms and contours, you will be left with a general aspect of the picture's light and dark zones. To organize and balance the masses of a painting, we must take a number of factors into account: the size of the zones in relation to others, the distance separating them, and the different degree of lightness or darkness that each of these zones possesses.

The two watercolor paintings reproduced on this page are excellent examples of compositional balance obtained by means of the balance of the masses.

Figs. 67 and 67A. Manel Plana, *Borredá Square*. Private collection, Burgos. This watercolor is a fine example of balance and compensation of masses.

66A

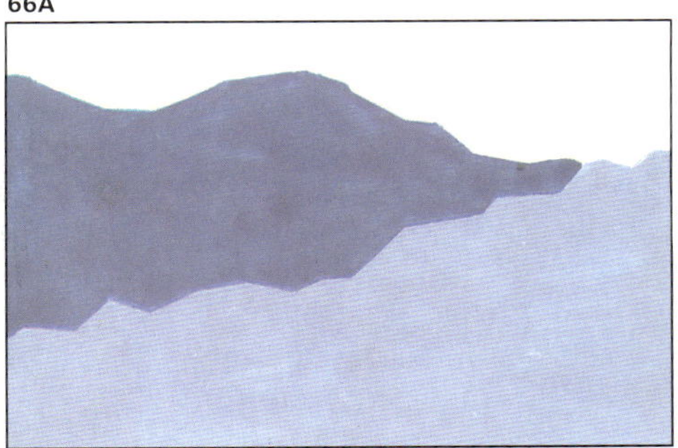

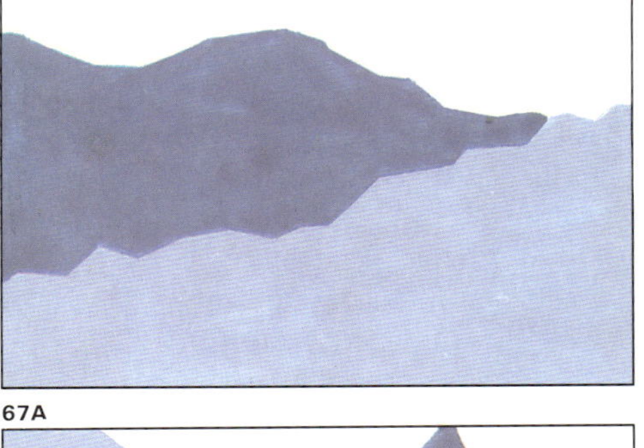

66

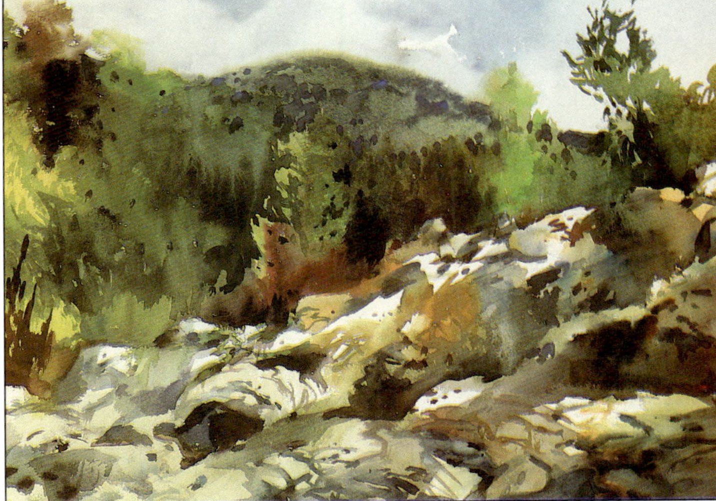

67A

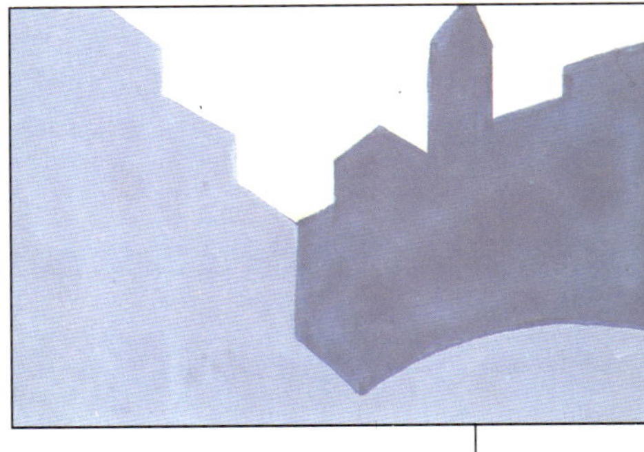

67

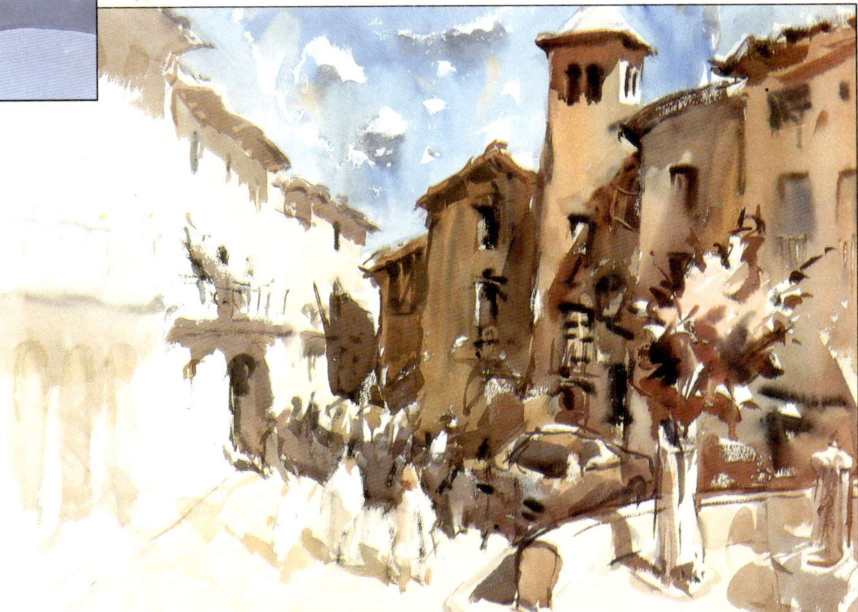

Figs. 66 and 66A. Vicenç Ballestar, *The White Rocks*. The foreground of this watercolor has been resolved with warm and light colors that form a great mass, contrasting with the darker background, painted with cool tones.

Composition in practice: Manel Plana paints a still life

68

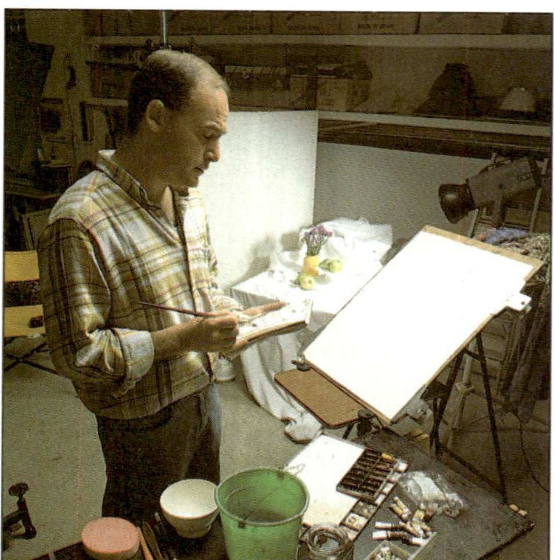

Fig. 68. Before beginning the actual painting, Manel Plana does studies in watercolor using the point of the brush, in order to consider all the possibilities the composition has to offer.

This is what the still life will comprise: two apples and two pears, a plate and a glass of water, and a small jar containing some dried flowers. A white tablecloth underlines the sobriety of the theme. Few objects, few colors. It's enough for Manel Plana.

Plana displaces one piece of fruit, moves the glass, and pauses; he contemplates the composition. He turns the glass over and places the plate on top of it: an improvised fruit bowl. A pear and an apple are placed in the fruit bowl and that's it. Plana begins to paint.

Before anything else, he does a sketch (fig. 68), a small study to act as a guide, a rough outline of the composition. Plana chooses to balance the masses, placing the small jar on one side and the fruit bowl on the other. The two pieces of fruit placed on the right break the symmetry of the arrangement.

Having decided on the composition, the painter stains the paper with confidence, almost without thinking about it. The forms appear among the color staings: an oval stroke expresses one of the fruits, a few green brushstrokes represent some leaves (fig. 69); and the tablecloth is interpreted with thick and agile strokes, us-

69

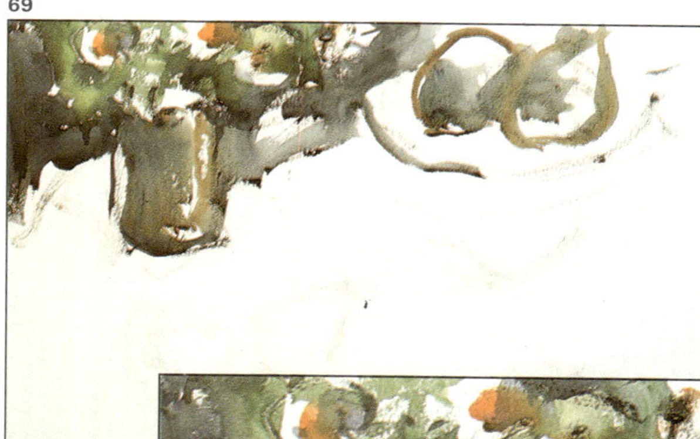

70

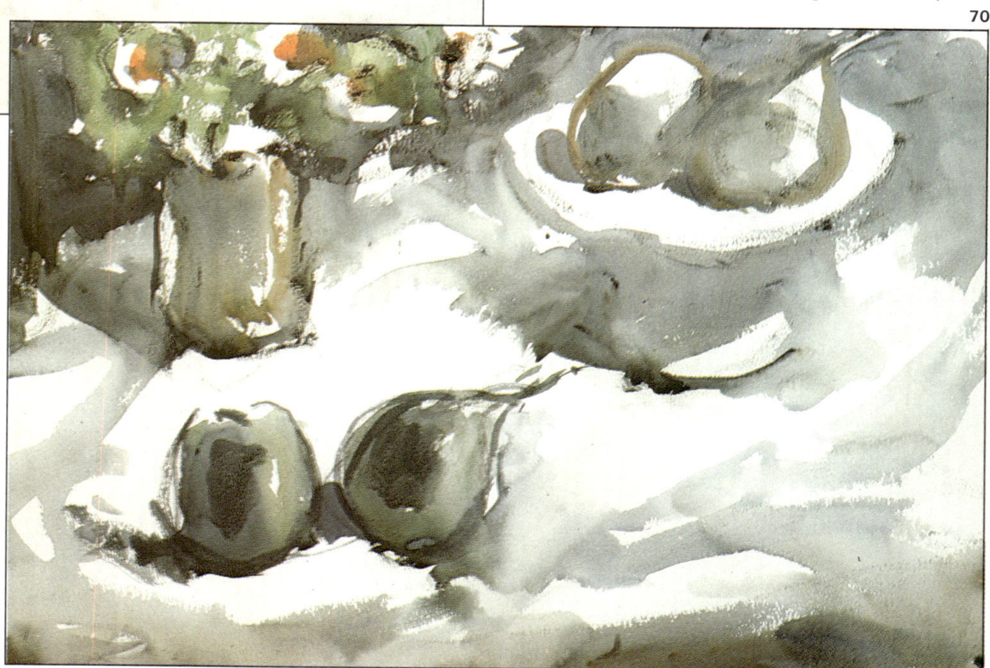

Fig. 69. The oblong format of Plana's first watercolor favors a horizontal composition. The artist has cropped the motif in a way that will place the fundamental masses in the top part of the paper.

Fig. 70. The lightness of the stains in the final product is characteristic of the painter's style.

ing a transparent, subtle gray that enriches the monotony of the white (fig. 70).

Plana takes up a new piece of paper and places it in a vertical position. He is ready to begin a new composition, from a new point of view. This time the still life itself occupies only a small area of the top part of the paper; Plana reserves the rest for the combination of lights and shadows on the part of the tablecloth hanging off the table. This second still life will be different from the previous composition: The flowers do not appear, and all the objects are much closer to the edge of the table (fig. 71). Note how Plana accentuates the rim of the bowl, even suggesting by use of highlights the existence of a slightly scalloped edge (fig. 72). (Observation and creativity come from the same hand.) A large stain outlines and expresses, in contrast, the tablecloth dangling over the table edge. The central white are is the scene of magnificent and brave brushstrokes, which give Manel Plana's painting so much energy and intensity (fig. 73).

71

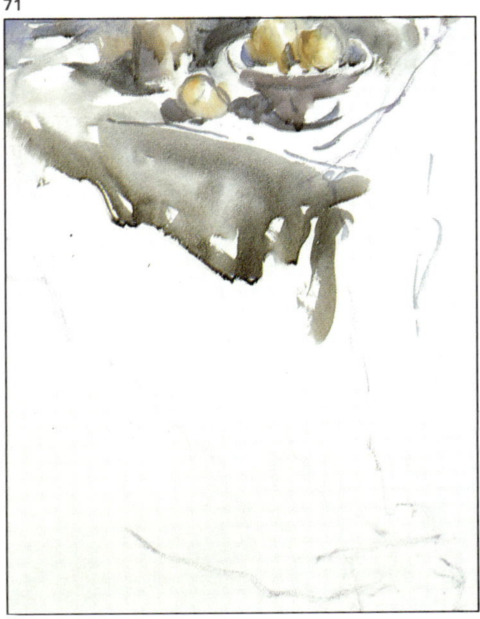

Fig. 71. The composition of this watercolor has been cropped from a totally different angle from the previous one. Here Plana devotes nearly all his attention to the tablecloth, with its creases hanging over the side of the table.

Fig. 72. Plana paints as if he were sketching, but after he applies some large brushstrokes, the time has arrived for defining the form with a fine brush.

Fig. 73. This is what the final result looks like: a splendid watercolor for its color harmony and free technique.

72

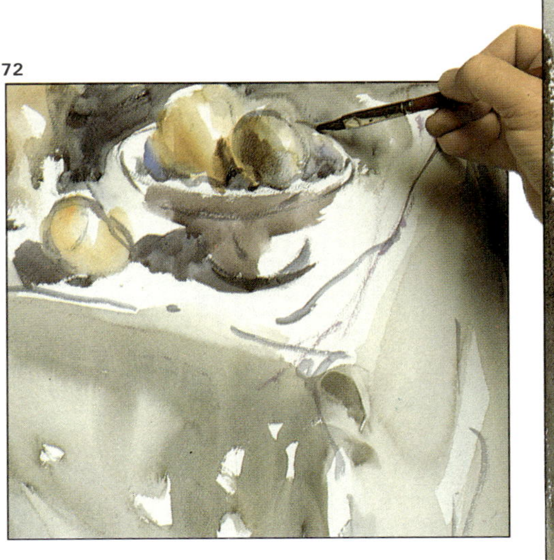

73

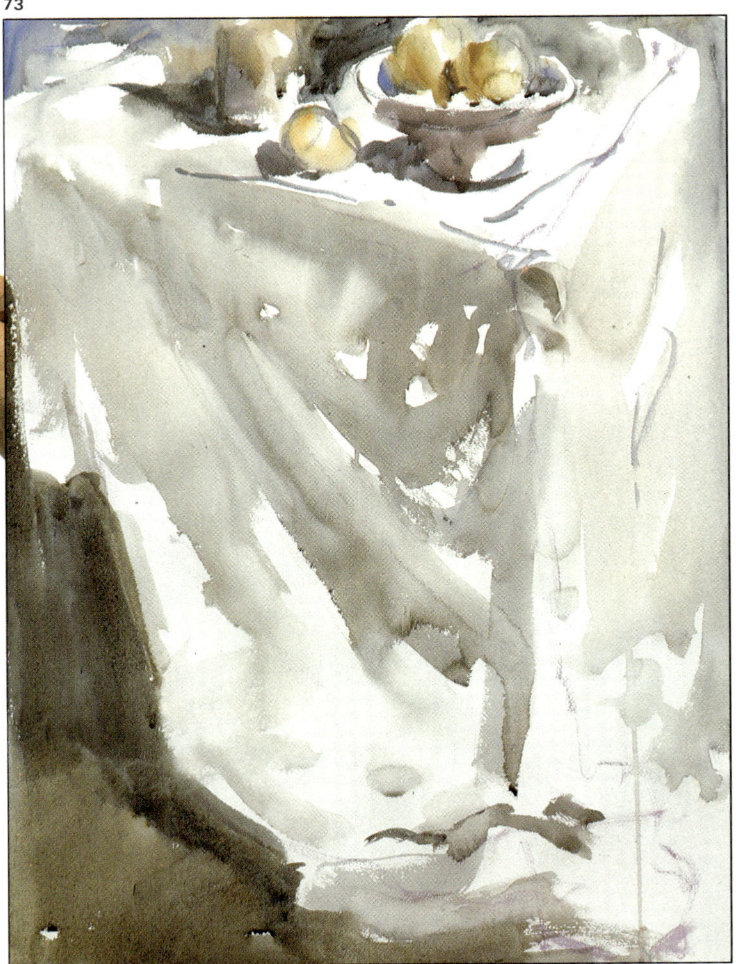

Choosing a theme

Until the nineteenth century, painting possessed a well-defined thematic repertory, and artists knew exactly what was worth interpreting. The artistic theme par excellence was the so-called historical painting, which involved the use of large formats to honor historical personages and their deeds. The nineteenth-century French writer Théophile Gautier defined these paintings as "monstrosities," because of their imposing format and theatrical nature. The scandal caused by the impressionist painting was mainly due to the fact that the themes were insignificant. The impressionists painted their immediate reality, exactly as it appeared before them. Anything was considered a potential theme.

The German romantic painter Caspar Friedrich said: "As long as it is felt, any aspect of nature can constitute an artistic theme." There is no such thing as a privileged theme, because the value of a motif lies in its effect on the sensitivity of the painter. The painter has to be awake, alert to everything that produces such an effect on him; this can happen with any subject.

Fig. 74. Vicenç Ballestar (1929-), *Boat in a Shipyard*. Private collection, Barcelona. What seems to be a rather unappealing theme can be converted into an original painting with great impact.

74

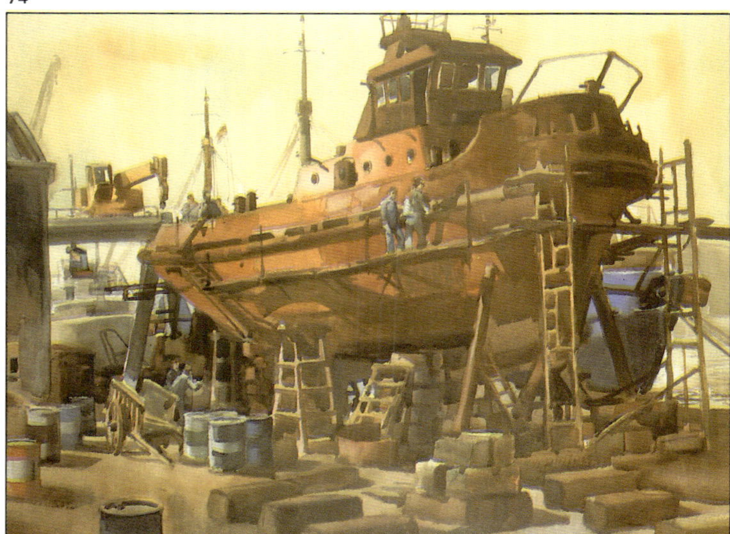

75

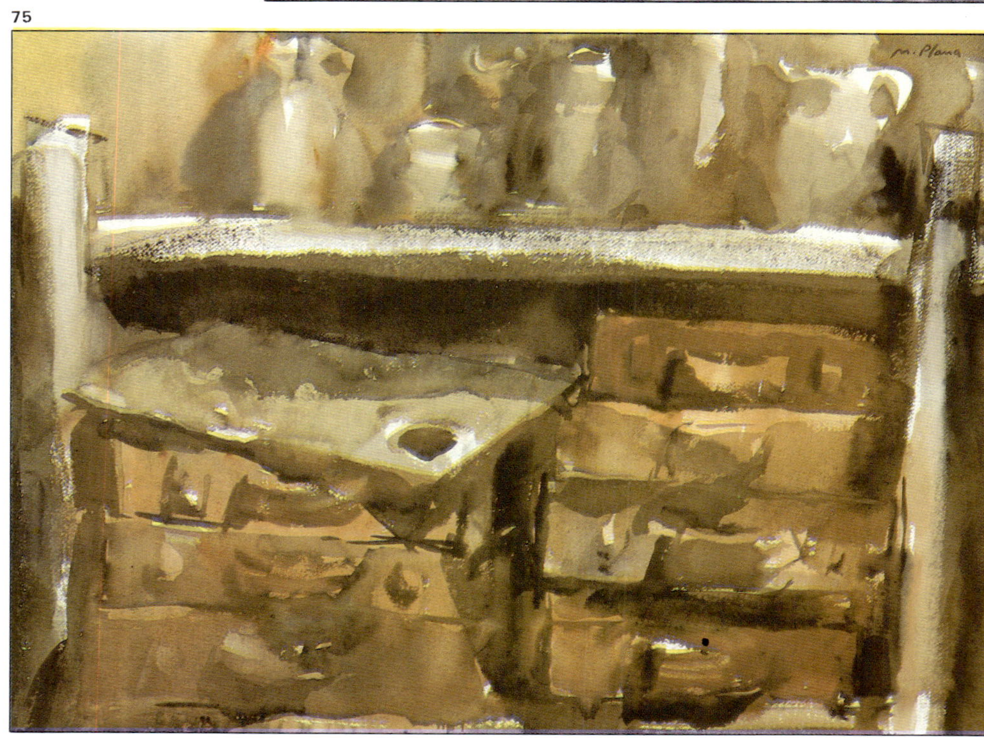

Fig. 75. Manel Plana (1949-), *Paintboxes in the Studio*. Private collection. It is not necessary to go far in search of attractive, suggestive themes. Plana painted this unusual "still life" in his own studio.

Finding the theme

76

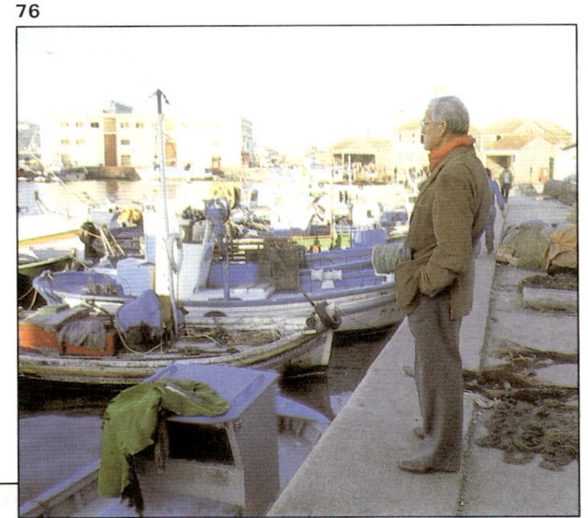

Fig. 76. The different possibilities of a theme must be studied carefully before you start to paint.

A fishing port, or even a commercial one, is a theme that is visually attractive and can stir the senses. Contemplating the panorama from the wharf, we see that the theme can be treated in very different ways, from which a great number of interesting subthemes can arise, such as boats, the sea and its reflections, the fishermen at work in the port, and so on. This is the moment that spurs creativity: walking around, discovering different points of view, new angles, and the varying possibilities of light effects. All this provides the artist with the possibility of creating a personal interpretation—in fact, when you mull over possibilities for paintings, you are already "painting." Before commencing, however, there are a series of basic factors that you must be aware of, without which nothing in the port can inspire you. We are talking about the basic knowledge of cropping or framing, lighting, and color contrast that we will shortly study.

77

78

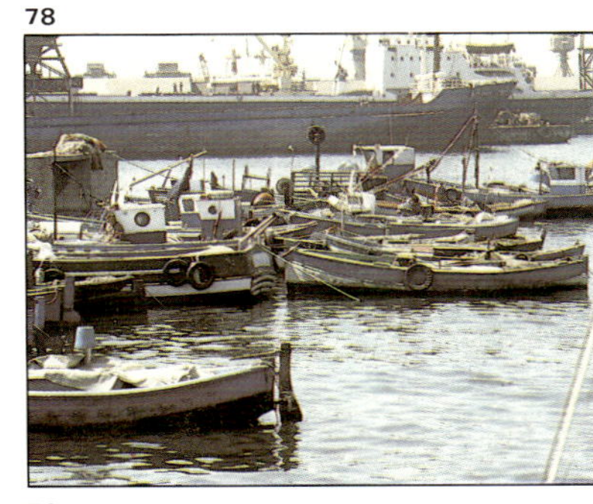

79

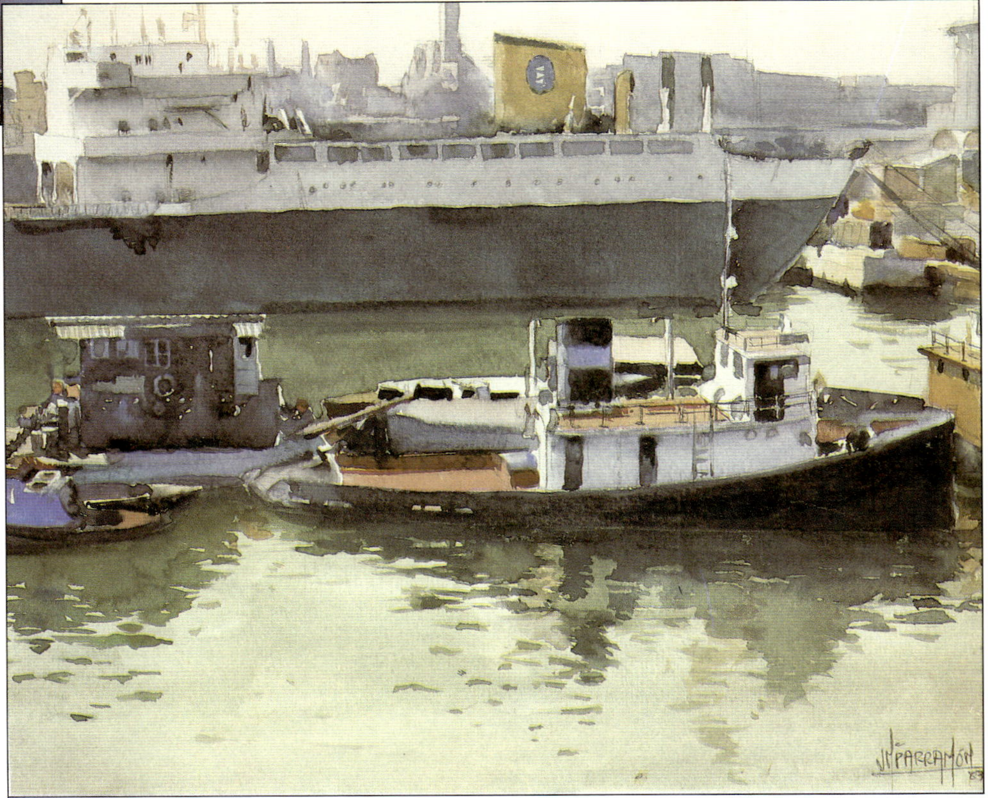

Figs. 77 and 78. A port can provide the artist with a multitude of pictorial themes: the boats, reflections on the water, the fishermen, and so on. The moment you start to look for the best composition or point of view—the moment you study the different effects of light or decide what color range would be best—you are using your creative resources to realize a personal interpretation.

Fig. 79. José M. Parramón, *Towing in the Port*. Private collection, Barcelona. Parramón has resolved this picture by using horizontal planes to organize the space in a clear and simple way.

The point of view

A natural motif consists of many motifs at the same time. Saint Victoria mountain was painted many times by Paul Cézanne, but every canvas is different; the profile of the mountain is never the same, the landscape around it changes from one picture to another; the point of view is different.

Knowing how to choose the best point of view from the countless possibilities is essential. It all depends on the work's visual beauty, given that every natural motif has a characteristic aspect, a facet that is most relevant and of greatest interest.

When you choose a point of view, the first thing to take into account is the distance between you and the model. If it is excessive, the theme will lose its impact, being lost in the vast space around it. If, on the other hand, the distance is too short, it will be easy to make mistakes in the proportions and sizes of the picture's elements, since your view is distorted by the lack of distance. Try to find the place that will enable your point of view to compose the painting correctly; don't hesitate to move around until you find the spot.

80

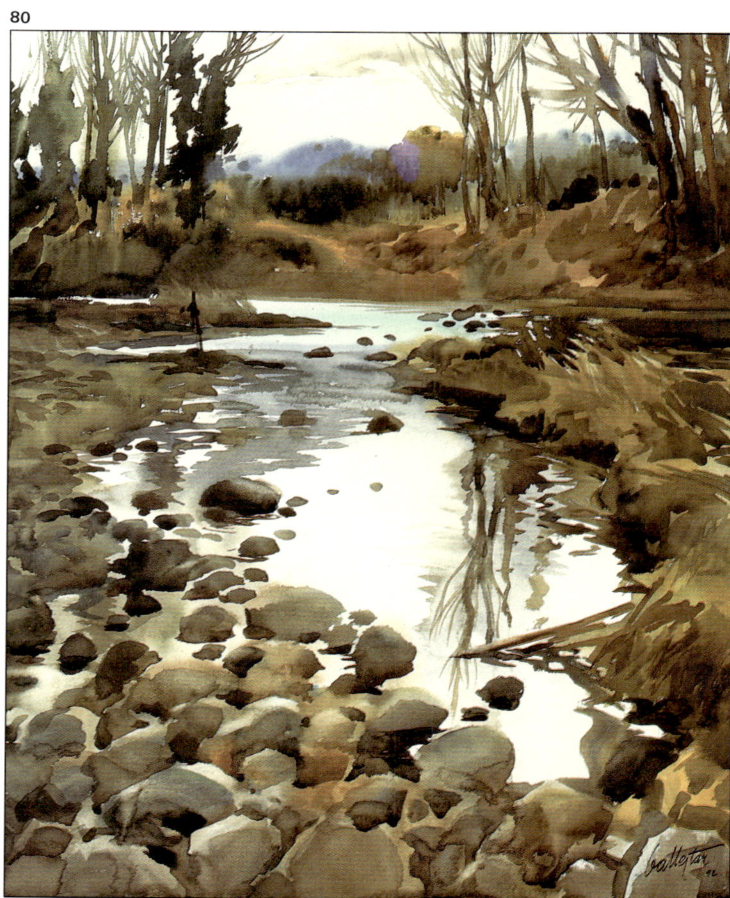

81

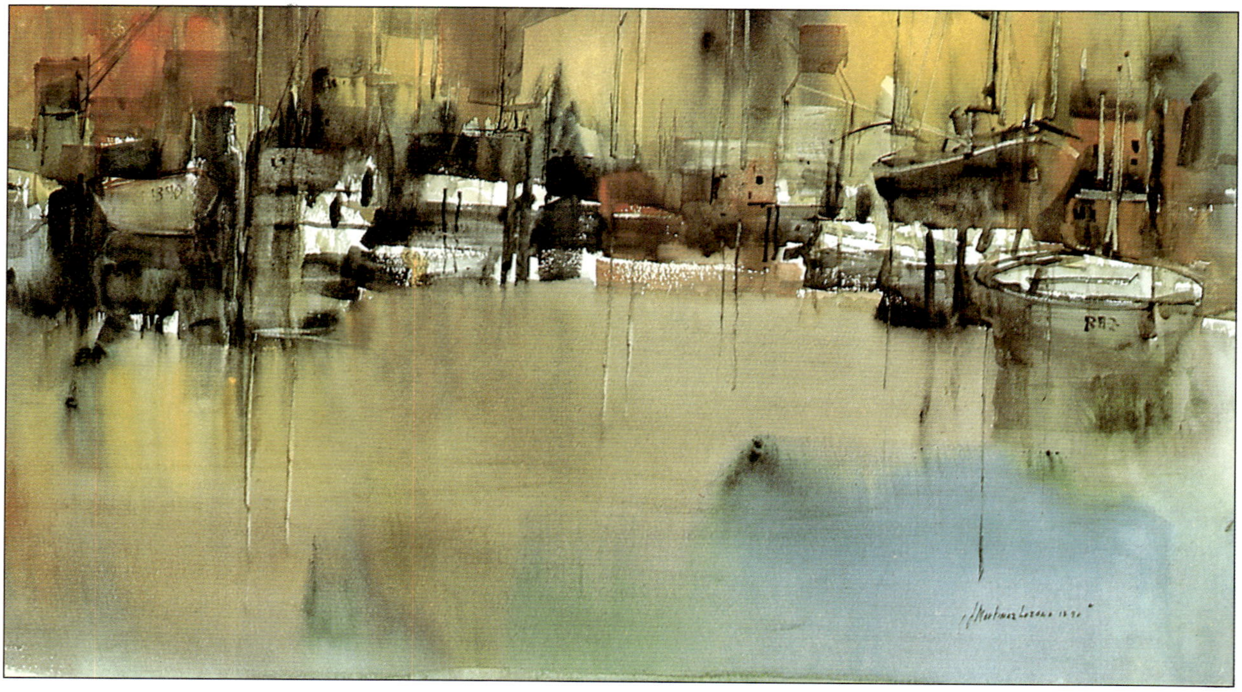

Don't be tempted to paint the first reasonable view you come across. When deciding on a point of view, you must also take into account the disposition of the different planes that make up your picture. Sometimes it is a question of situating an object in a strategic place. For example, in a landscape painting, a tree situated in the foreground is an ideal reference point from which to establish the other distances of the composition; Cézanne repeatedly used this technique. Look for unconventional creative points of view with a striking foreground, such as from a higher elevation. The examples on these pages give you some ideas about how to do this. Ballestar uses a vertical format (fig. 80) to obtain a point of view in which the foreground takes on the greatest importance; this enables him to compose the watercolor on the basis of the succeeding planes, thus achieving depth in the picture. Martínez Lopez (fig. 81) highlights the importance of the sea's surface and its reflections by painting from an elevated point of view.
Elevated points of view allow countless expressive possibilities. In the case of an urban landscape painted from a certain height, such as this one by Plana (fig. 83), the use of diagonal lines that form the streets produces a panoramic sensation of great pictorial interest.

Fig. 83. Manel Plana (1949-), *Zorilla Square*. Private collection. Plana reinterprets the most traditional themes in a totally personal way, as in this urban landscape painted from an elevated point of view.

82

83

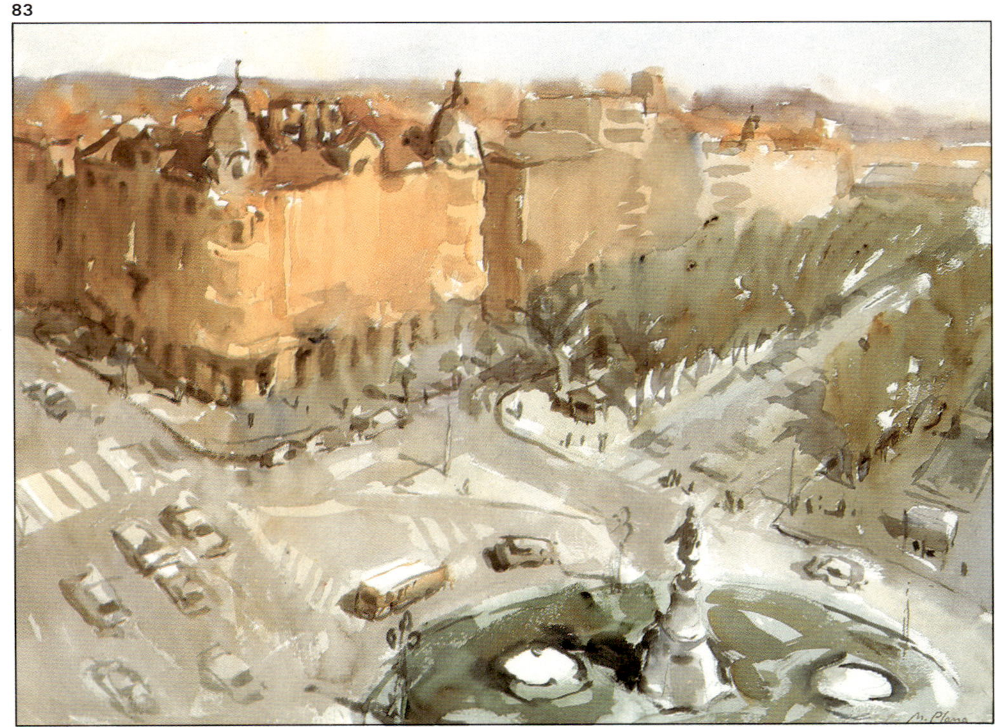

Fig. 80. Vicenç Ballestar (1929-), *River Ford*. Private collection, Barcelona. The artist chose the point of view at the same time he was organizing the composition's different planes.

Fig. 81. Martínez Lozano (1923-), *Seascape*. Private collection. By elevating the horizon line, Martínez Lozano accentuated the importance of the sea in the foreground.

Fig. 82. Martínez Lozano, *The Village of Llançà*. Private collection. A landscape interpreted from a bird's-eye view allows the forms, perspective, and atmosphere to be dealt with using less conventional means.

The direction of the light

There are four kinds of light: frontal lighting, frontal-lateral lighting, lateral lighting, and backlighting.

In frontal lighting the light illuminates the model from the front and reduces the shadow to a minimum; this produces a sensation of less volume and depth in the model, but on the other hand, accentuates the local color. This is the type of lighting that favors colorism—that is, the relevance of color in detriment to the volume and chiaroscuro.

Frontal-lateral lighting proceeds from a 45-degree angle, highlights the model's volume, and gives it a more natural relief. This type of lighting is excellent for representing lifelike forms. Lateral lighting provides a great deal of contrast between the model's illuminated side and the one in shadow, thus producing an intense, dramatic effect that is always present in baroque tenebrist works. It is ideal for practicing chiaroscuro and tonal values. We talk of backlighting and semi-backlighting when the model is situated between the light source and the observer, creating a silhouette of the model against the background. This type of lighting produces a loss of volume and leaves the subject surrounded by a romantic halo of light.

Figs. 84 to 87. Here are four classic possibilities of lighting that notably change the appearance of this bust of Socrates: frontal lighting (fig. 84); frontal-lateral lighting (fig. 85); lateral lighting (fig. 86); and backlighting (fig. 87).

84

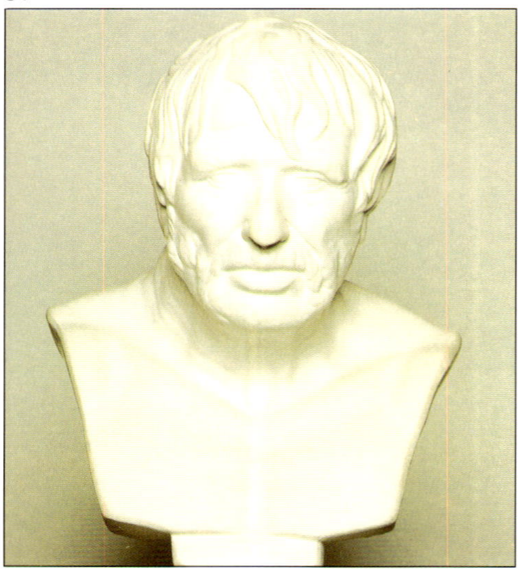

85

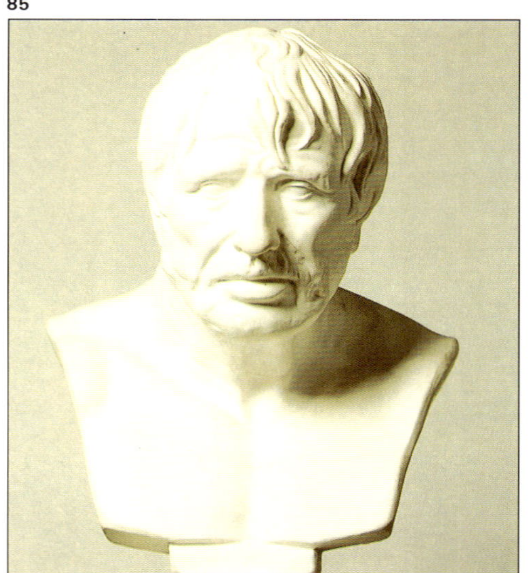

86

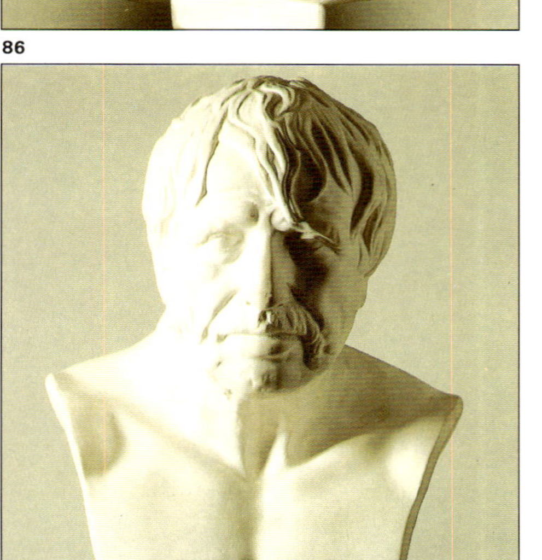

87

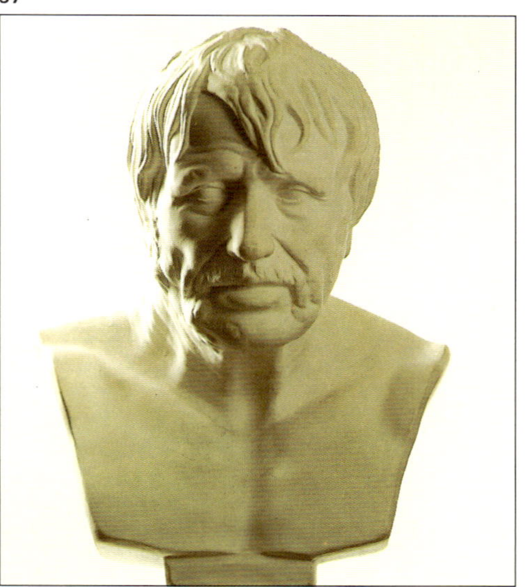

The quality of the light

Figs. 88 and 89. Direct light hardens the model's forms and accentuates the contrast of tonal values (fig. 88), while diffuse light on the same model brings out the volume without contrasts, softening the contours and transitions of the chiaroscuro.

The model will appear differently according to the intensity of the light that illuminates it (soft, intense, weak, and so on). For this reason, the interpretation of the values, the contrast, and the chiaroscuro differ greatly from one type of lighting to another.

Direct lighting concentrates its beam directly onto the model, clearly highlighting the model's forms, profiles, and details, and thus eliminating chiaroscuro to a large extent. Generally speaking, any type of artificial lighting, such as spotlights, bulbs, and screens, can be considered direct lighting as long as they are beamed directly onto the subject. Diffuse lighting illuminates the model by softening its contours and the borders between lighted areas and those in shadow. It is the light of a cloudy day, for example, or a source of indirect artificial light, softened by a screen.

There is another type of light that can also be considered for its quality: zenithal lighting, the best kind for drawing or painting. This light illuminates the model from a 45-degree angle, from a height of approximately 6½ feet (2 meters. This type of lighting can be achieved with both artificial and natural light, by way of a window through which direct sunlight does not penetrate. Finally, there is another factor to take into account when illuminating the model. The *quantity* of light (whether small of great) can change the model's appearance considerably, giving it a sensation of intimacy when the lighting is particularly weak, or a sensation of vitality and action when it is intense.

88

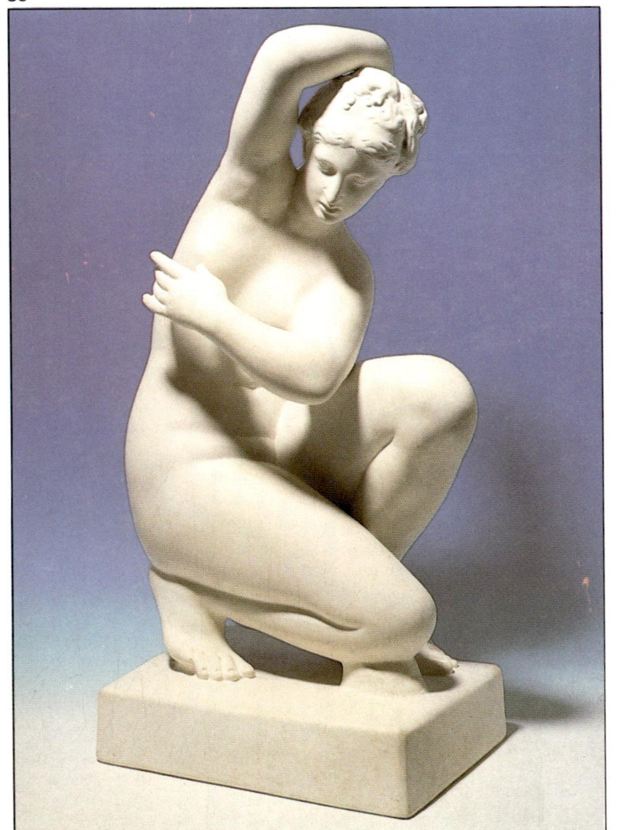

89

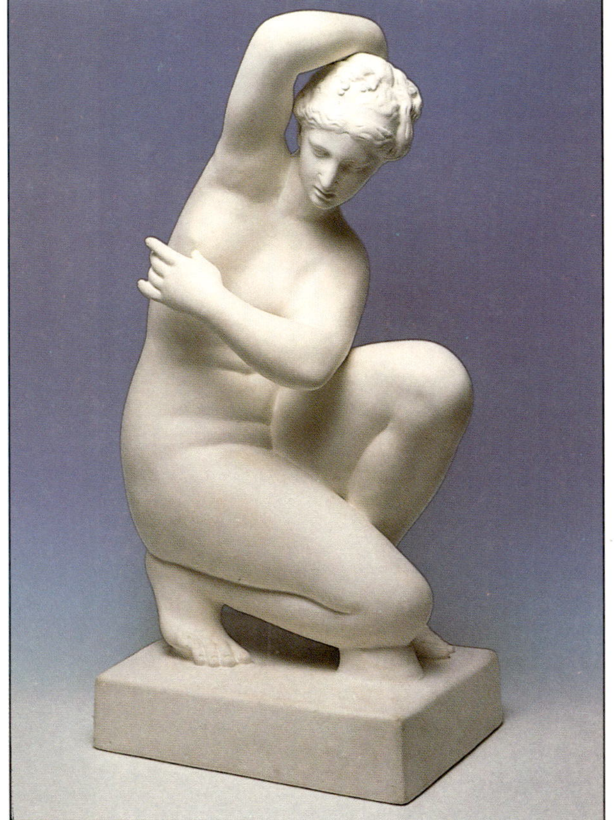

Expression with light

Light can be a formidable means of expression because of its inherent psychological associations. There is a series of very general associations between different types of light and feelings or moods. When we study the illumination of a picture, we have to take these psychological implications into account, which when well used can produce a powerful expressiveness in our works.

The most important aspect of such a psychological interpretation lies in the direction of the light. Frontal lighting, as we have already said, is the best way of highlighting the local color of the objects, and at the same time it flattens them, depriving them of volume. This increases the expressive impact of the color. When color takes the leading role, it acquires a more subjective significance. This type of lighting best serves the expressionist and colorist styles, in which the color contrasts themselves construct the painting.

When a balance between color and form is desired, the most adequate types of illumination are frontal and lateral lighting; the first is ideal for expressing the forms in all their volume. It gives your subject balance and serenity, which "support" the theme, that is, explain it as near to reality as is possible. So frontal lighting is perfect for depicting what is seen, in the most objective and accurate way possible.

Something similar occurs in lateral lighting, except that there is a far greater chiaroscuro emphasis. This type of painting is called value painting. It is present in Baroque painting (Caravaggio, La Tour, and so on), as well as in academic painting.

The main characteristic of backlighting and semi-backlighting is their greater emphasis on atmosphere rather than on the model itself. With the model in the shade or in a light penumbra (partial shade), the poetic sense of the painting's forms are highlighted. Light directed from unusual angles (such as from above or below) provokes effects of great drama and expressiveness. Light from above impregnates the model with "mysticism" (think of the religious paintings of Murillo, Zurbarán, or El Greco); while light from below creates a sensation of mystery, terror, or magic. Both means of illumination produce a certain supernatural atmosphere.

Fig. 90. El Greco (1541-1614), *The Adoration of the Shepherds*. Prado Museum, Madrid. El Greco's personages are very strange in appearance thanks to the direct light, presumably from the Christ child, which modifies and deforms their features.

90

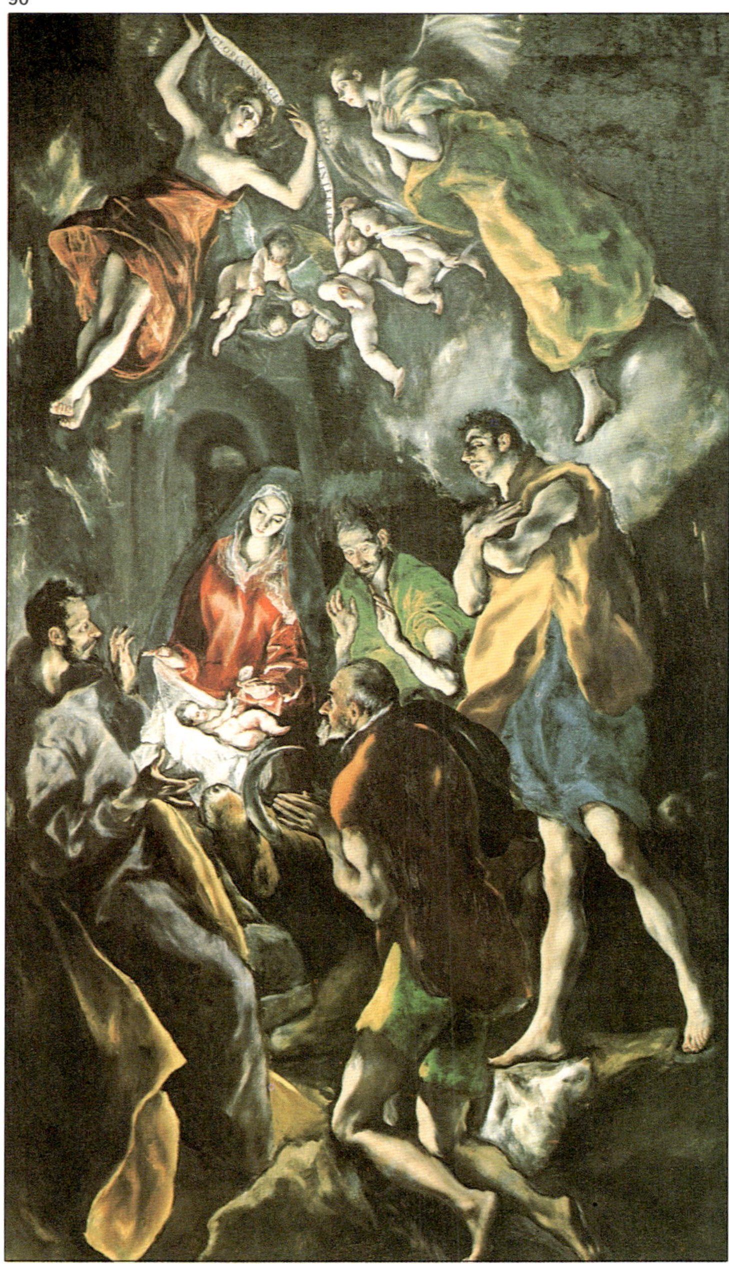

Fig. 91. Vicenç Ballestar (1929-), *Nude Woman*. Private collection, Barcelona. The deep contrasts between light and shadow are the starting point for evaluating the tones in this figure.

Lighting plays an important role in the watercolors reproduced on this page. Contrasts between light and shadow such as those that appear in Ballestar's works (figs. 91 and 92) are perfectly normal in reality. The artist has used his skill to darken them in order to obtain expressive effects: the projection of the landscape's depth and the evaluation of the volume of the figure. The motif chosen by Plana (fig. 93) is a fine example of a combination of lights. The artist has done a creative job of achieving a truly phantasmagoric atmosphere.

91

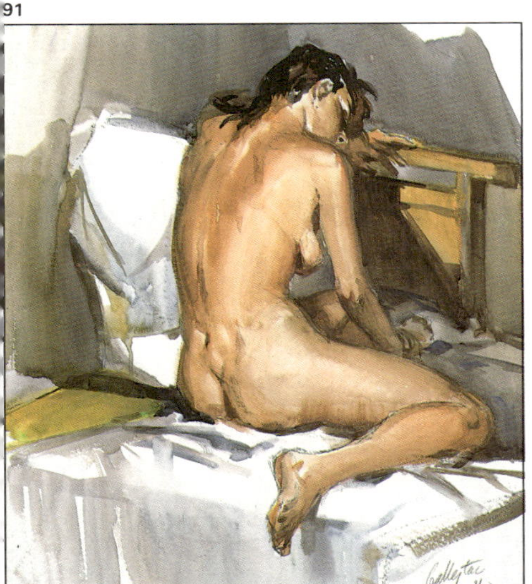

92

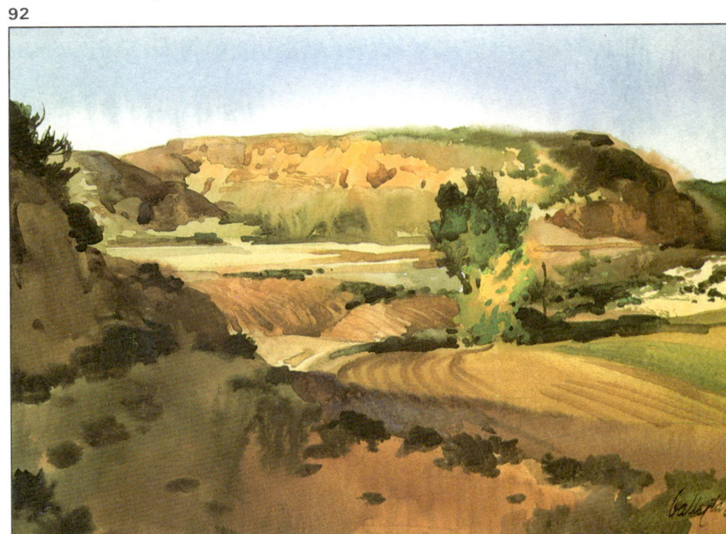

Fig. 92. Vicenç Ballestar, *Yellow Landscape*. Private collection, Barcelona. Succeeding planes of light and shadow are essential for providing a sense of depth in a landscape.

93

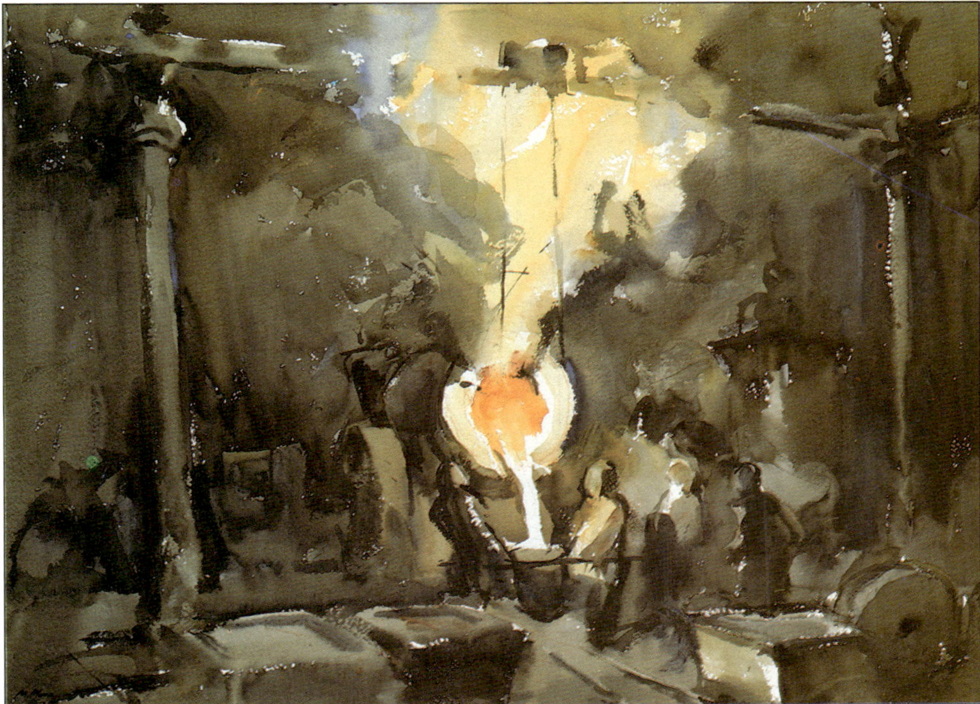

Fig. 93. Manel Plana (1949-), *Foundry*. Private collection. Plana uses this unconventional theme to exploit its gestural and colorist lighting effect.

Contrast and atmosphere

Contrast is the convergence of tones of varying intensity. When representing a space (a landscape, for example), the hierarchy of the light and dark planes produces the effect of depth. These planes contrast among each other, producing a characteristic effect of mutual contrast.

Contrast contributes to providing the picture with a three-dimensional air, but the sensation can be rather cold and crude if the atmospheric effect is not taken into account. In painting, the idea of atmosphere refers to the representation of the air that exists and circulates around all the objects that surround us. In the writings of Leonardo da Vinci, compiled in his famous *Treatise on Painting*, we find constant references on how to achieve this atmospheric feeling. Leonardo comments: "If you finish the more distant objects too much, and with too much detail, they will appear to be near instead of far. Represent them as they are and do not finish them too much."

Leonardo advises us to respect and represent the ever-lessening appearance of distant things in order to achieve an air of depth. With regard to atmosphere—the contrasts, contours, and so on—we should take various factors into account:

— Place the strongest contrasts in the foreground; in that way the forms will be more accentuated and will create a feeling of advancing toward the spectator.

— Gradually gray the tones of the objects that grow farther away. At the same time, avoid dark contrasts, since tones tend to lose their intensity, becoming ever more blue and gray, according to how much atmosphere intervenes between them and the viewer.

Remember that the contours of the objects gradually lose their definition with distance, making them more blurred. On the other hand, the objects of the foreground are clear and well defined.

94

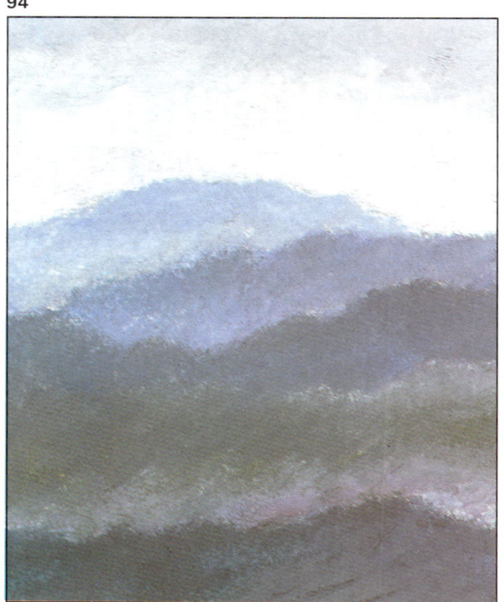

Fig. 94. The representation of atmosphere is based on a color gradations of the foreground, middle ground, and background: the farther they are from the viewer, the more toned down the colors.

95

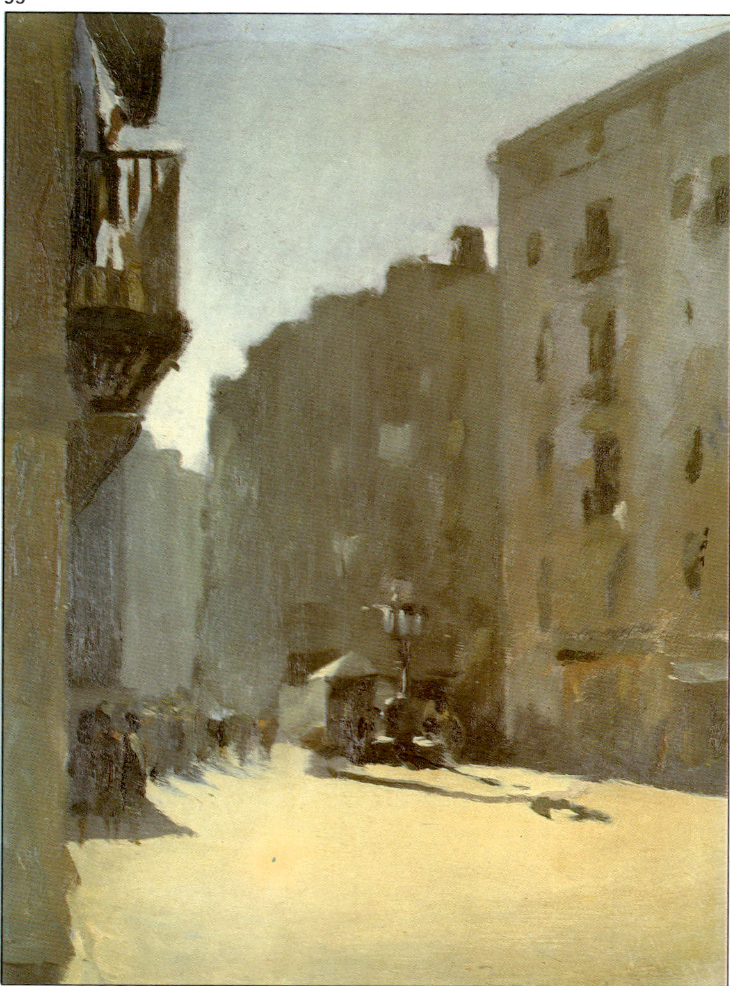

Fig. 95. José M. Parramón. *Ripalda Street*. Private collection, Barcelona. This work combines the principles of contrast (the effect of backlighting on the façades of the background) and atmosphere.

Fig. 96. Martínez Lozano (1923-), *Port*. Private collection. Intense contrasts also permit a profoundly spatial pictorial expresion.

Fig. 97. Manel Plana (1949-), *Rocky Landscape*. Private collection. The contrast between the background and foreground has been realized inversely: it is the foreground that appears relatively undefined. However, the result produces a sense of depth all the same.

96

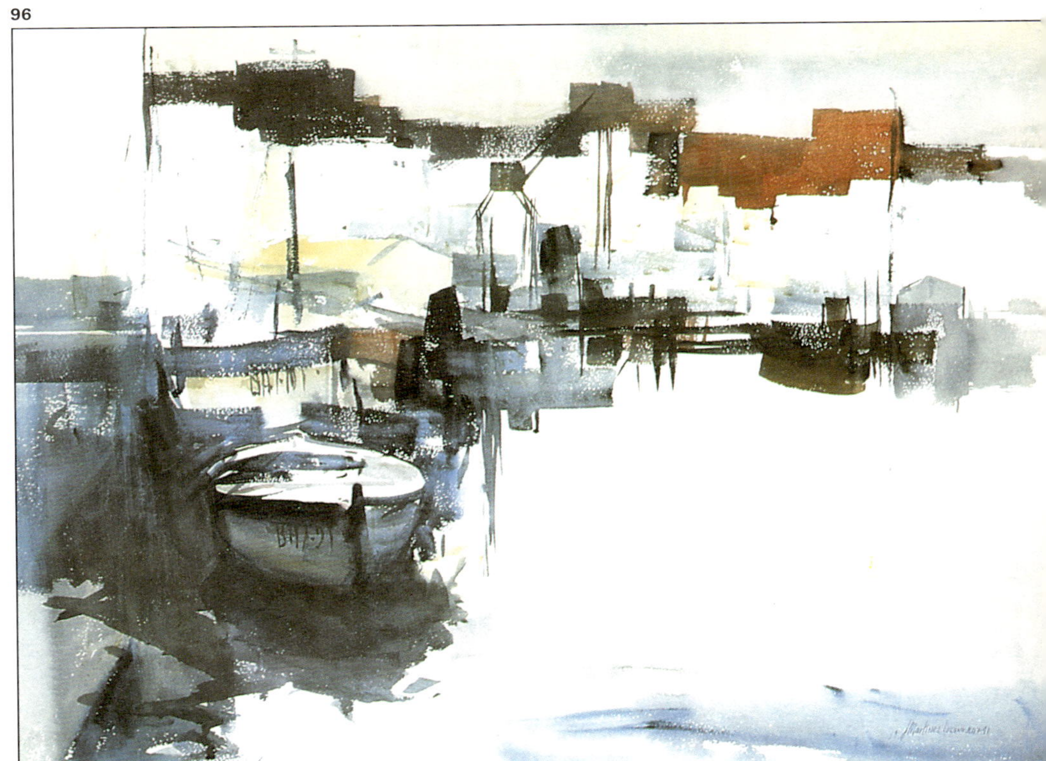

97

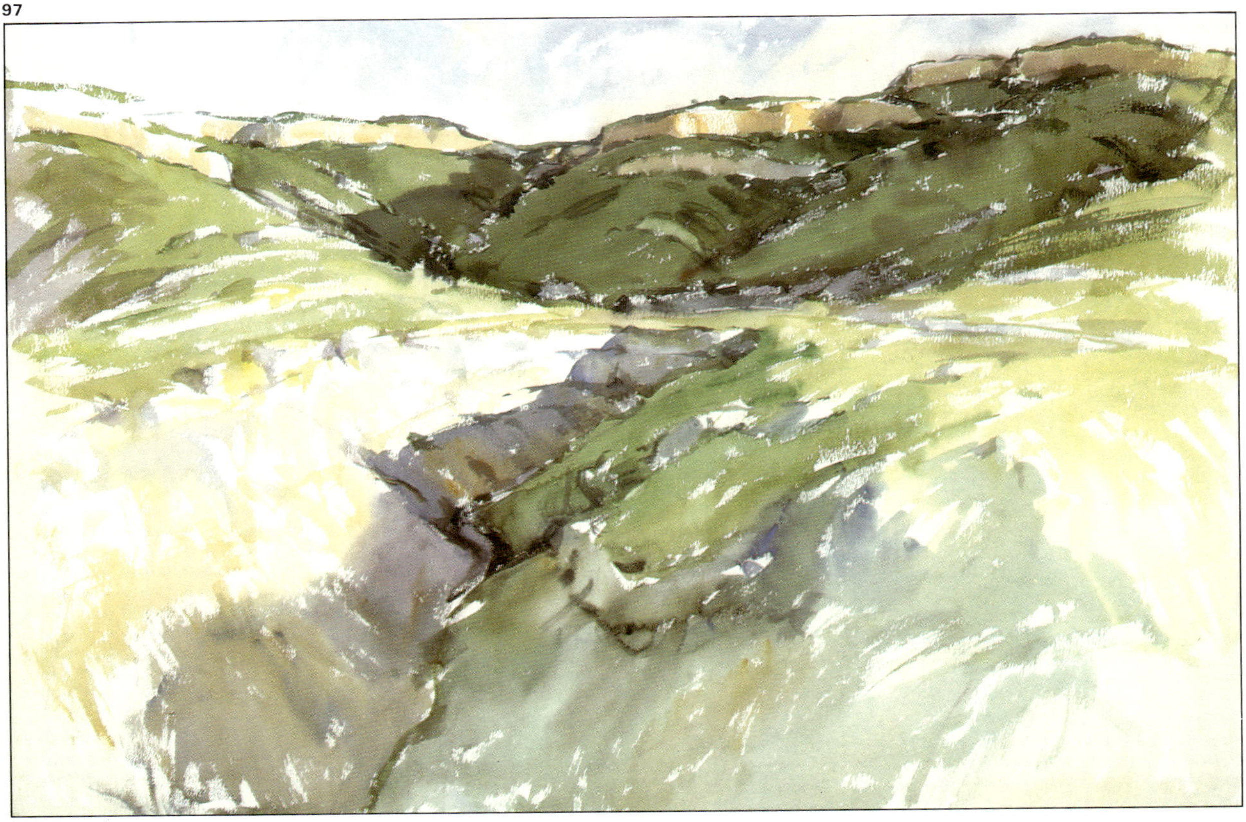

Cropping the image

98

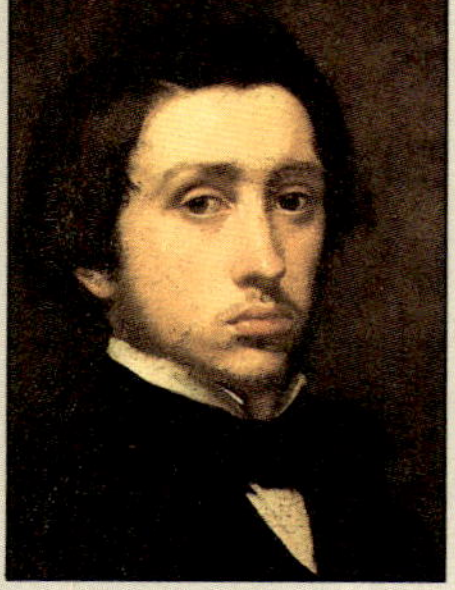

Fig. 98. Edgar Degas (1834-1917), *Portrait of the Artist*. Orsay Museum, Paris.

99

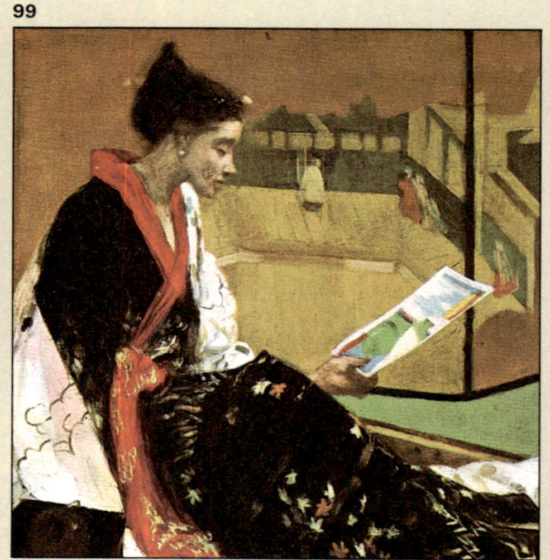

100

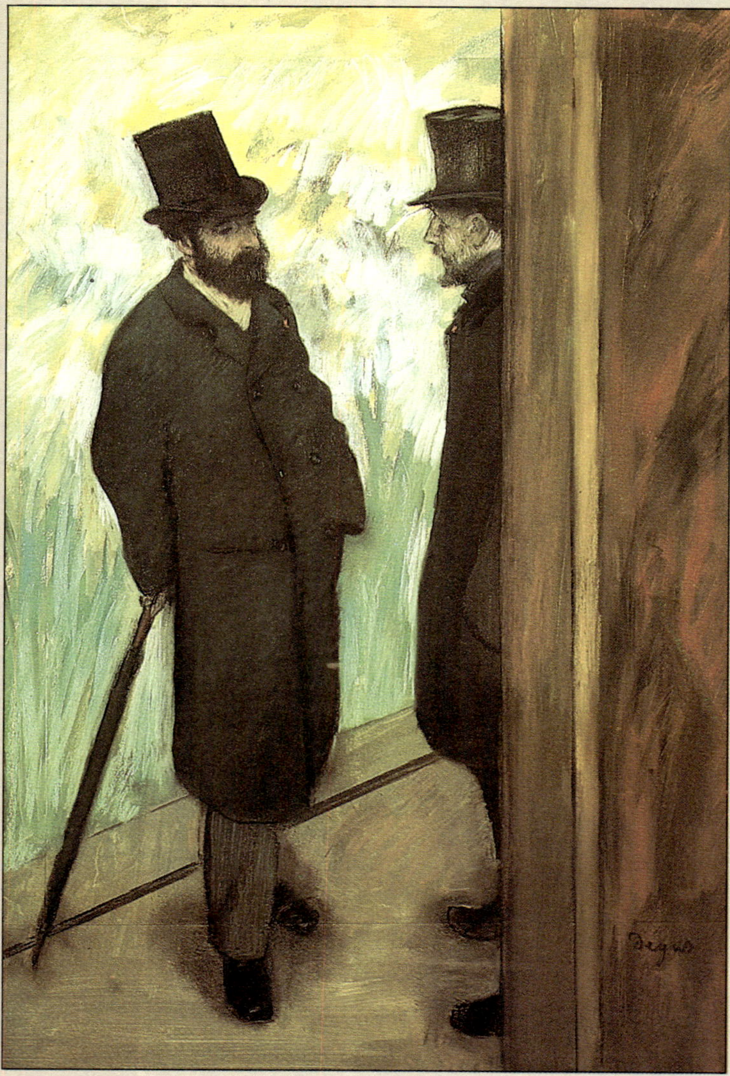

During the last part of the nineteenth century, Japanese art and decoration were very much in fashion in Europe. Artists collected prints containing Japanese drawing techniques, and sometimes even Japanese themes, as was the case with a number of drawings by Whistler. The flat inks, the silhouetted forms, and, above all, the compositional style began to make their mark in European painting. This distinct style in composition had one very revolutionary impact on western art: cropped images. Until the appearance of *Japonisme*—the name by which the tendency was known—artists tended to situate the picture's theme or motif in the center of the canvas. The surrounding areas were reserved for secondary elements and the background. The influence of Japanese prints gave way to a new concept of how to fit a theme onto paper or canvas. Edgar Degas was extremely enthusiastic about this novelty and was the painter who achieved the most brilliant results. His paintings reproduced on these pages demonstrate his variety and originality in composition. A door, a column, and, occasionally, the border of the painting itself would abruptly cut off the figures, producing a dynamic, attractive, and very realistic effect, rather like a snapshot. This way of cropping the motif became a characteristic style of Degas's work. On one occasion, the artist gave to his friend Manet a picture he had painted of the painter and his wife. Madame Manet appears in it playing the piano. Some time later, when Degas was visiting his friend's studio, he saw that his picture had been vertically cut. The only parts of Madame Manet that could be seen were her back and half a head. Degas was furious and tore the canvas off the frame with the intention of painting it again, but he never did. Perhaps both painters mutually accepted such a brusque way of cropping the image.

101

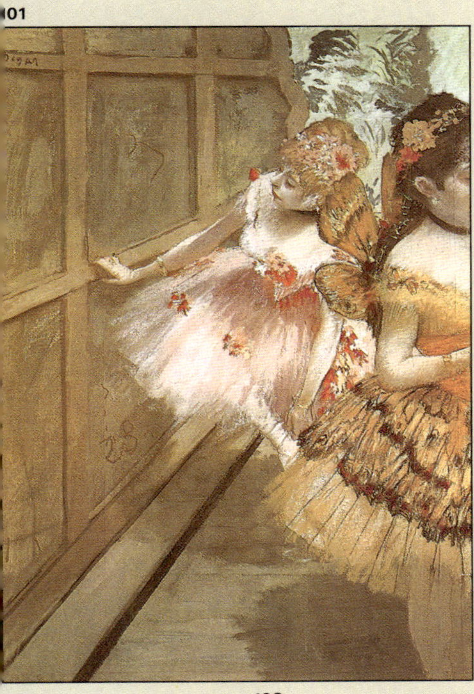

Fig. 103. Edgar Degas, *Monsieur and Madame Manet*. Municipal Art Museum of Kitakyushu. Although the boxing of this painting seems characteristic of Degas, it was not painted like this. Manet cut off a piece of the work. When Degas saw what his friend had done, he angrily took the painting away to repaint it, although he never did. Who knows, perhaps he liked this new composition after all.

102

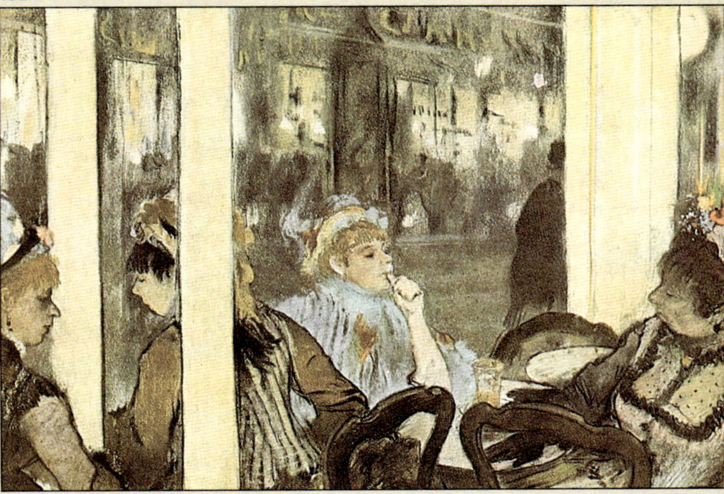

103

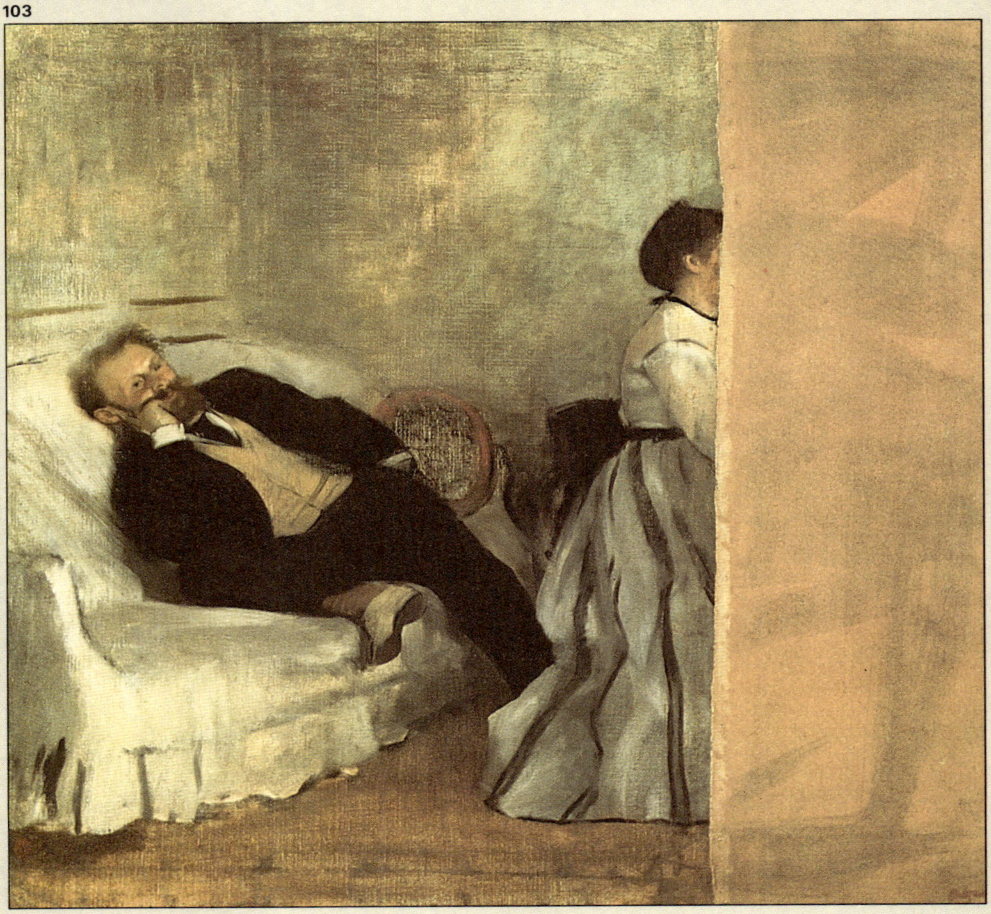

Fig. 99. James Whistler (1834-1903), *Caprice in Purple and Gold*. Freer Gallery of Art, Washington. Several European painters were influenced by Japanese prints.

Fig. 100. Edgar Degas, *Portrait of Friends on Stage*. Orsay Museum, Paris. *Japonisme* introduced a new concept of cropping images.

Fig. 101. Edgar Degas, *Ballerinas in the Wings*. Norton Simon Foundation, Pasadena, California. In his ballerina themes, Degas used composition never before seen.

Fig. 102. Edgar Degas, *Women on the Terrace of a Café*. Orsay Museum, Paris. Many of the scenes painted by Degas resemble snapshots reproducing an immediate reality.

Photography as an auxiliary medium

Painters were not indifferent to the advent of photography during the middle of the nineteenth century. The ease with which this revolutionary visual medium reproduced reality enabled people to see the world from countless—and until then unknown—different aspects (freezing movement, aerial shots, unusual angles, and so on). Photography deprived the representation of reality of any subjectivity and intention. The result was a cold and faithful reproduction that people were not accustomed to. It was the impressionists who were most influenced by the photographic medium: Renoir painted scenes of movement, such as *Dance à la Moulin de la Galette*, undoubtedly inspired by photographs; Degas painted his dancers and women in the bath, using a purely photographic frame. Since then, photography and the plastic arts have continued to have a fruitful relationship.

This proves that, directly or indirectly, photography has an influence on painting, and can even be used as an important auxiliary medium. A photograph can be a source of inspiration for a painting, or at least a reference. It would be more correct to consider photography as a complement to the art of painting, for studying a theme or composition, and so on. You don't need to have a "professional" camera; an ordinary single-lens-reflex camera with a basic lens (50 mm) will enable you to get good-quality prints or slides. But remember that photography is only an *auxiliary* medium, a complementary tool. It is best to combine painting from nature with some possible touching up in the studio using a photograph of the model. Using photographs is also justifiable when it is difficult to paint the theme from nature, such as a crowded street or fair, or because of its short duration, such as dawn or dusk. But remember too that painting exclusively from a photograph often results in paintings of a flat tendency, without relief (just as it is seen in the photograph), losing all the vitality that can be achieved only from viewing it in person from nature. The artist must try to *interpret* a photograph, in the same way he or she freely interprets reality.

Fig. 104. Photography is totally justifiable when it is difficult to paint a theme from nature. It is best to take several photographs of the motif to obtain a good interpretation of the theme.

104

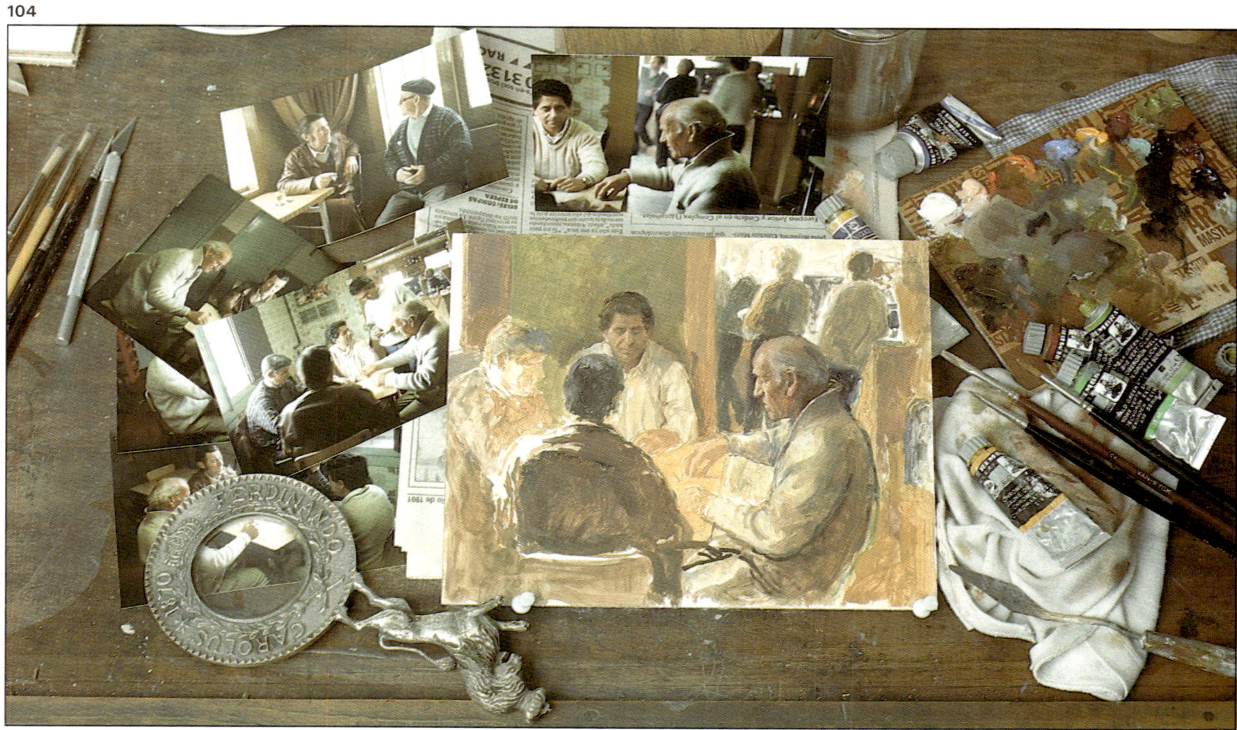

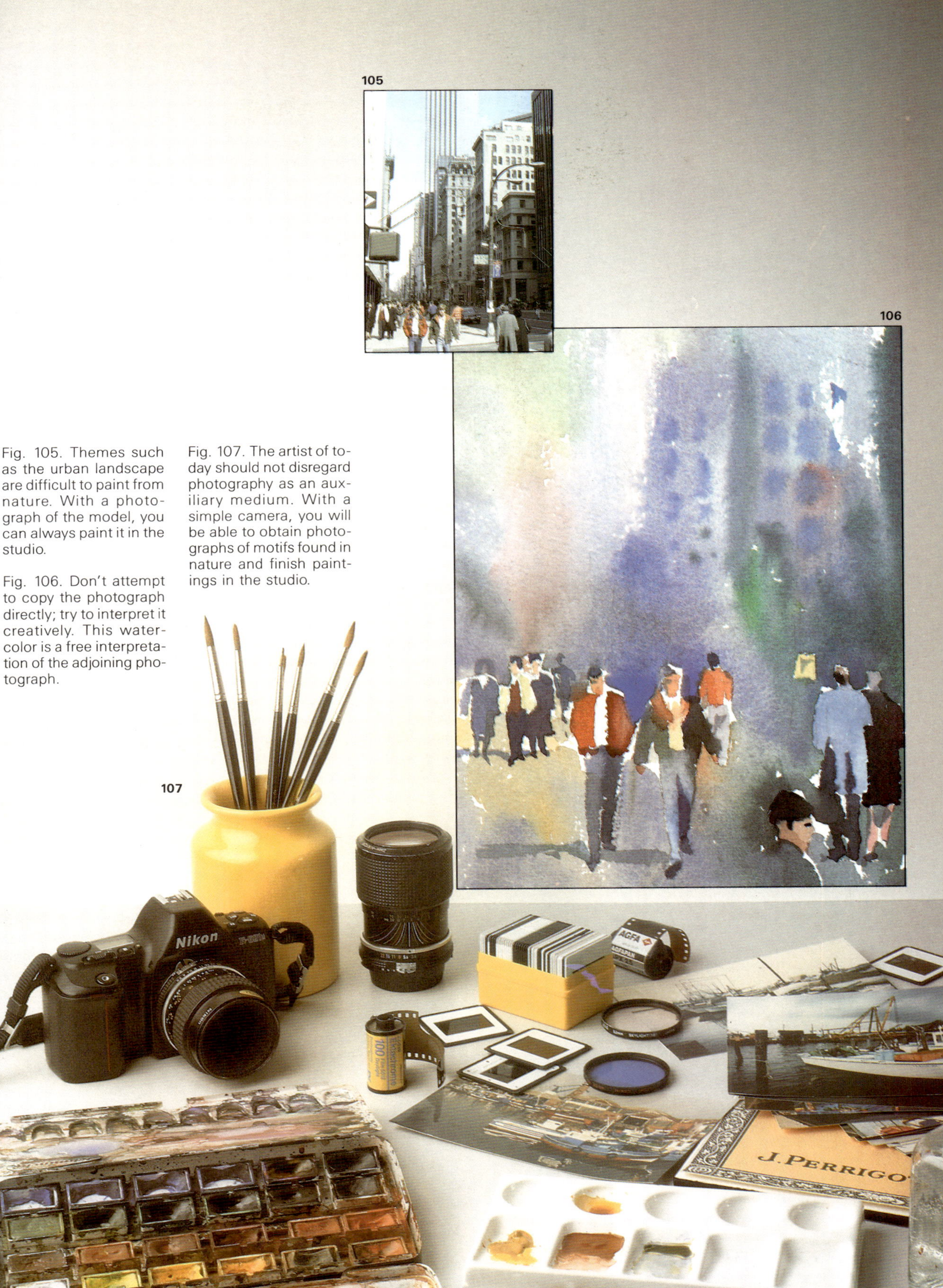

Fig. 105. Themes such as the urban landscape are difficult to paint from nature. With a photograph of the model, you can always paint it in the studio.

Fig. 106. Don't attempt to copy the photograph directly; try to interpret it creatively. This watercolor is a free interpretation of the adjoining photograph.

Fig. 107. The artist of today should not disregard photography as an auxiliary medium. With a simple camera, you will be able to obtain photographs of motifs found in nature and finish paintings in the studio.

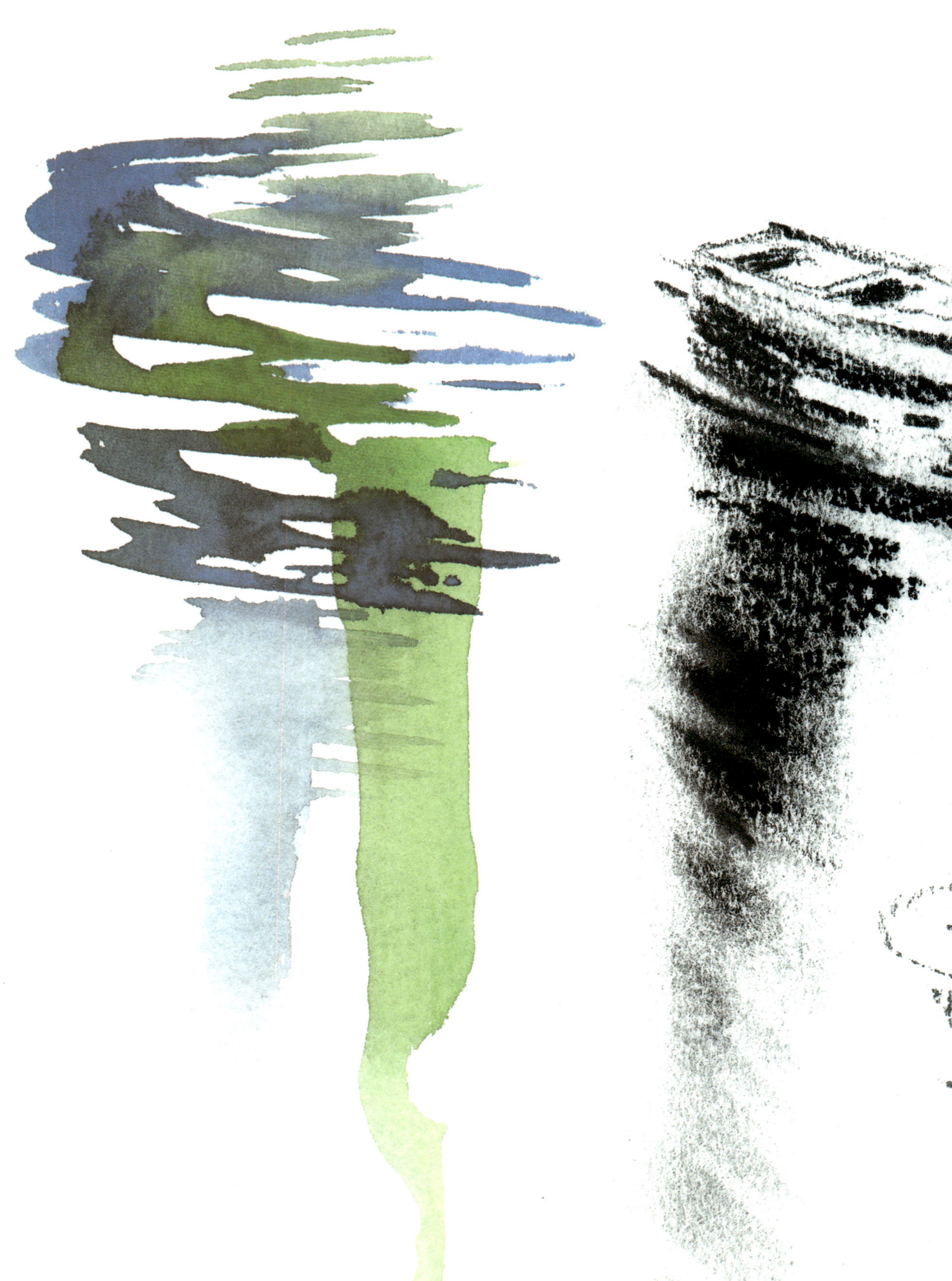

Watercolor painting requires confidence and accuracy. It allows no doubts or hesitation. The painter must have a clear idea from the start, before painting. This is possible only if the pictorial potential of the motif has previously been explored through sketches, preliminary studies. This chapter deals with sketches, studies, the interpretation of the theme, the fit of the shapes into the drawing. These are basic and essential concepts, rooted in experience and in the daily practice of the great watercolor painters.

The sketch: the first step toward creative watercolor

The importance of a preliminary sketch

The artistic virtues of watercolor painting, its grace and charm, depend on sureness of touch. As you already know, watercolor painting does not lend itself easily to corrections or retouching. Each brushstroke is final, and the result must appear spontaneous, carefree, and inspired. It is hardly surprising that inspiration does not always come when the artist needs it and cannot be relied on. The only possible approach is to study the subject and draw numerous preliminary sketches.

Sketches are a means of broaching the subject in search of the eventual results—a rehearsal for the definitive watercolor. When making a sketch, the painter synthesizes the most essential aspects of the subject taken as a whole, leaving details and nuances aside, making a "first draft."

Fig. 108 (preceding spread). Sketches by Vicenç Ballestar.

Fig. 109. Manel Plana (1949-), preparatory sketch. Private collection.

Fig. 110. Manel Plana, *Plaza Real*. Private collection.

109

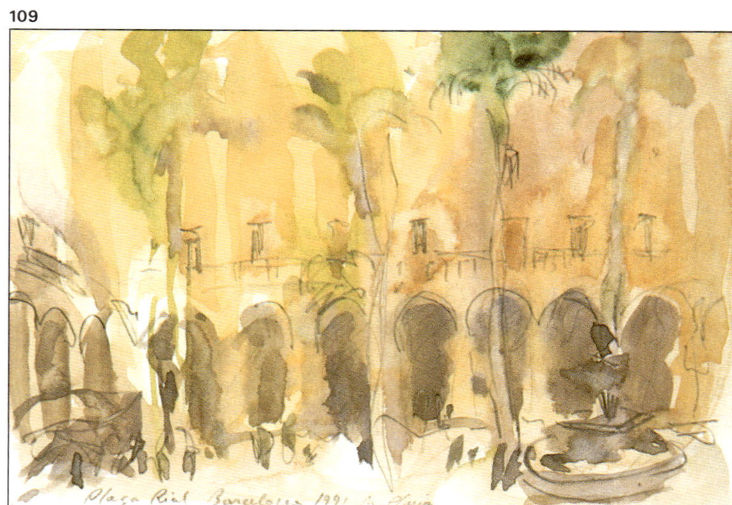

110

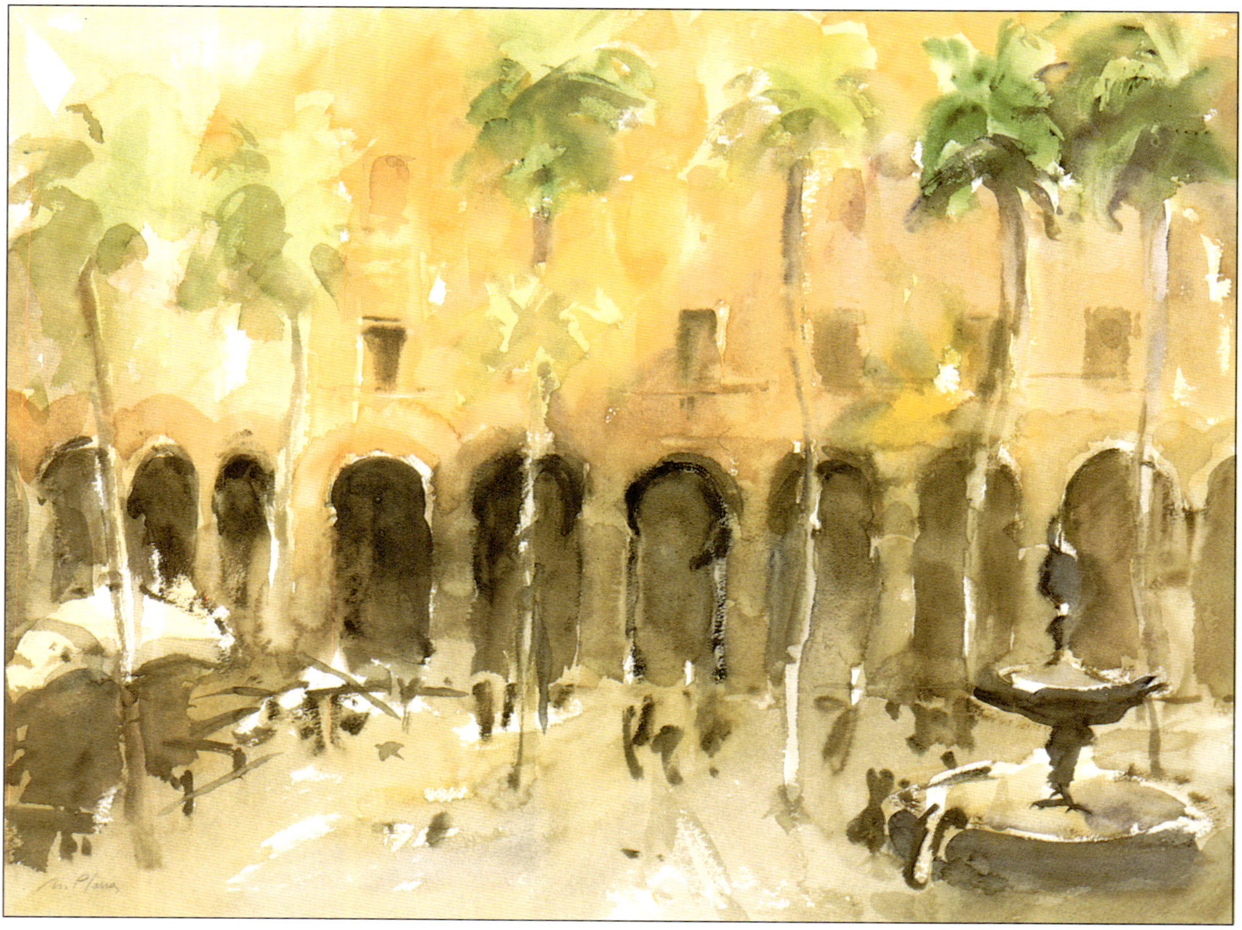

A constant concern for artists is how to hold onto the first impression they receive of a theme. Cézanne called it the "small sensation," that first impulsive encounter that stimulates the artist to paint and interpret a theme. This first impression is what is captured in sketches. In fact, watercolorists will occasionally consider certain sketches as finished pieces of work rather than other, more elaborate ones.

Look at the sketches on these two pages and compare them with the definitive works; see how the sketches approach and resolve certain pictorial concerns that appear in the finished paintings. All this is achieved with a minimum of means: simple brushstrokes, use of color, and composition.

111

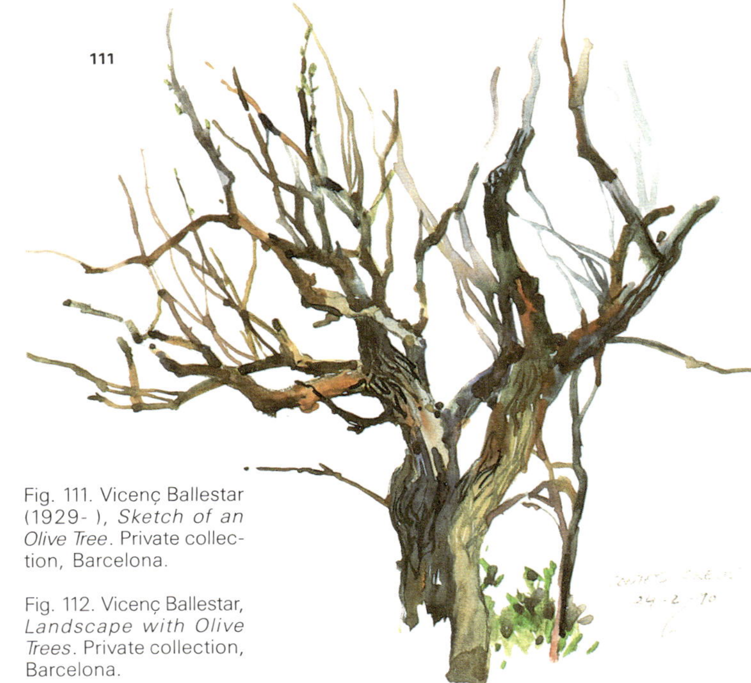

Fig. 111. Vicenç Ballestar (1929-), *Sketch of an Olive Tree*. Private collection, Barcelona.

Fig. 112. Vicenç Ballestar, *Landscape with Olive Trees*. Private collection, Barcelona.

112

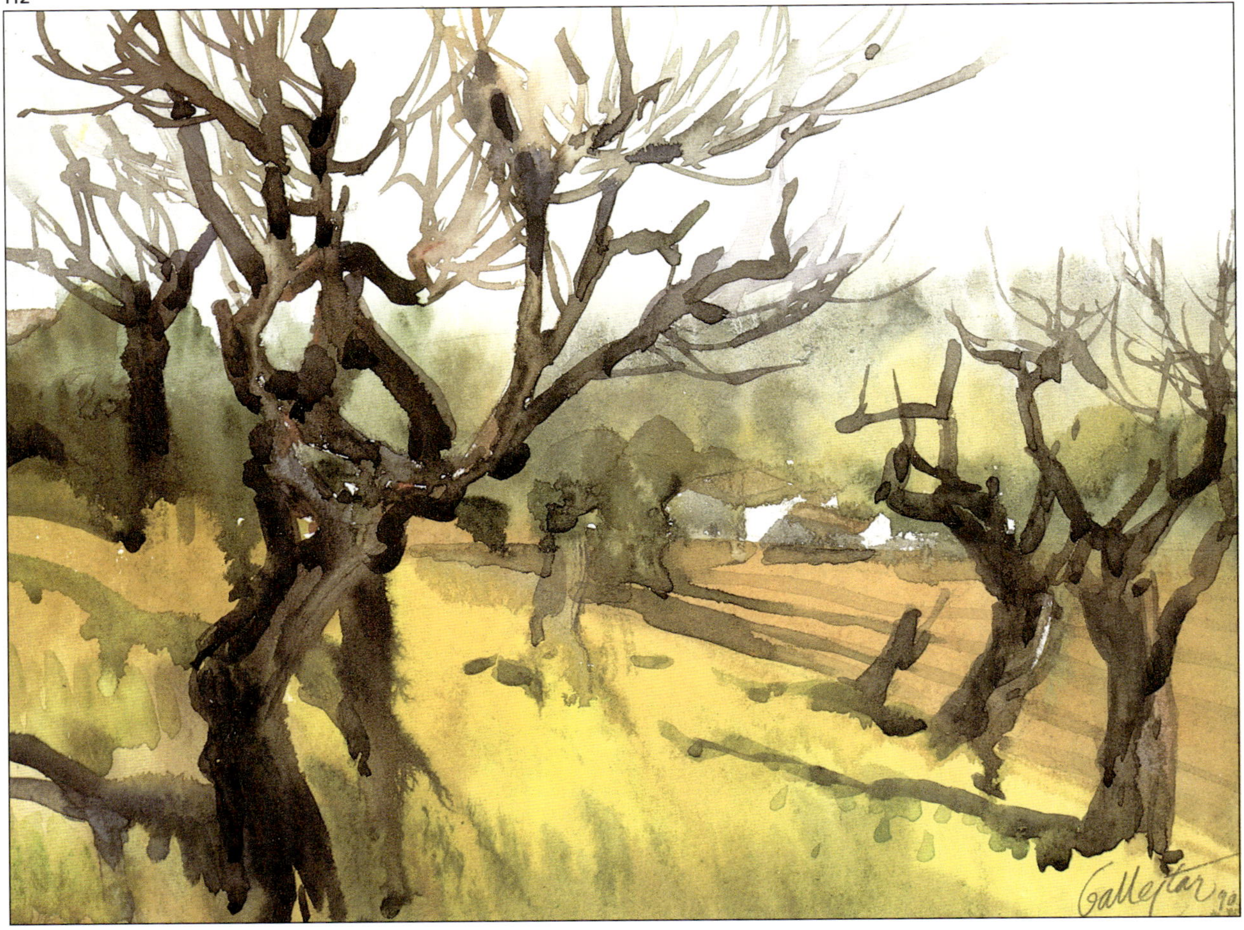

Martínez Lozano's creative interpretation

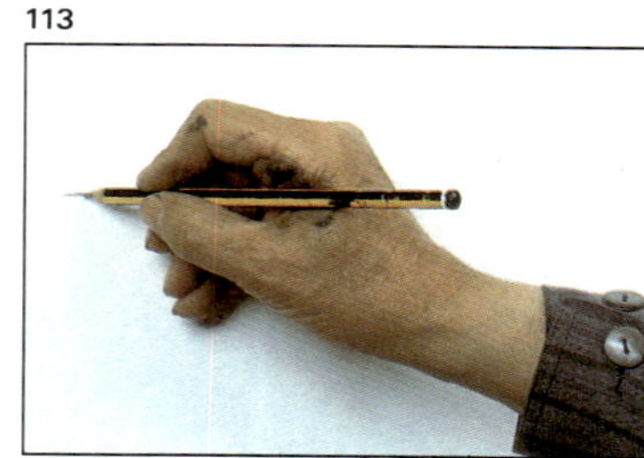

Fig. 113. Lozano intuitively draws the horizon line, along the golden section of the paper.

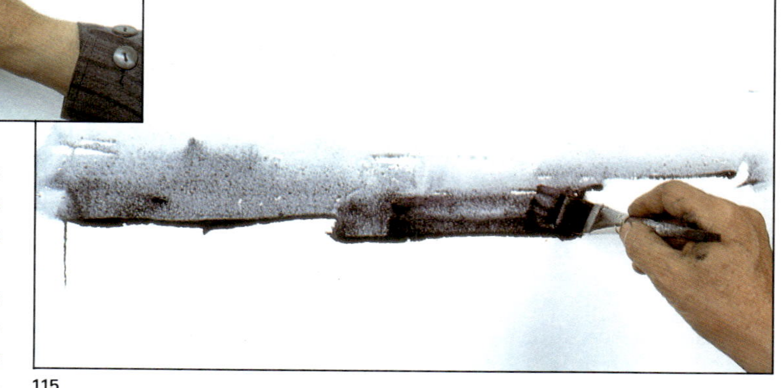

It is when we watch Martínez Lozano paint a watercolor—a seascape in this case—that we begin to understand the concept of creative interpretation.
The artist's extraordinary artistic sense reveals itself even before he begins to paint. Lozano draws a line on the white paper with a pencil: the horizon line. This line, drawn without preparation, corresponds to a golden section of the paper, to within a few millimeters! While we measure the paper to check it, Lozano smiles wryly, as if it were not important.
After dampening the paper with a wide paintbrush, Lozano applies broad, irregular areas of gray, that converge to form an abastract wash across the lower part of the paper. These areas are, of all things, the sky. Yes, the sky. Once the color has spread downward, the artist turnes the paper upside down (figs. 115 and 116). We can now see the sky in these colors, a splendid slate-colored stormy sky of extraordinary realism.
Lozano has resolved the sky with apparent ease. Now he paints the boats beached on the right of the painting. To do this, he overlays dark, detailed brushstrokes. The shapes begin to appear among the confusion of colors. With the pointed handle of the brush he paints the masts and the mooring ropes. The boats suddenly stand out clearly. The painter does not imitate or copy reality; rather, he suggests it by providing numerous visual clues that the observer recognizes and reconstructs for himself. This is clearly seen in the final result (fig. 119), a fine example of creative interpretation.

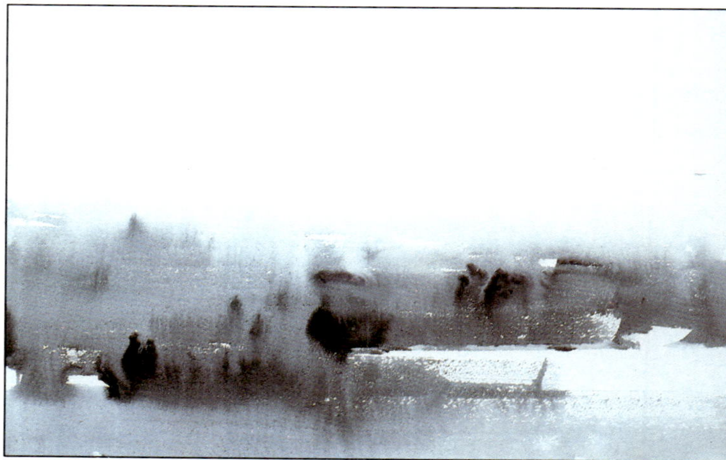

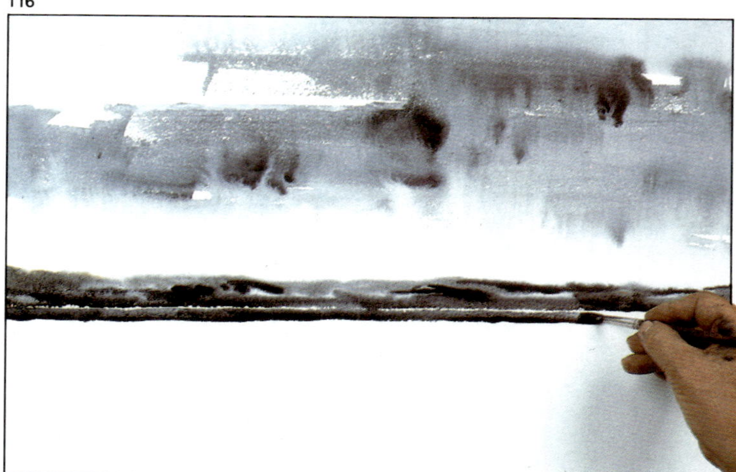

Figs. 114 and 115. The artist applies the wash of the sky with the paper turned upside down to make use of the water as it runs down.

Fig. 116. Underneath the horizon, Lozano paints another wash to express the expanse of the sea.

118

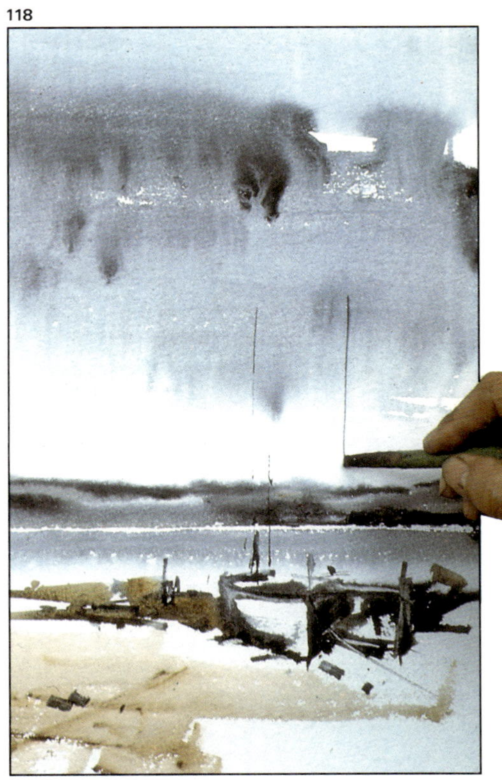

Fig. 117. Against the finished background of the sky and the sea, Lozano paints dark brushstrokes to build up the shapes of the boats.

Fig. 118. With the pointed end of the brush dipped in color, the artist draws the masts of the boats.

Fig. 119. This is the finished watercolor. It really looks as if it were painted from nature; nobody would say it is purely studio work.

117

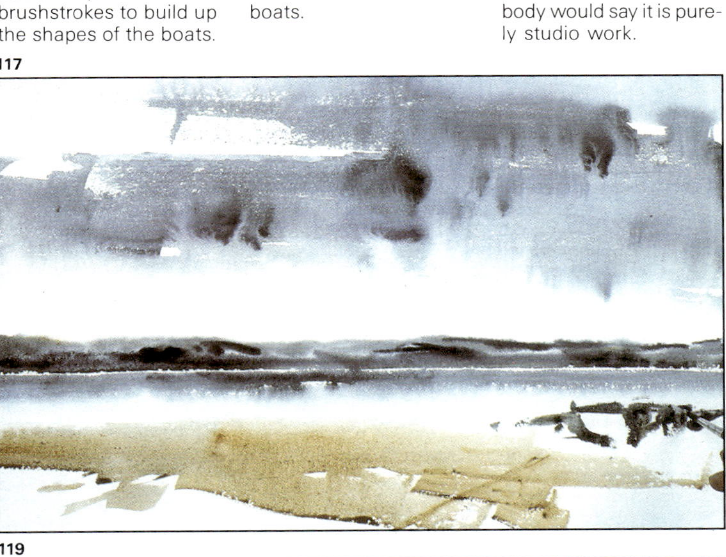

119

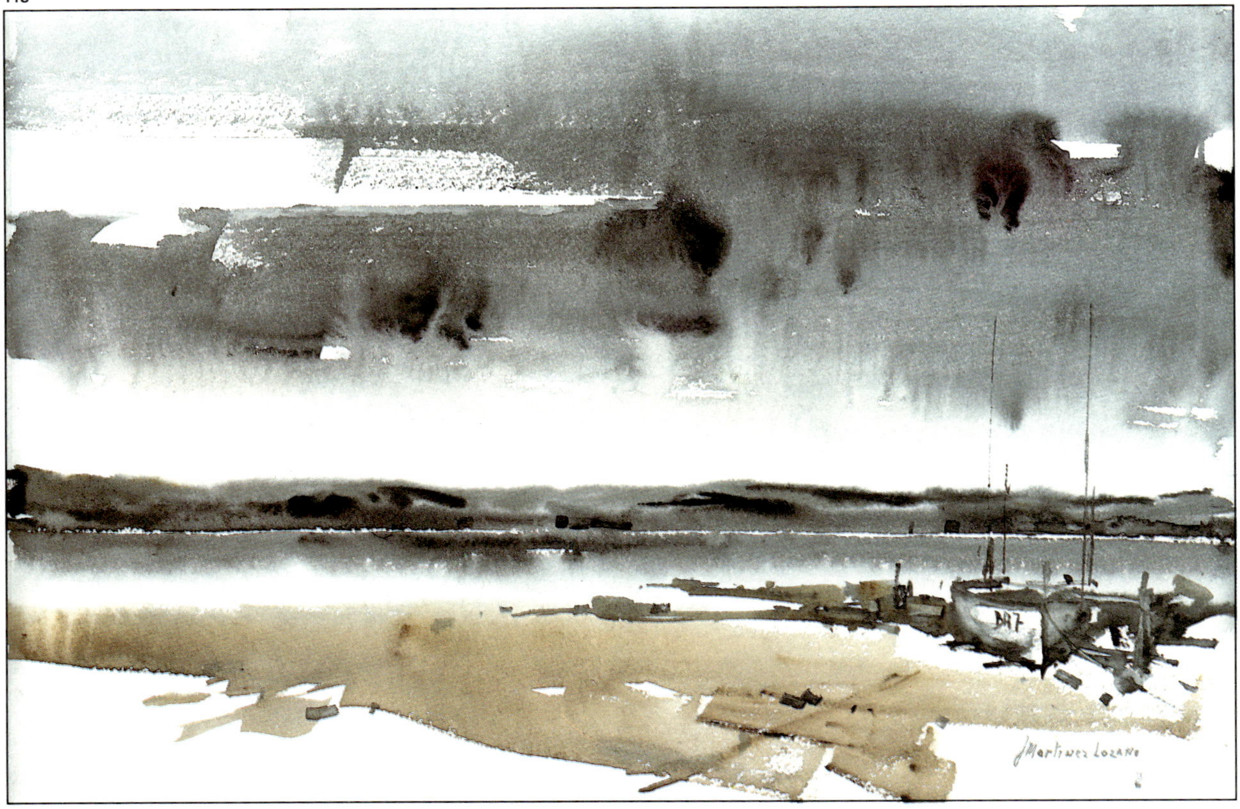

Structuring and blocking in

120

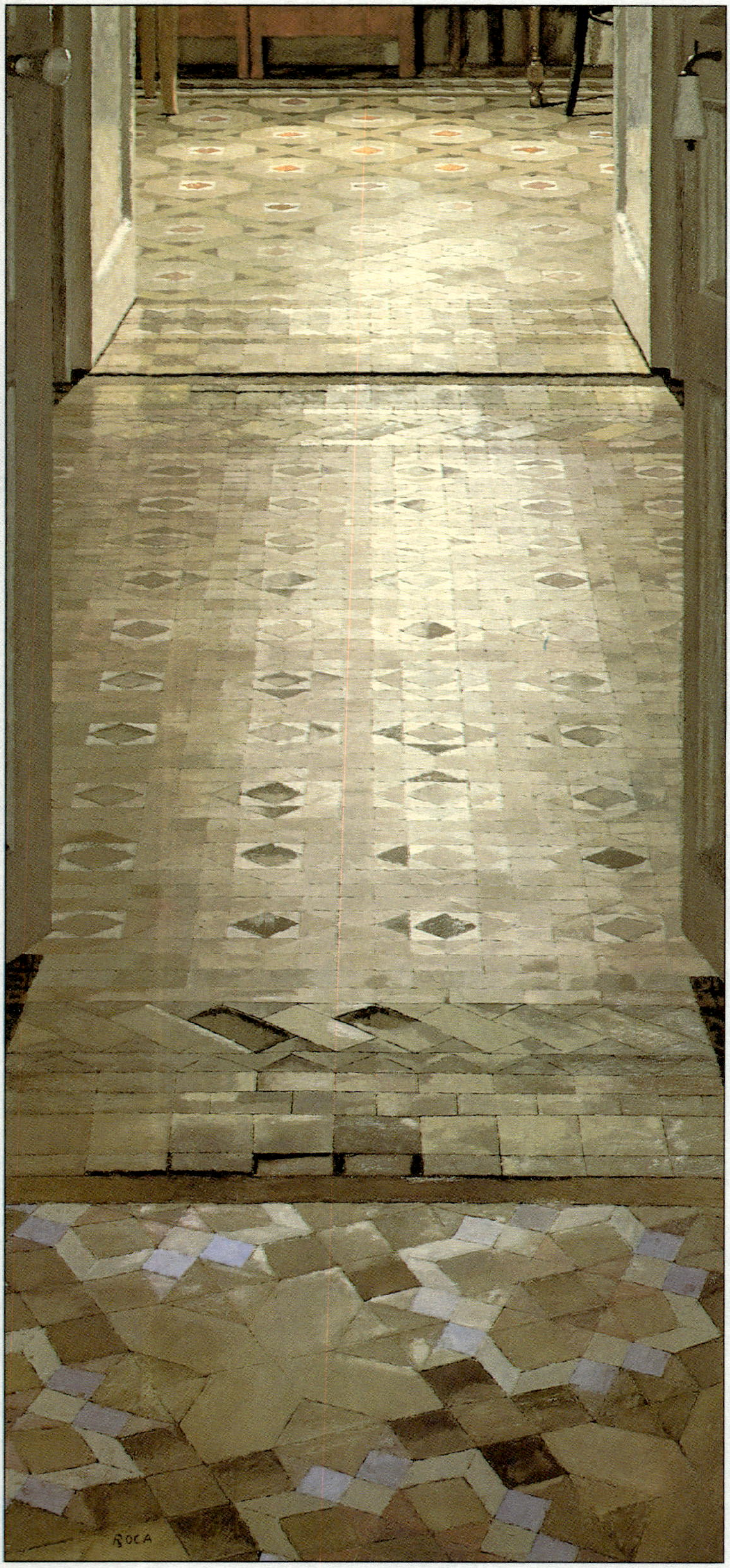

Watercolor requires a good command of the most basic principles of drawing: how to structure shapes, give them the proper proportion, fit them into a composition, and so on.

In order to study and illustrate these ideas we turn to an exceptional artist: Josep Roca-Sastre. Let me introduce him. It is no exaggeration to say that Josep Roca-Sastre is one of the most important of today's painters. His many international exhibitions and, above all, the undeniable quality of his work bear witness to this fact. His interior work, such as that shown in the illustration (fig. 120), has made him famous. These paintings are sharply realistic with a fascinating delicate balance of color and a solid composition. The artist was kind enough to invite us into his studio. Looking through the folders there, we came across a good number of admirable drawings from his formative years. You can see a selection of them here.

Looking at these works reminds us of a famous saying of Cézanne's: "In nature, everything is modeled after three basic shapes: the cube, the cylinder, and the sphere."

In a certain way, Roca-Sastre's paintings are the practical interpretation of this idea. They can serve you as valuable examples of how to capture reality in a simple, clear way. If you are able to draw a cube, a cylinder, and a sphere, you can draw natural shapes. Before doing anything else, you must analyze the basic structure of the model starting with a flat geometrical shape (a square, a circle, a triangle) that enable you to understand the basic shape of the model. This is called *blocking in* a drawing. Then you

Fig. 120. Josep Roca-Sastre (1928-), *Mosaic*. Private collection, Barcelona. Roca-Sastre has chosen an intimist theme and brought out the quiet beauty of this tiled floor with great accuracy.

Fig. 121. Josep Roca-Sastre, *Woman's Head*. Artist's collection, Barcelona. This magnificent ink drawing shows a fine interpretation of volume starting from simple geometric shapes.

can go on to analyze the volume, based on the simplest of its structures. In figure 121 we can see how he has resolved the drawing of a woman's head using spheres and cylinders, while the blocked-in neck and upper chest suggest two superimposed rectangles. Study these drawings by Roca-Sastre; they are not only a perfect example of our subject but also beautiful in themselves.

121

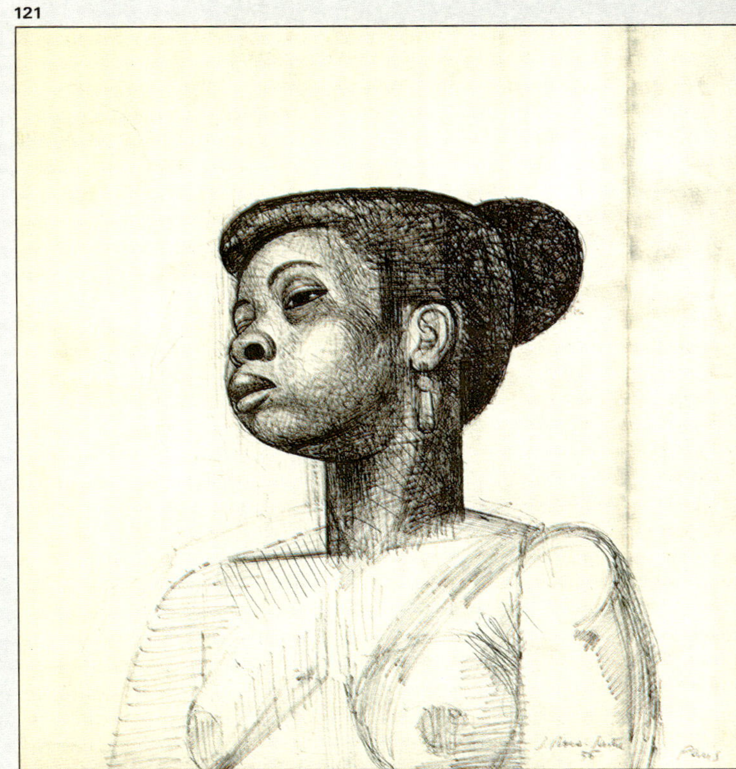

Fig. 122. Josep Roca-Sastre, *Still Life with Oil Lamp*. Artist's collection, Barcelona. The composition of this still life is resolved using geometric figures that balance out and complement one another.

Fig. 123. Josep Roca-Sastre, *Study of a Figure*. Artist's collection, Barcelona. This study of a figure has been accomplished using only the most essential lines and shapes, avoiding all superfluous detail.

22

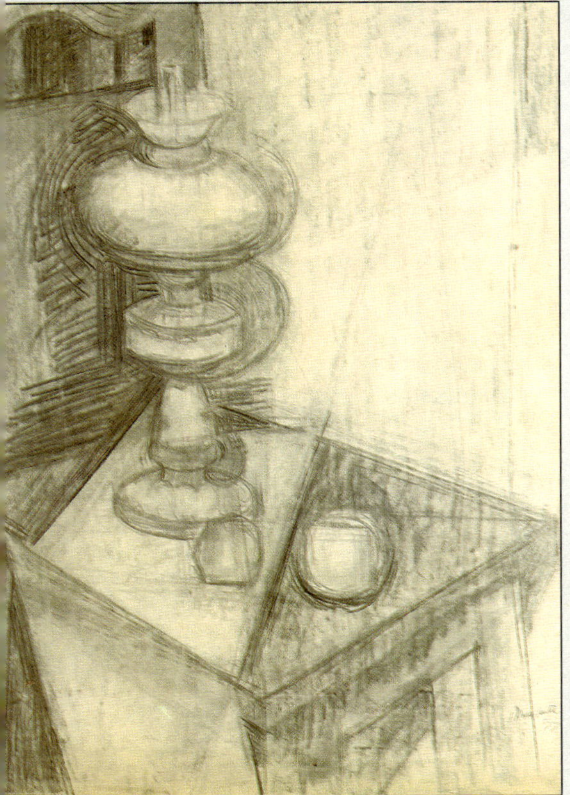

123

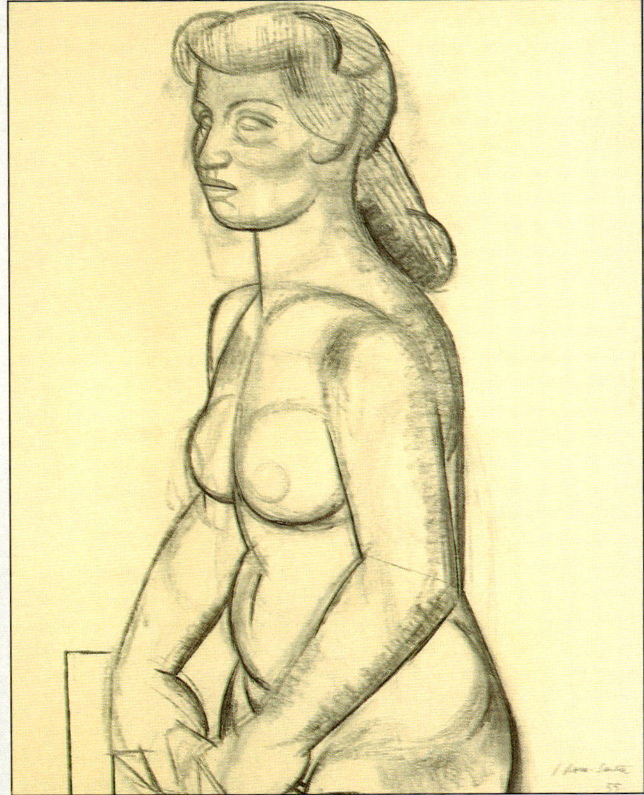

Calculating sizes and proportions

Fig. 124. Josep Roca-Sastre (1928-), *Study of a Figure*. Artist's collection, Barcelona. The lines making up the framework of this drawing result from the process of blocking in the figure.

Fig. 125. Josep Roca-Sastre, *Study of a Figure*. Artist's collection, Barcelona. In order to study figures in movement, Roca-Sastre simplifies the basic forms using lines, circumferences, and cylinders.

Fig. 126. Josep Roca-Sastre, *Profile of a Figure*. Artist's collection, Barcelona. Here is another example of a solidly composed figure made up from lines and regular shapes.

Another factor to bear in mind when drawing is to calculate the dimensions and proportions of the model. You must begin with a detailed and systematic study, because we obtain the sizes and proportions from this observation of reality. When we talk of proportion, we are referring to the harmonic relationship between each of the different parts of the model and the model as a whole. Anyone can see when a figure is out of proportion because, for example, the head is too large or small in comparison to the rest of the body; it is not in harmony with the whole. The problem of proportion can arise when we want to draw a model on a smaller scale (that of the paper) while maintaining the sizes and relationships of the life-size figures. Mentally calculating sizes and proportions requires some practice. The first step is to put the visual information in order, comparing certain sizes with others. There are several tricks in drawing that make these calculations easier. One is to take a pencil or the handle of a brush as a reference to compare the width and length of the model or a part of it. Hold out the pencil before you and position it so that you can measure the model against the pencil. Repeat this as often as necessary, comparing certain sizes with others while you are drawing. Another way of calculating the proportions is to draw reference points and lines to correlate certain parts of the drawing with others. Let's look at an example by Roca-Sastre (fig. 124). The painter has built up the figure from straight lines forming a framework that helps to correlate certain points with others, using parallel, perpendicular, or diagonal lines. In other drawings (fig. 125 and 126) the artist has structured the figures using straight lines and circumferences that simplify and define both the volume and the movement of the bodies. In figure 127, we can see certain lines that do not actually exist. One divides the torso into two halves, lending it volume; the arm

124

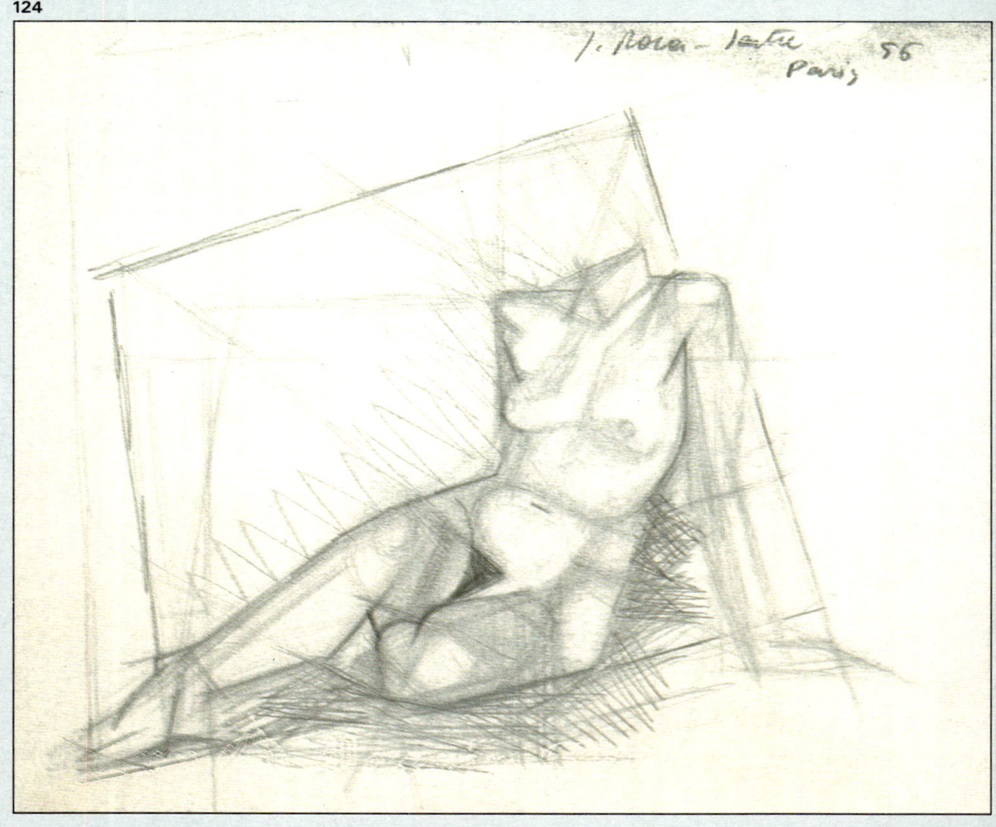

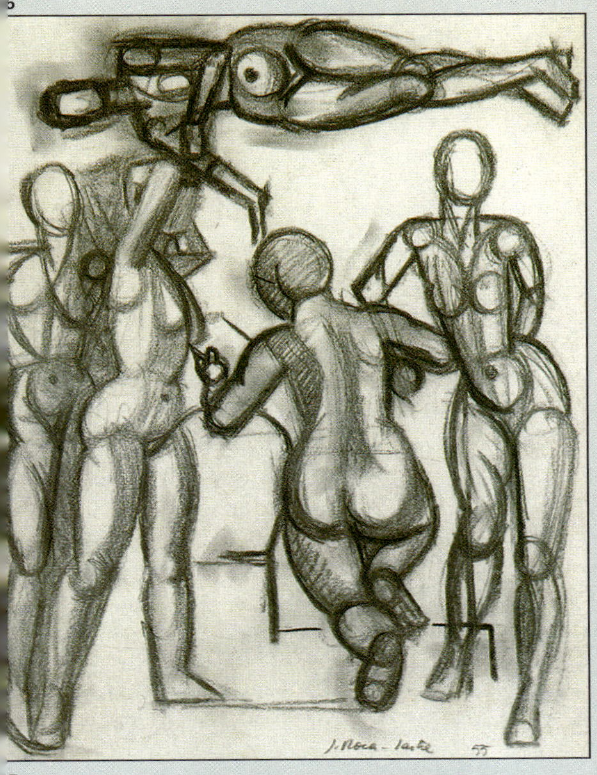

126

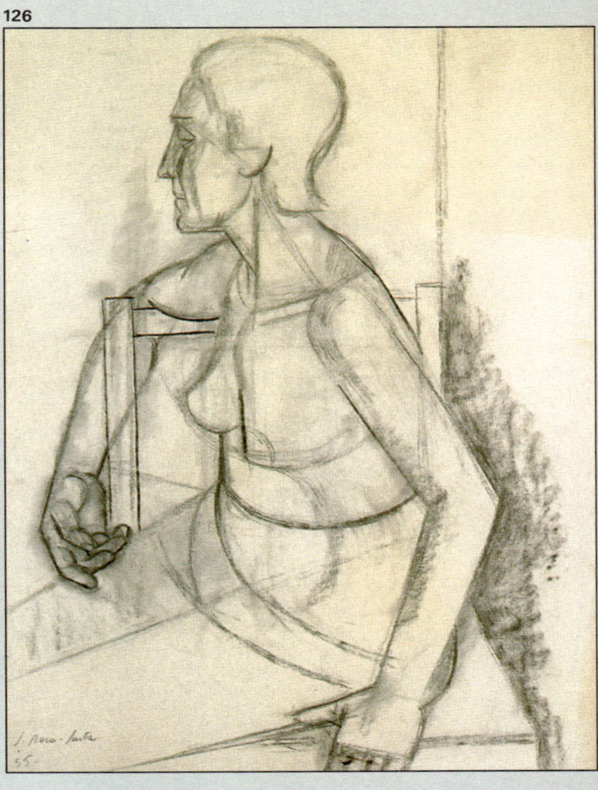

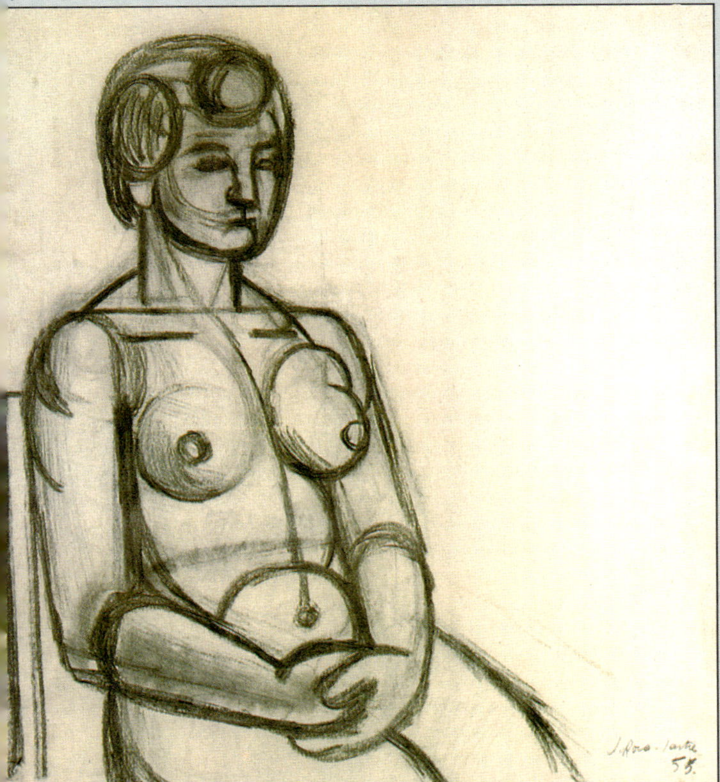

and the forearm are like two cylinders placed almost at right angles. I recommend that you study Roca-Sastre's drawings carefully. They are interesting and provide ideas for understanding all these factors.

Fig. 127. Josep Roca-Sastre, *Study of a Figure*. Artist's collection, Barcelona. In this drawing we can clearly see how the artist has introduced lines that relate some parts of the figure with others in order to define the proportions.

Linear drawing

Fig. 128. Charles Reid (1942-), *Study in Gouache*. Private collection. Courtesy of Watson-Guptill. In this gouache painting, the ink lines define the composition based on the main areas of light and shade.

Fig. 129. Charles Reid (1942-), *Peasant*. Private collection. Courtesy of Watson-Guptill. Reid has emphasized the sensation of sunlight with a range of rich, vibrant colors. A line drawing that summed up the main features of the model permitted the artist to concentrate on the colors when he applied the paint.

128

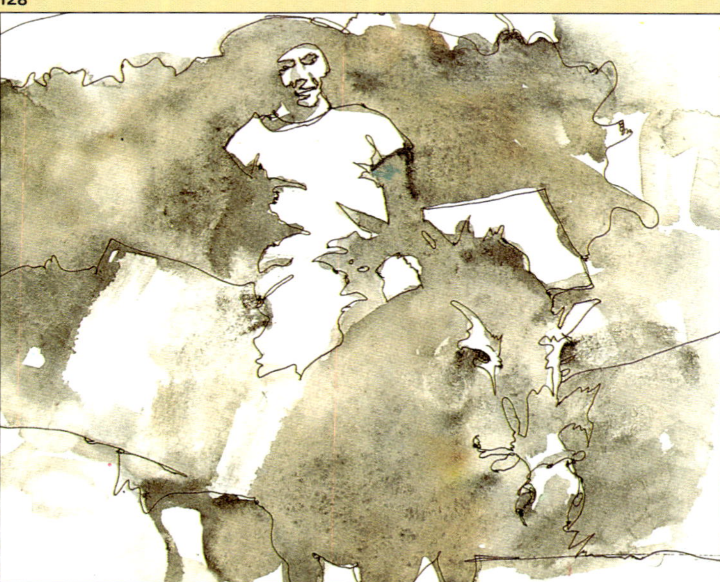

129

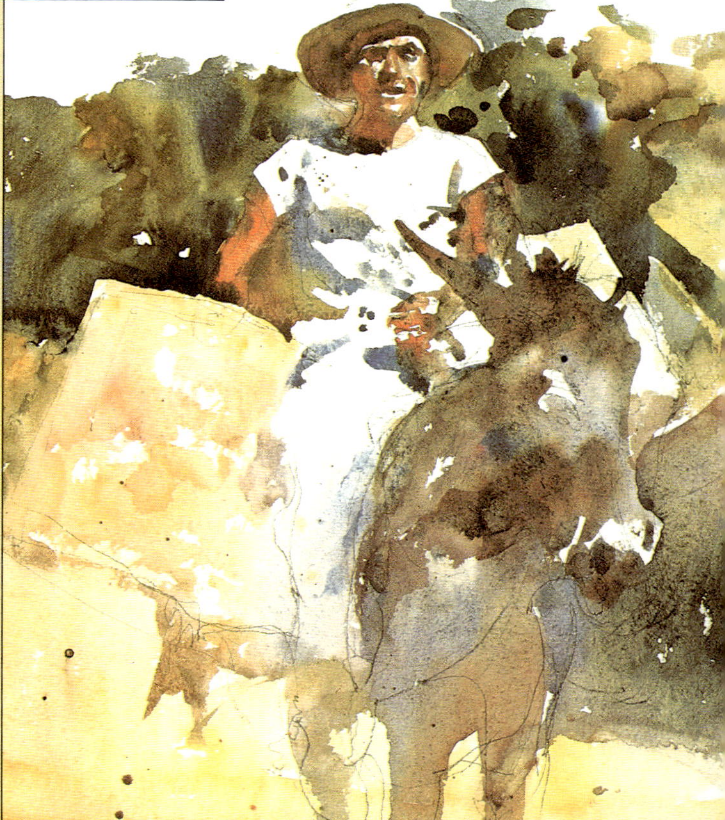

Now we are going to discuss a practical exercise that makes for greater firmness and fluency in drawing; it is also particularly well suited to watercolor painting. This is linear drawing, done freehand without blocking it in first. I suggest that you use a medium that cannot be erased, such as a ballpoint pen, fountain pen, or fine felt-tip pen. In this type of drawing, the most important thing is to define the structure and basic details of the model using *only* lines—that is, without any shading or modeling. This kind of drawing requires a good ability to synthesize, as it aims to explain in a simple yet accurate way the shape and volume of the objects *without any shading or modeling*. You may wonder why this kind of drawing is the best suited to watercolor painting. For two reasons: first, because watercolor is a concise, direct technique. When painting in watercolor, you focus mainly on obtaining hues, tonalities, and colors, using only the brush. Therefore, the objects in the composition must be carefully and accurately positioned and outlined in the preliminary drawing (now using a pencil, as the ink may run with the water.) Without a prior drawing, you must continually reconstruct the composition, and this diverts you from you basic aim: to make the best use of all the expressive resources that can be achieved with color.

Second, because of the transparency of watercolors. In watercolor painting, the play of light and shadow is achieved using color, not pencil. If the pencil drawing contains shading in blacks or grays, all the watercolors painted on top of them will become dirty and lose their luminous quality.

I recommend that you practice line drawing until you become reasonably adept. Begin by drawing anything that you may have in front of you now. Do not aim to draw a perfect sketch, but rather a sketch that is harmonious and pleasing when taken as a whole. Observe the model while you draw, without lifting the pen from the paper so as not to lose continuity. Pay as much attention to the background as to the main motif so that they relate to each other. And don't worry if the proportion is not always accurate, because this can even introduce a certain charm and personality into the drawing.

Fig. 130. The theme of urban landscape in watercolors requires a preliminary sketch to define the composition in a clear, accurate way.

Fig. 131. Andrew Freeth (1912-1986), *Grandma and the Boys in Trafalgar Square*. Private collection, London. Freeth has used a light, anecdotal style to express the bustle of a busy city square.

130

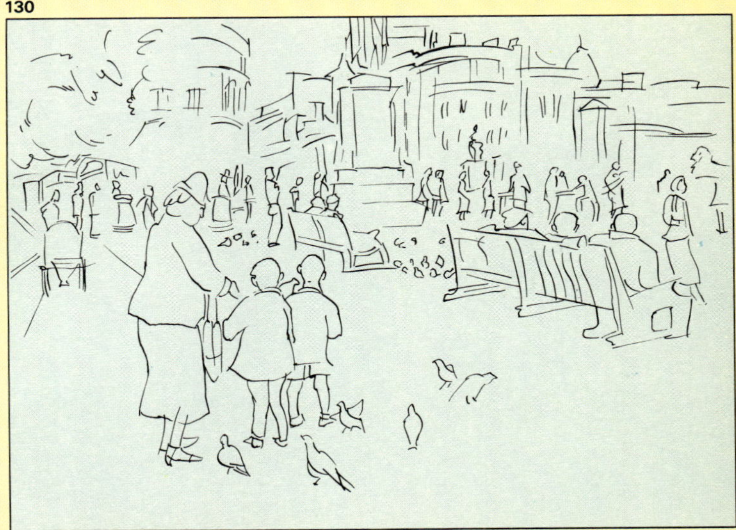

131

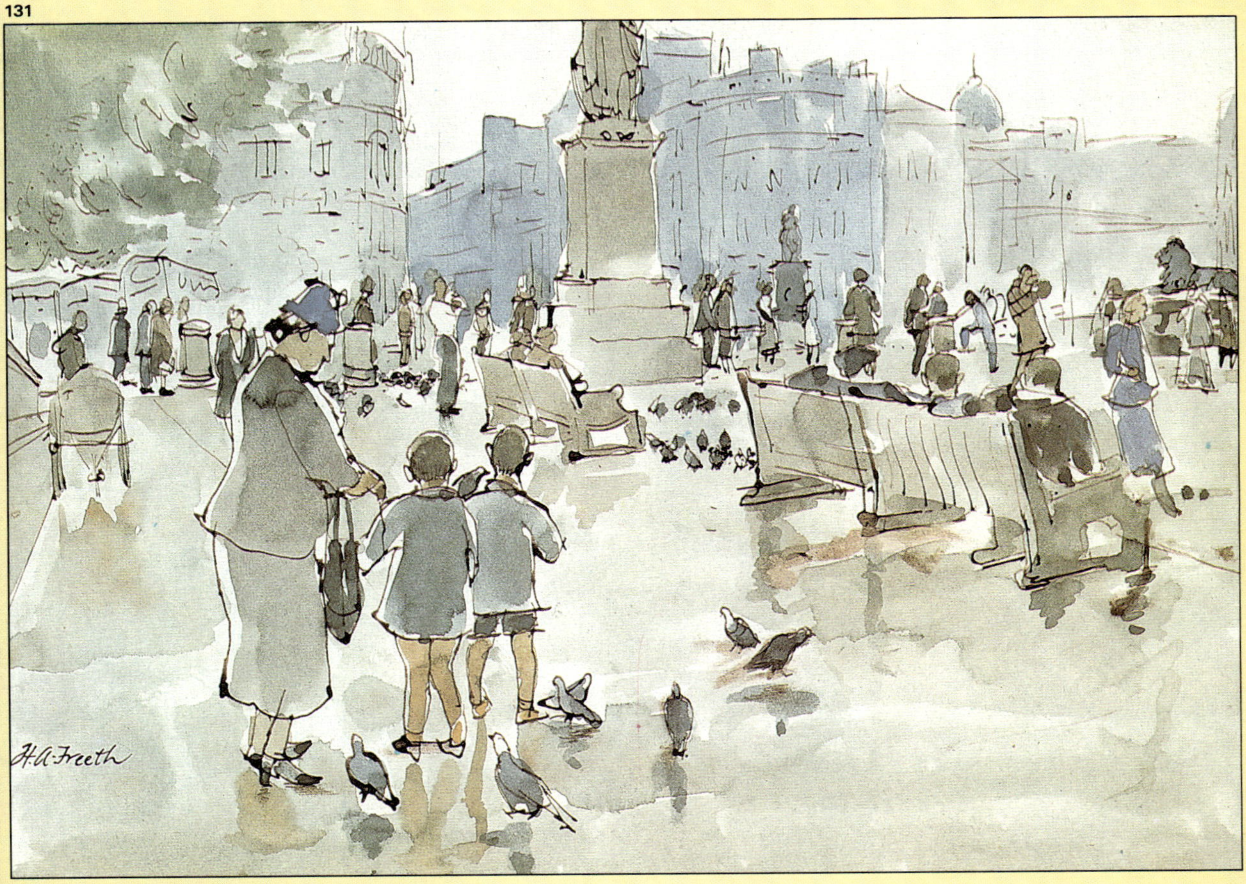

Watercolor sketches

132

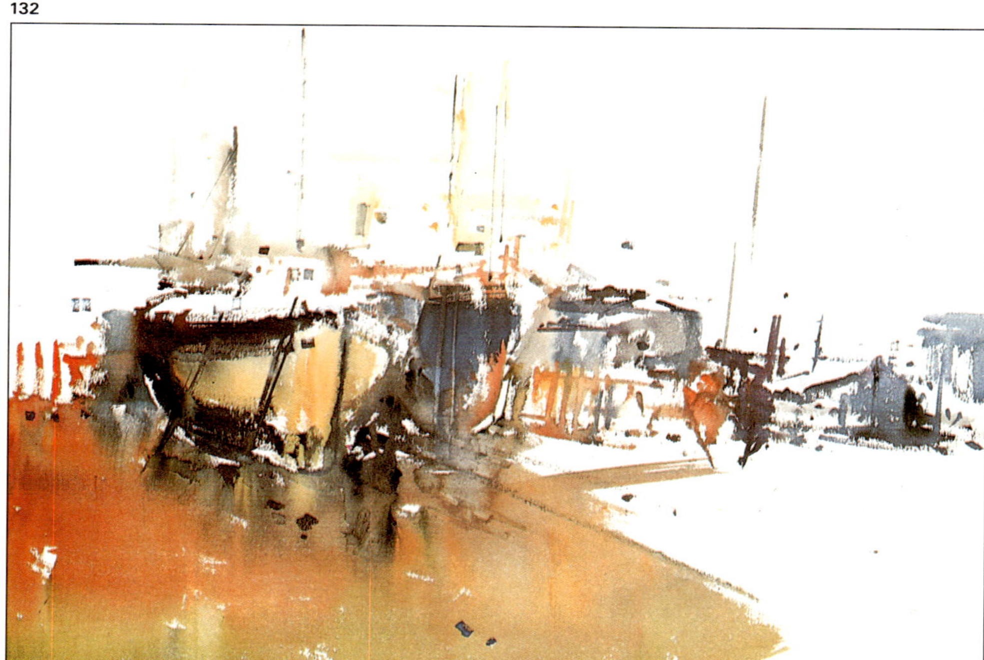

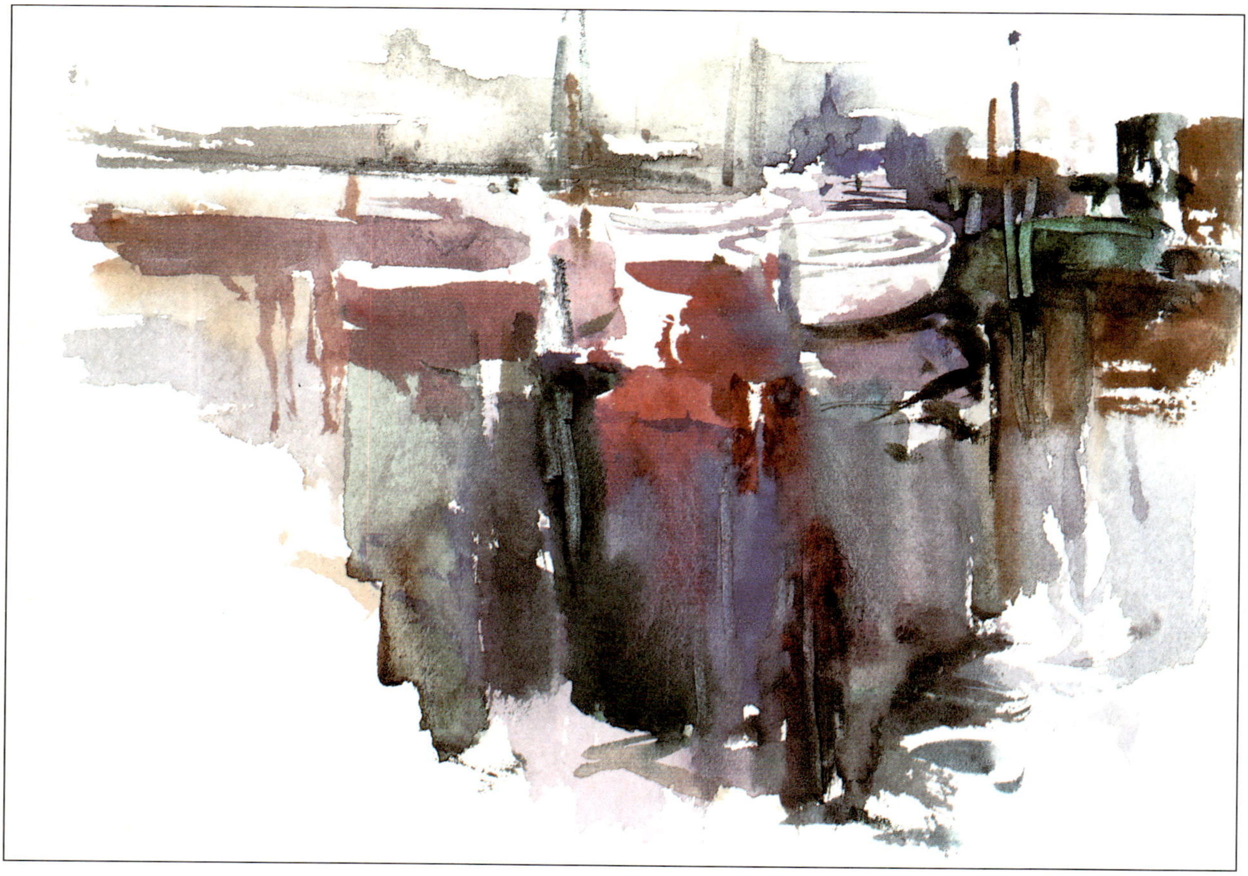

Fig. 132. Josep Martínez Lozano (1923- ?), *Boats*. Private collection. A visually pleasing scene, whether common or uncommon, is a good reason for doing a watercolor sketch.

Fig. 133. Josep Martínez Lozano, *Reflections in the water*. Private collection. In this sketch, the artist has captured the momentary effect of the reflections and lights on the water's surface.

133

With the same ease that a quick pencil sketch can be drawn, it is also possible to paint a quick watercolor sketch. If you have not yet had the chance to do this, I strongly recommend that you try it. All you need is a small notepad, two or three colors at most, a brush, and water. Take these materials outside in the street, in the countryside, or wherever you like. Practicing watercolor sketching will enable you to paint more freely and enhance your ability to observe and synthesize reality. If you have ever been able to see the sketches of established painters, you will certainly have come across small "masterpieces" that with a few brushstrokes bring together specific ideas (the effect of a certain type of lighting, a particularly interesting composition, a given range of colors, and so on).
Some watercolor sketches are a basic means of studying and approaching the different aspects of a theme (light, composition, and so on) while others are merely anecdotal. Make quick sketches of scenes or people that have captured your attention during a trip to the countryside or the beach, or while you are strolling along the street.

134

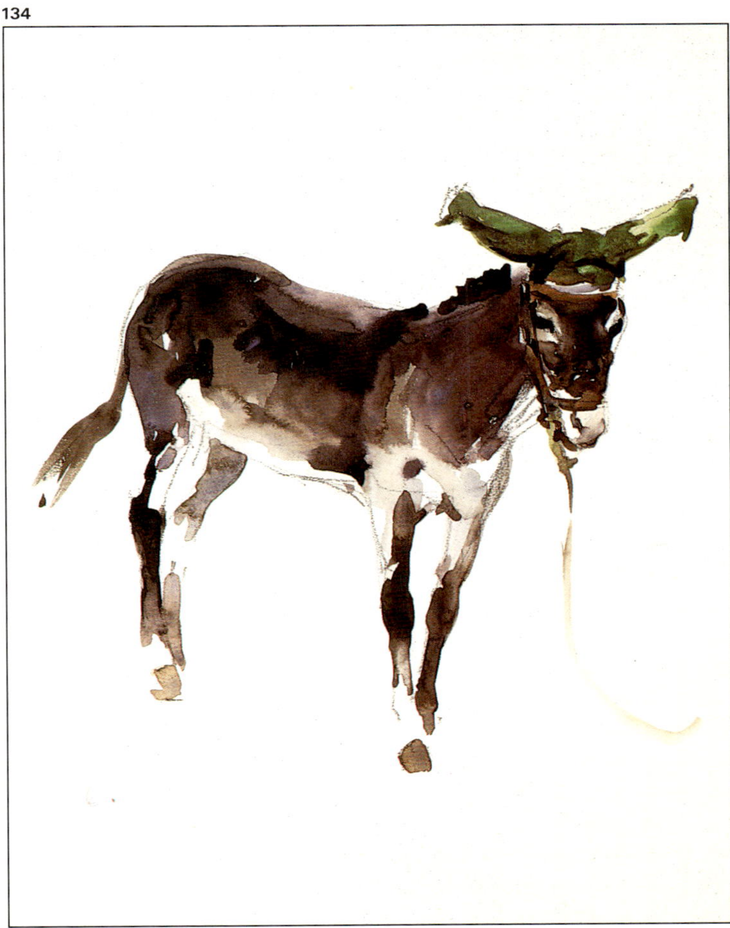

135

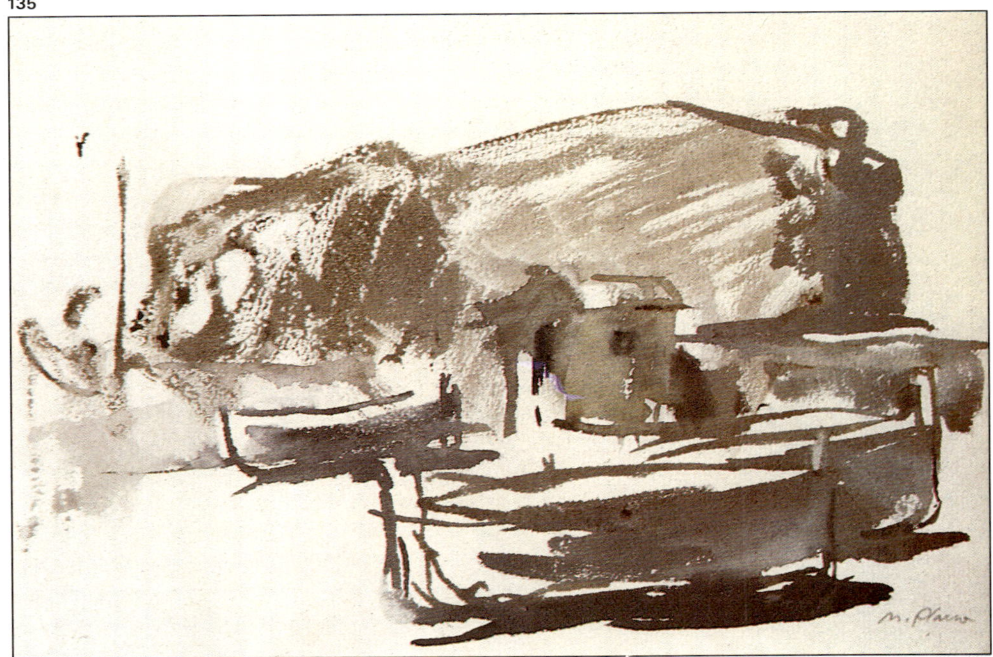

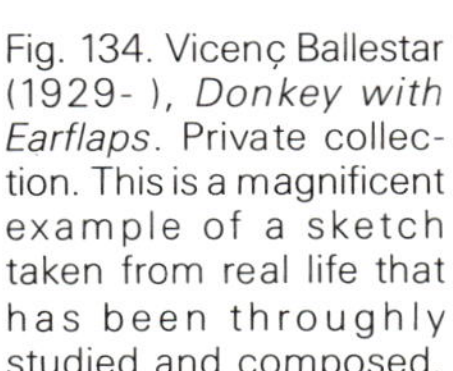

Fig. 134. Vicenç Ballestar (1929-), *Donkey with Earflaps*. Private collection. This is a magnificent example of a sketch taken from real life that has been throughly studied and composed.

Fig. 135. Manel Plana (1949-), *Boats on the Shore*. Private collection. Sketches like this one capture the essence of the motif with the scantiest of means: several lines, values, and a mere indication of color.

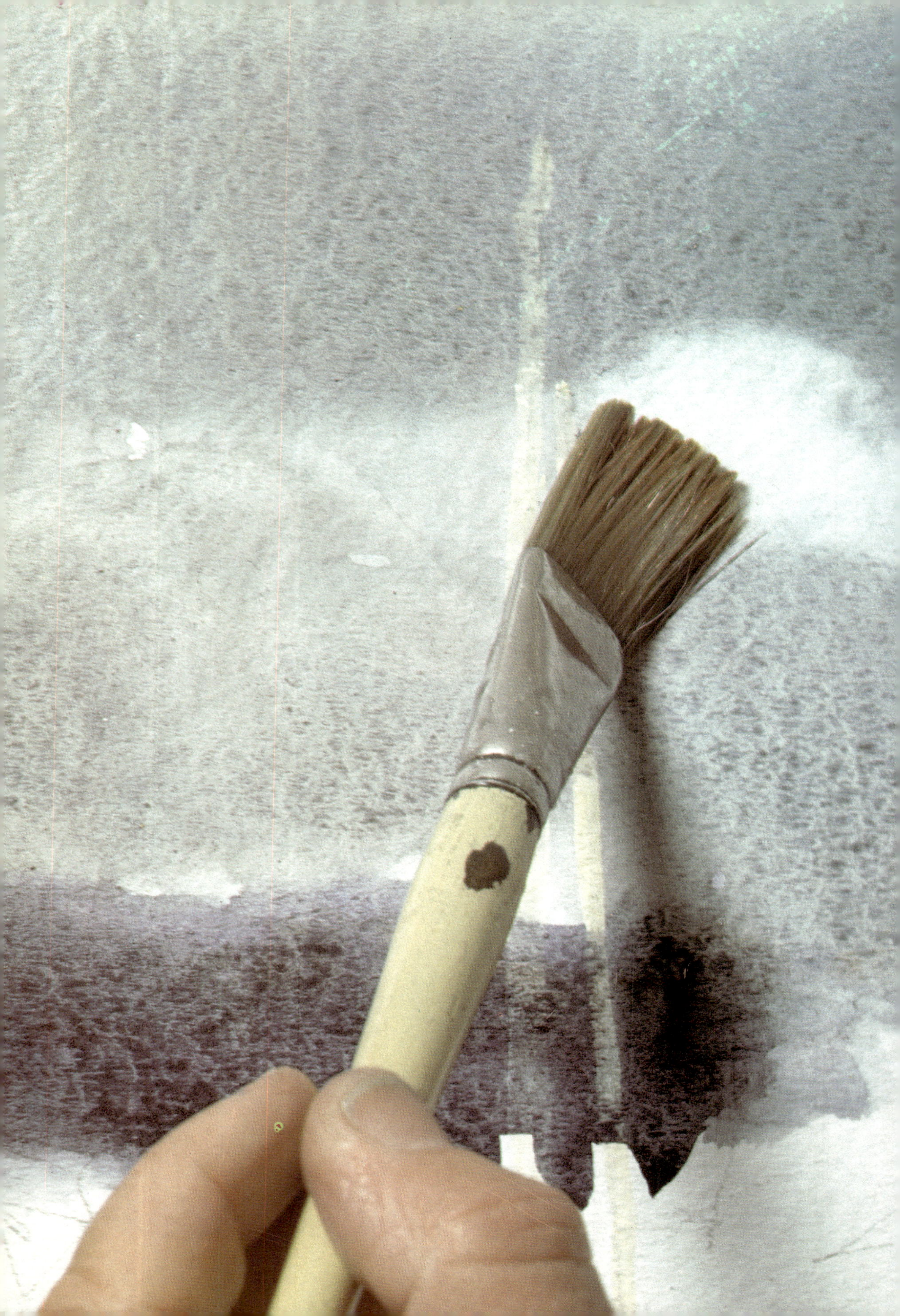

Watercolor, as a pictorial technique, is based on objective technical principles; creative work is impossible without a knowledge of these techniques. Wash is the basic technique for watercolor painting. This chapter discusses wash, together with all its related techniques and tricks of the trade that are essential for the development of creativity in watercolor.

Wash as a technical and creative exercise

Washes and gradations

137

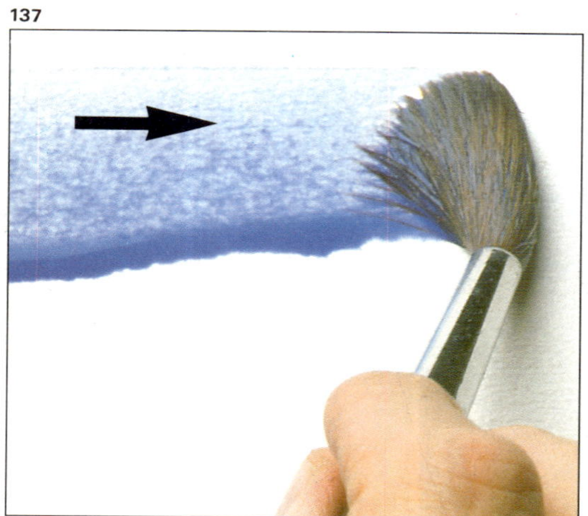

138

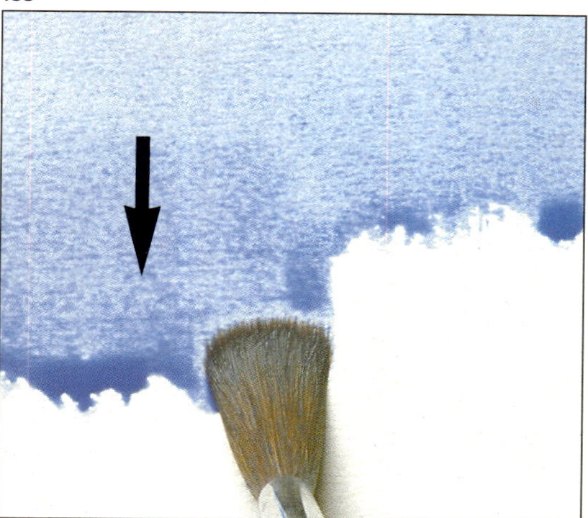

139

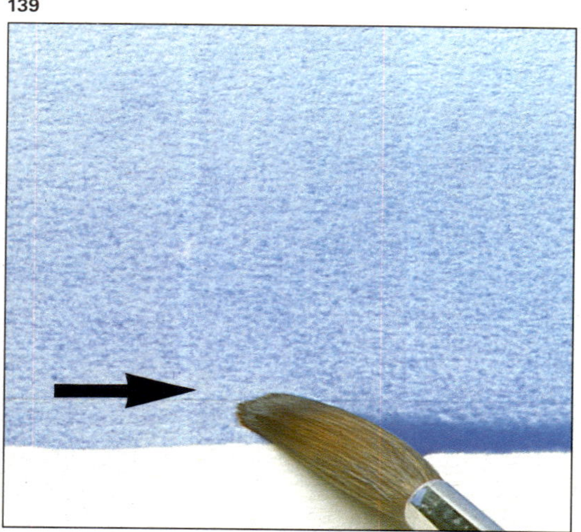

140 140A 140B

On this page we see two basic exercises in the use of watercolor. Take a piece of thick watercolor paper, a drawing board, watercolor paints, plenty of water, a pan to dilute the color, a roll of absorbent paper, and two sable brushes, nos. 8 and 12. On the left of the page you can see the wash; it must maintain an even tone, so paint from top to bottom with the board slightly tilted, dragging the color along but without letting it dry. Otherwise this would result in a ''hardening'' of the color (figs. 141 and 141A). Figures 140, 140A, and 140B show a gradation. The ''secret'' of gradation is to increase the amount of water in the color solution. This should produce an even, progressively lighter tone until is merges with the white of the paper.

141

141A

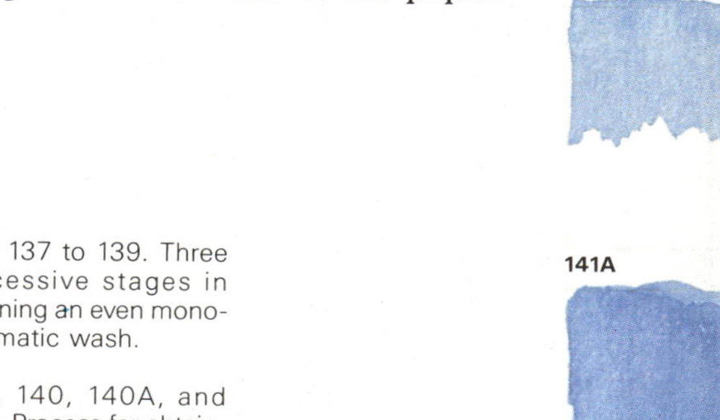

Fig. 136 (preceding spread). Vicenç Ballestar absorbs the color of the sky in a watercolor landscape.

Figs. 137 to 139. Three successive stages in obtaining an even monochromatic wash.

Figs. 140, 140A, and 140B. Process for obtaining a gradation, working from the saturated color (fig. 140) until it totally fades away (fig. 140B).

...wax, salt, water, turpentine

The following exercises should be done on moistened paper. In order to moisten it, use a wide brush that can hold a lot of water, or even better, a small sponge. A sponge is always handier, quicker, and more efficient. Well, the paper is now moist and you have dissolved the right amount of color in the pan. Painting a wash on damp paper (fig. 142) is very simple. Just place the well-charged brush on the damp area and spread the color evenly from top to bottom. You must be careful that any wrinkles in the paper caused by overmoistening do not accumulate paint, because when they dry out, these areas will look darker than the rest. To paint a gradation of color on damp paper (fig. 143), you don't need to increase the water in the pan; just spread the brushful of color from top to bottom, letting the color become lighter as it fades into the moisture on the paper. When blending colors on damp paper (fig. 144), apply the lightest tone first (yellow in this case). Then apply the darker color, working toward the middle of the light color. Paint in the same way as you did for a single-color gradation, letting the darker color blend into the lighter tone. This change in tone must be gradual.

142

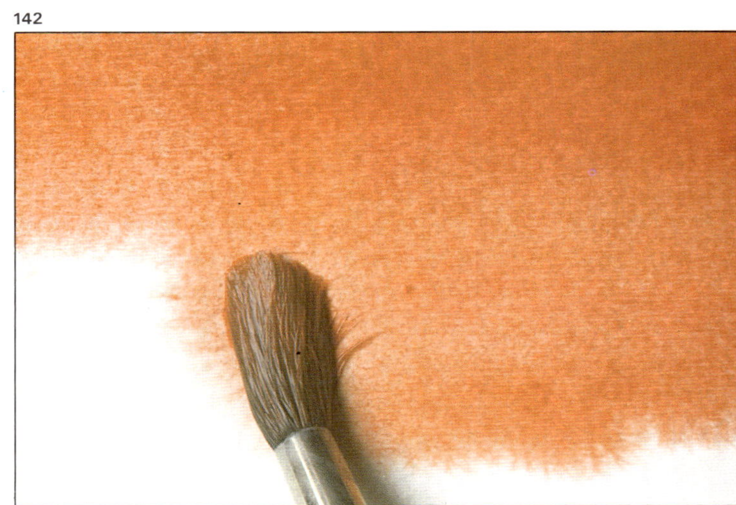

143

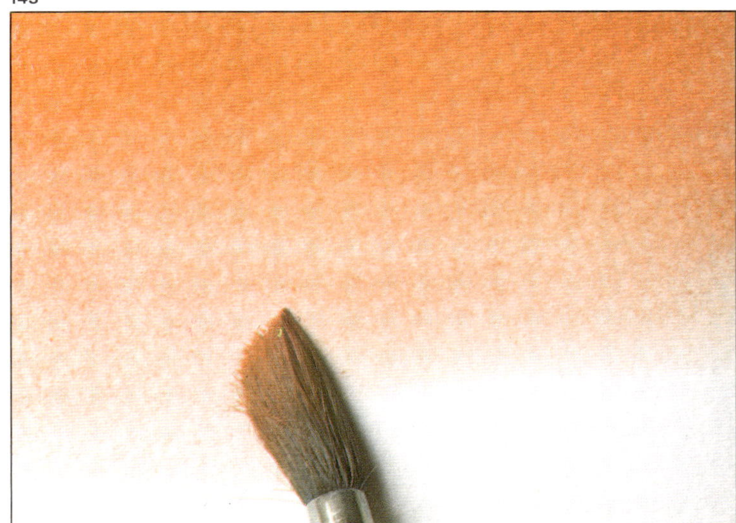

144

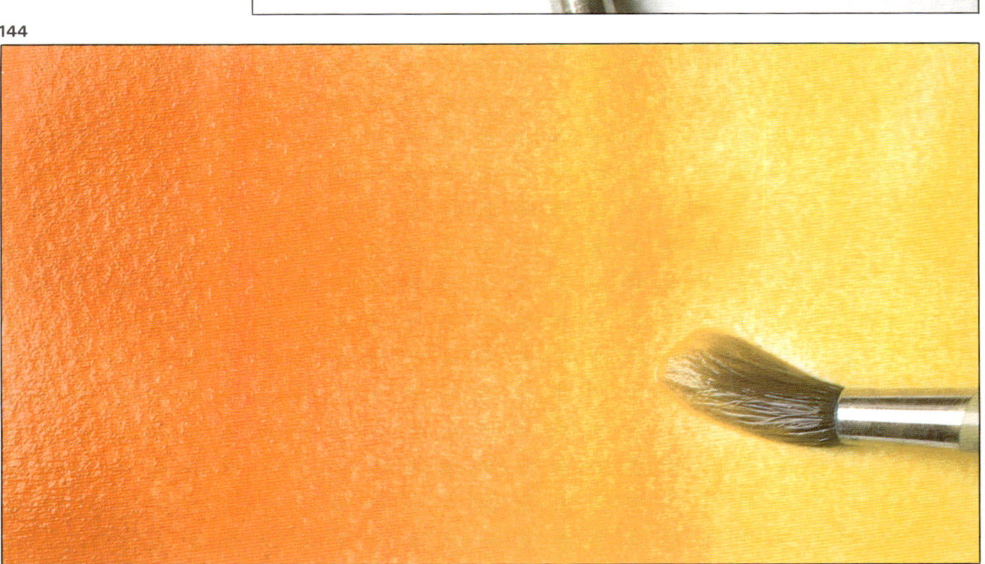

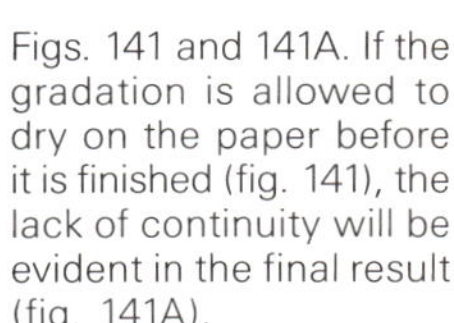

Figs. 141 and 141A. If the gradation is allowed to dry on the paper before it is finished (fig. 141), the lack of continuity will be evident in the final result (fig. 141A).

Fig. 142. Painting a wash over previously moistened paper.

Fig. 143. Painting a graded wash on moistened paper.

Fig. 144. Wet blending of two colors.

Reserving, absorbing, scraping...

Figs. 145 and 145A. Masking fluid for reserving whites must be applied before painting the detail you wish to leave white (fig. 145). When the watercolor is finished, the masking fluid can easily be removed with a crepe eraser (fig. 145A).

Fig. 146. White areas can be opened up on a damp watercolor by using a clean, damp brush to absorb the color.

Fig. 147. Lines such as the one in this illustration can be achieved by scraping the handle of the brush on the still damp color.

Fig. 148. Some watercolor painters use their fingernails to obtain white lines in the wet watercolor.

Fig. 149. Razor blades enable you to impart texture to the surface of a color when it has already dried.

Watercolor painting has its tricks and different resources. We have chosen the most interesting ones to illustrate the explanations on these pages.

Reserving whites with masking fluid (figs. 145 and 145A) allows you to keep back the white of the paper in very small, narrow areas. Apply the masking fluid using an old brush (the gum it contains may spoil a brush) to the area you wish to leave white. Once it has dried and after the watercolor has been painted, removed it with a crepe eraser. Whites can also be obtained from a watercolor that is still damp by absorbing the color with a clean, damp brush.

The handle of the brush can be used for producing lines that reveal the white of the paper (fig. 147). Broader lines can be made by using your fingernail (fig. 148). In neither case should the paint be dry. Scraping with a razor blade (fig. 149) produces textured surfaces with a lighter tone than the color being removed.

145

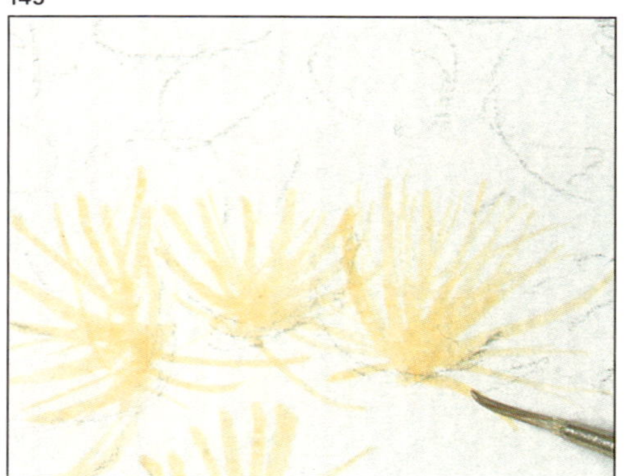

145A

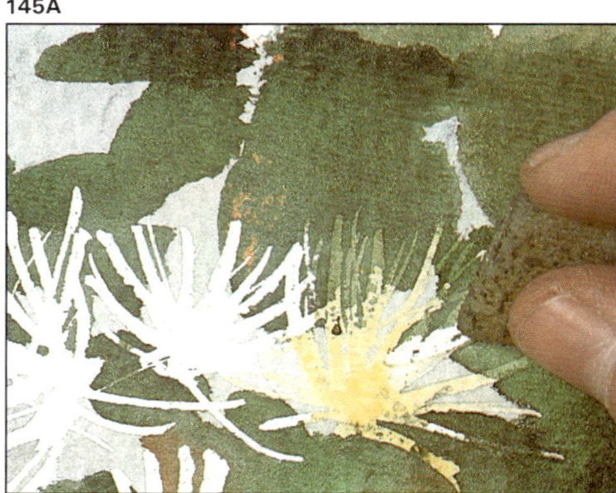

146

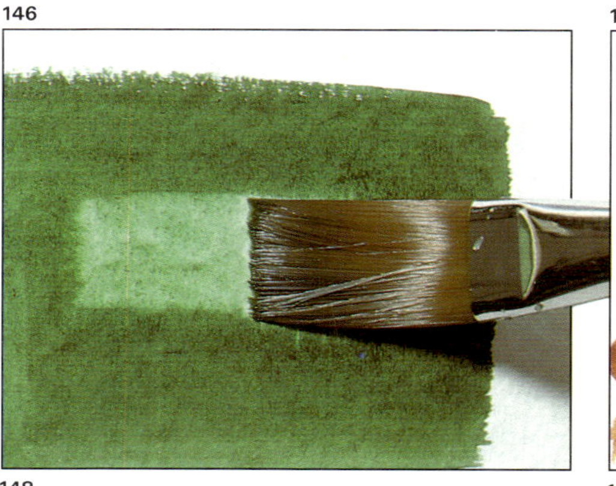

147

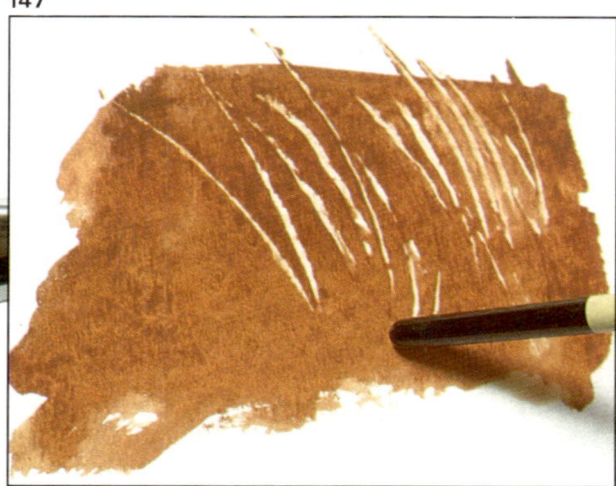

148

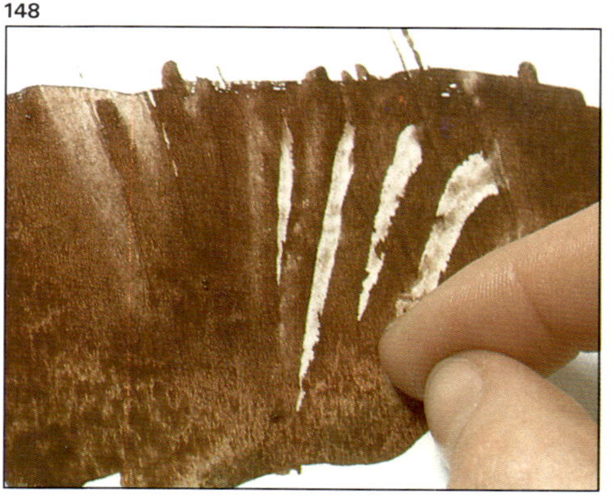

149

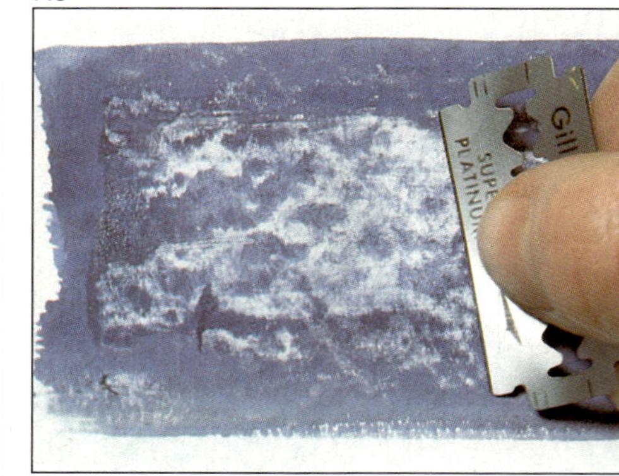

Fig. 150. Lines and textures obtained with sandpaper.

Figs. 151 and 151A. Lines obtained by applying white wax.

Fig. 152. Texture produced by sprinkling salt on the damp color.

Scraping of dry paint can be done with sandpaper, laid flat onto the paper or rubbed with one of the corners (fig. 150). A textured effect can be obtained by drawing lines on the paper with white wax before starting to paint (figs. 151 and 151A). Another interesting textured effect can be produced by sprinkling salt onto the wet patch of color (fig. 152).

In order to open up a white space in a dry, painted area, place water on the chosen space (fig. 153) and then rub it with a dry brush (fig. 153A), repeating the process as often as necessary.

Sprinkling water (fig. 154) and turpentine (fig. 155) on the damp patch of color produces textured, mottled effects when the color dries.

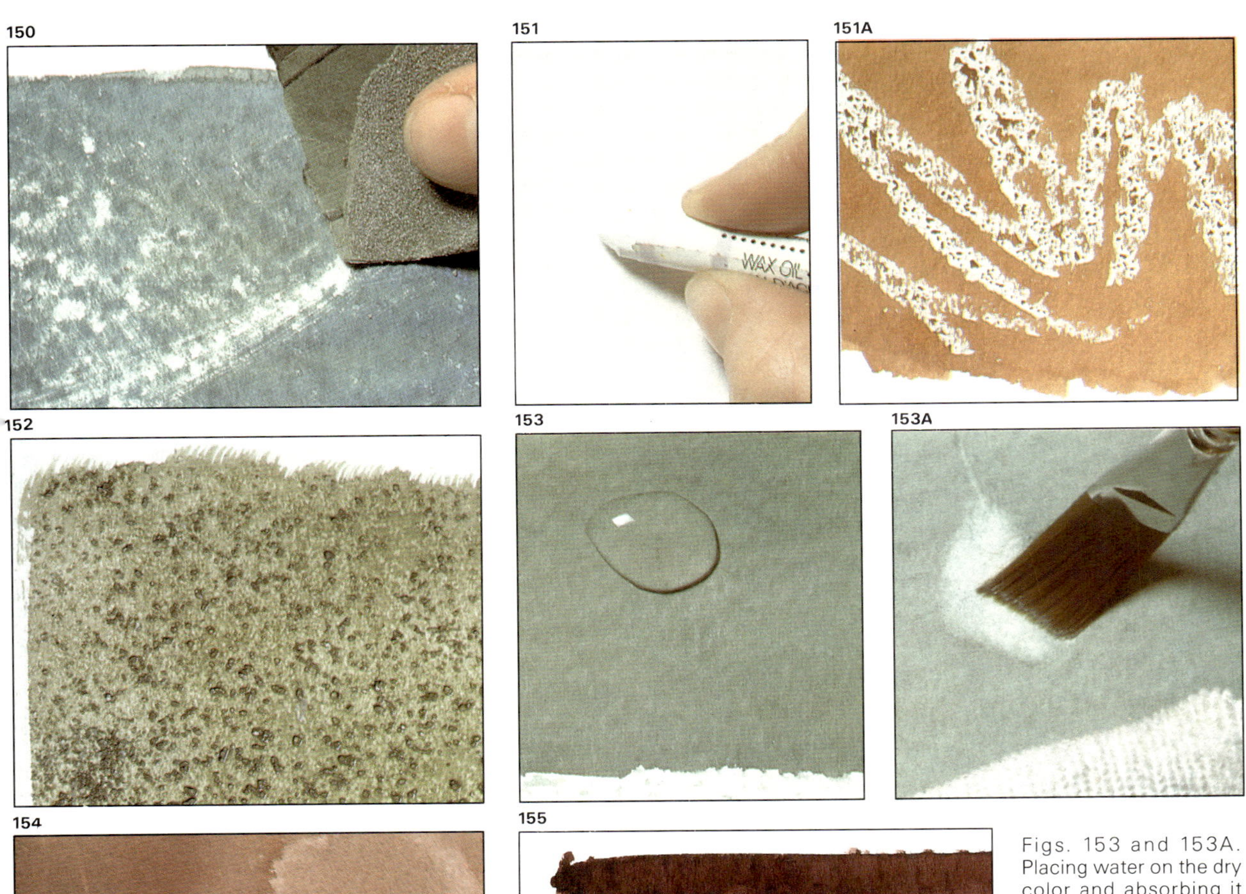

Figs. 153 and 153A. Placing water on the dry color and absorbing it with the brush is another way to open up white space, as in these two illustrations.

Figs. 154 and 155. The effect obtained by sprinkling water (fig. 154) and turpentine (fig. 155).

Ballestar shows how to apply technical resources

In order to create the landscape shown in figure 162, Ballestar has applied the resources and techniques displayed on this page. The chosen motif lends itself well to these kinds of tricks. The mud and puddles of the lane are ideal for intense pictorial creation. The damp, gray sky, the branches of the trees—both call for the use of special techniques. Please observe the process of elaboration used by Ballestar in the illustrations, together with their respective explanations.

Fig. 157. Scraping with the handle of the brush. In order to "open up" these whites, Ballestar briskly rubs the handle on the still wet paint.

Fig. 158. Reserving whiles. We cannot paint a light color over a dark one in watercolor; we must always paint from a lesser tone to a darker one. Ballestar has planned ahead the whites and lighter colors he wishes to reserve.

Fig. 159. Absorbing color with a cloth. To soften the intensity of the color while it is still wet, Ballestar presses a cloth onto the area. He obtains some very interesting textures with this method.

Fig. 160. Scraping with utility knife. The artis scrapes the color with utility knife when th paint has dried.

Fig. 161. Spattering wate or paint. This techniqu allows you to achieve a almost pointillist effect Ballestar wets the brus in water and flick droplets onto the paint ing using his finger.

Fig. 162. This is th watercolor obtained fro putting all these tech niques into practice.

156

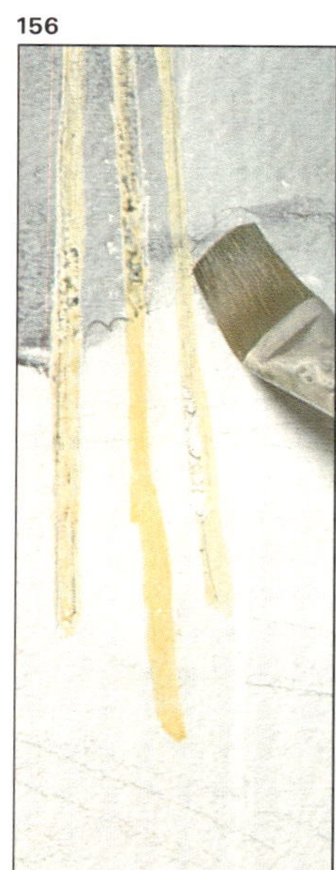

Fig. 156. Delicate white lines reserved with masking fluid. Ballestar paints some parts of the drawing he want to keep white with masking fluid. He can then paint around and over the fluid. When the watercolor is dry, he removes the masking fluid with a crepe eraser, obtaining a perfect white.

157

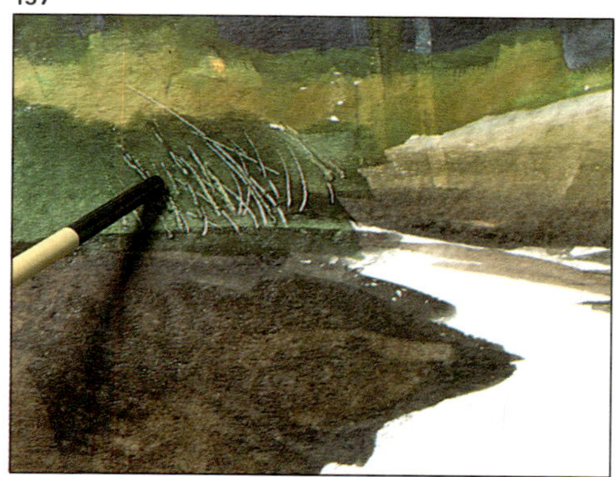

158

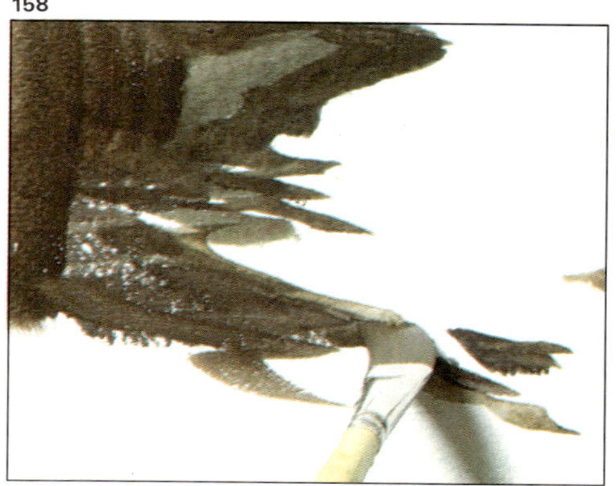

159

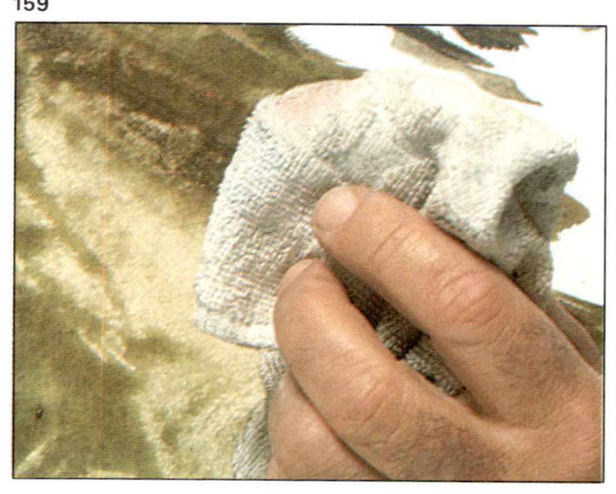

160

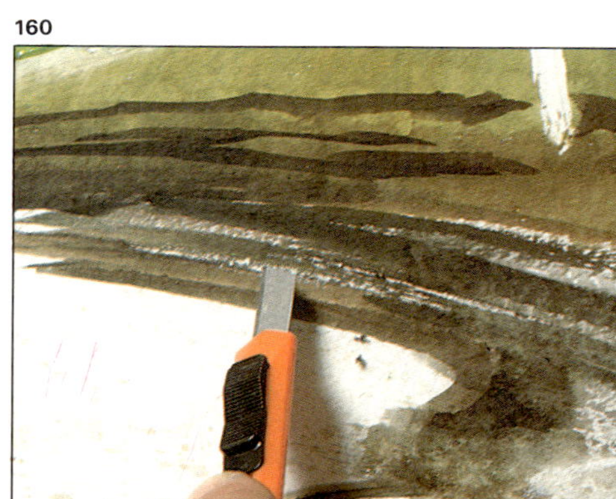

161

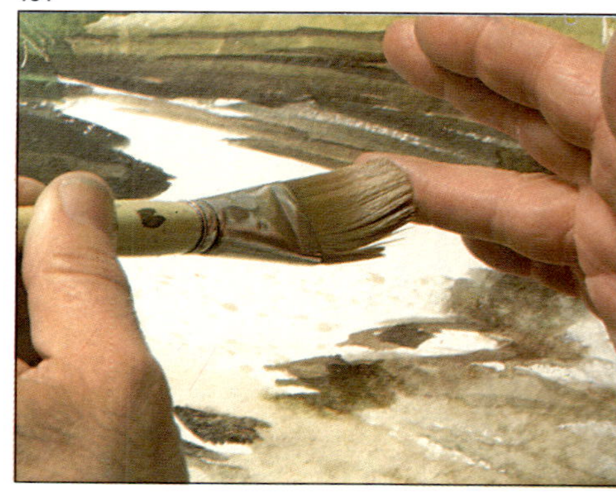

62

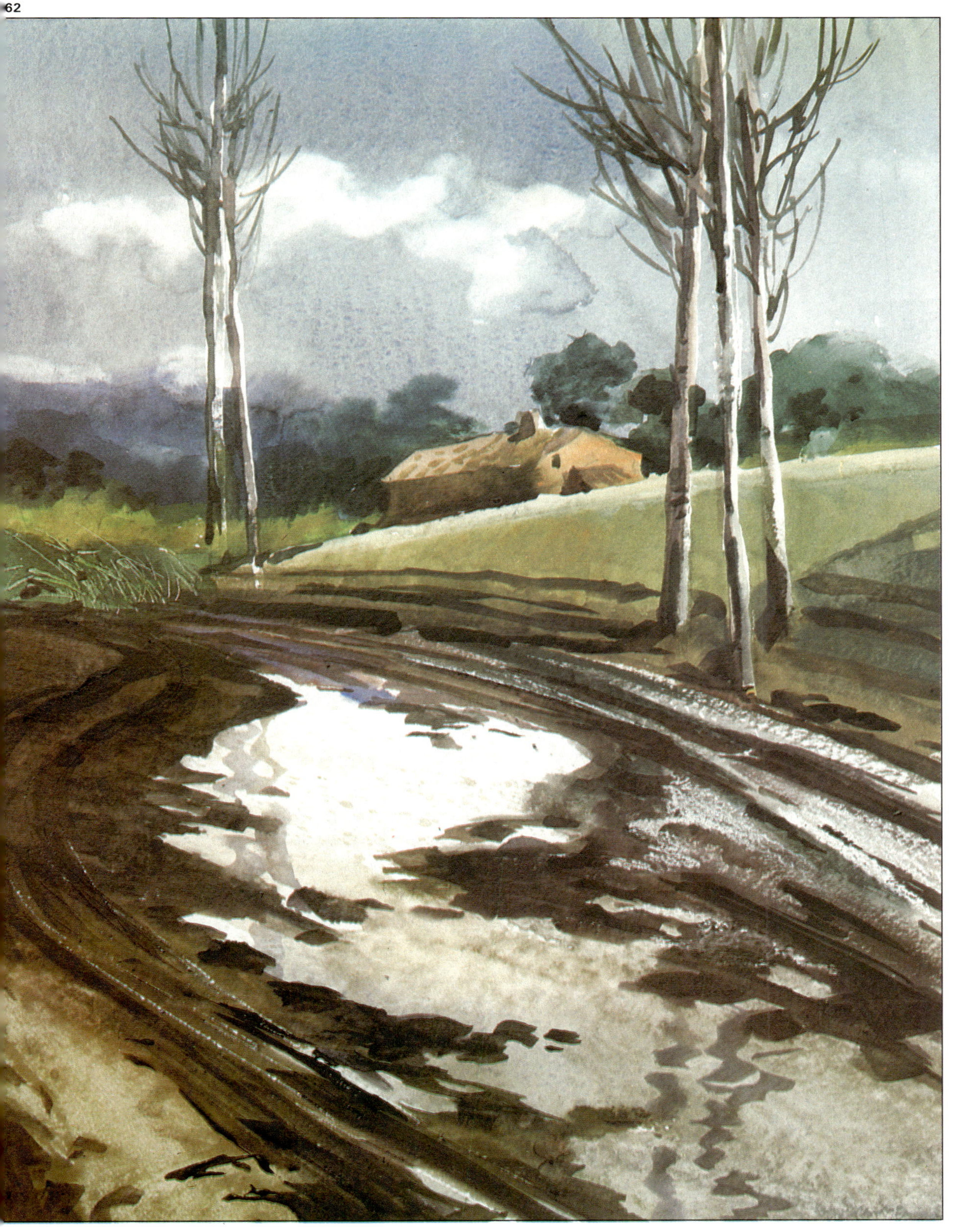

Shape and color as creative factors

163

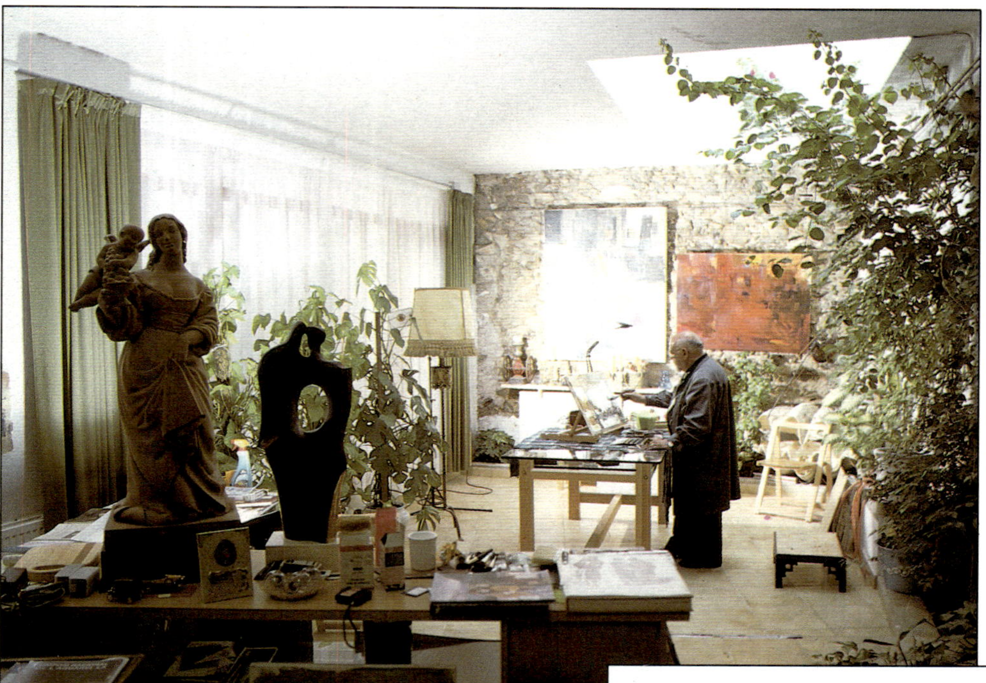

Fig. 163. This is Martínez Lozano's studio—an enviable place that is ideal for painting watercolors.

Fig. 164. The first strokes of this watercolor seem random and apparently meaningless. The important thing for the moment is the intensity and vividness of the colors.

Fig. 165. The colors begin to merge and form a whole. The theme begins to appear.

164

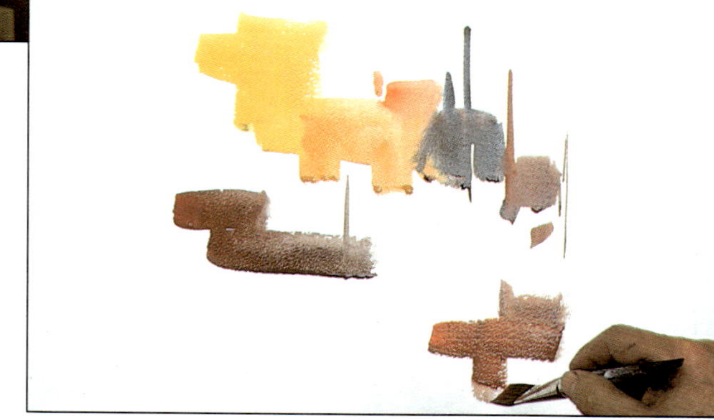

Josep Martínez Lozano's studio, as you can see (fig. 163), is ideal for painting. It is bright, spacious, comfortable, and, above all, full of objects that have a special significance for the artist, the objects that encourage him to paint watercolors. Martínez Lozano is about to display his capacity for creation and invention. He expresses it thus: "Colors and... whatever appears!" Actually, Lozano is well aware that the result will be guided by him, however spontaneous the process may appear. And that, in short, is watercolor painting: vivid patches of color applied with firmness, boldness, as if it were an abstract painting. These patches of color overlap, mix, and become richer until they capture the overall theme and then work down to the detail. The artist improvises as would a musician with a perfect command of his instrument.

165

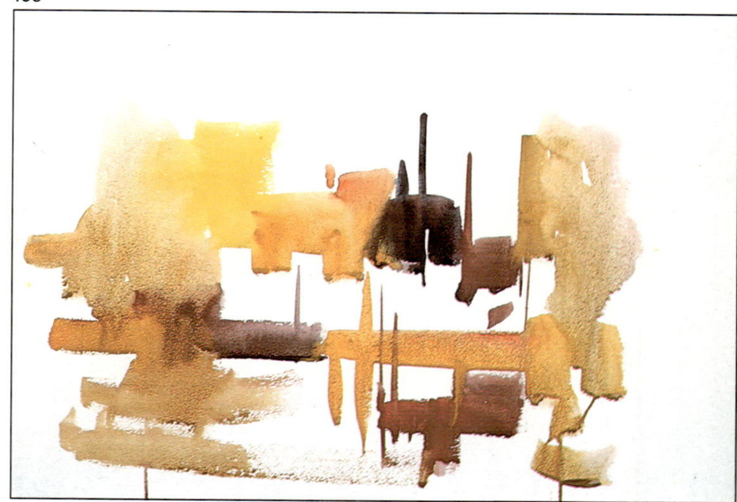

This procedure is reminiscent of Picasso when he said, "Before painting I have a certain idea of what I want, but it's a very vague one." It is the color itself, the rhythm of the shapes, the balance of light and shade that determine Lozano's work. The theme—the seascape—is just the "certain idea" that Picasso referred to: the framework of shapes and color. Lozano has marked out the shapes of this seascape incorporating the mast and their reflection in the water: a traditional theme dealt with using truly creative shapes.

166

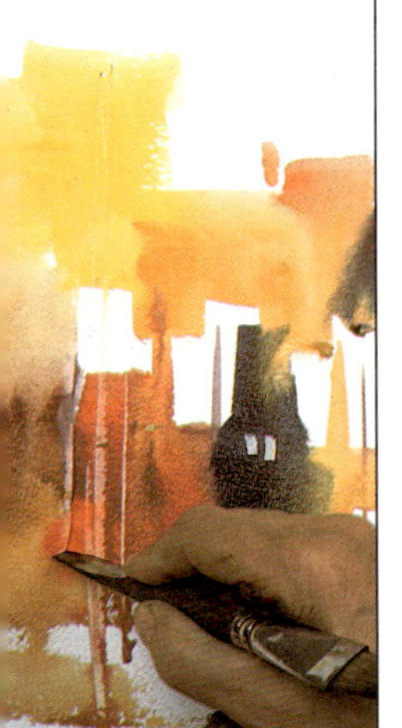

167

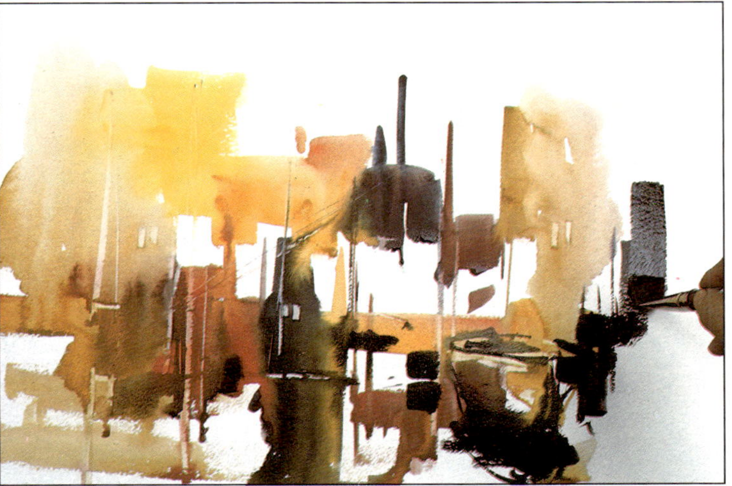

Fig. 166. With the pointed end of the brush dipped in paint. Lozano draws vertical lines that suggest the masts of the boats.

Fig. 167. What before seemed to be an almost abstract composition is becoming a port flooded with light, reflections, and above all, shimmering color.

Fig. 168. This is the finished work. Notice that the boat on the right is essential to appreciating the scale and the proportion of the work as a whole.

168

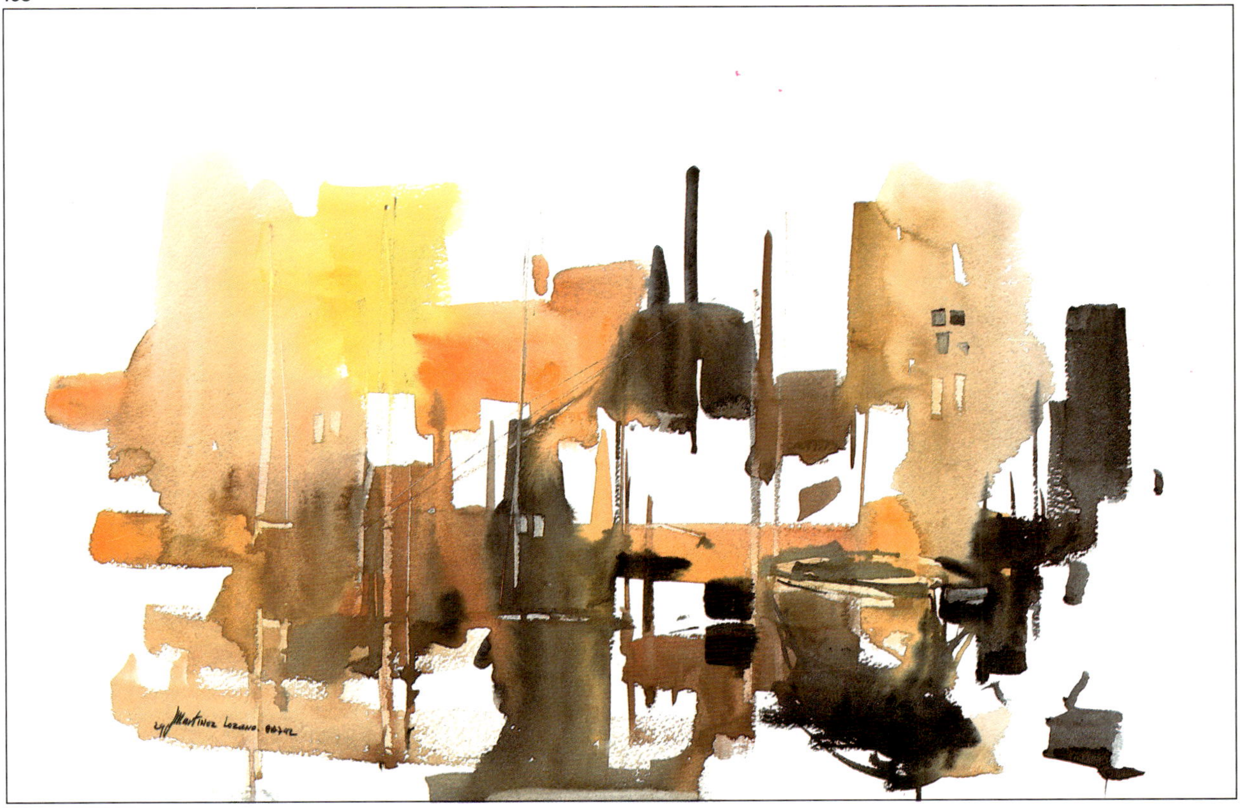

Range of commonly used colors

169

The watercolorist's palette has changed considerably throughout history. The English painters of the eighteenth century—Cozens, Girtin, and Turner, for example—used a very limited assortment of colors: five or six at most. In fact, there are three strictly essential colors for painting: red, yellow, and blue, which when mixed can produce all the remaining colors. But the watercolor painter need not be so thrifty. Let us take a look at the most commonly used colors in watercolor painting.

The boxes of watercolors sold in art supply stores usually have a range of between six and fourteen colors. In general, most manufacturers coincide in their assortment of colors. This choice is not random, but corresponds to the colors most in demand.

A professional artist's palette usually contains a limited number of colors. With experience, painters gradually "whittle down" the number of colors they use to those that best suit their particular style. The colors that appear in most assortments and most palettes are cadmium lemon, cadmium yellow deep, yellow ochre, cadmium red, alizarin crimson, emerald green, ultramarine blue, and ivory black. These colors, which we might call the basic colors, are usually complemented with a sienna, another blue (cobalt or Prussian), and another green or gray (like Payne's gray). These are also fairly common, although each painter has his or her own preferences. Actually, there is nothing to stop you from using any other color out of the vast assortment on the market. The colors mentioned here are merely a recommendation based on personal experience and that of the manufacturers.

The color chart

Fig. 169. Assortment of colors commonly used by the professional artist.

Fig. 170. A color chart comprising 36 different tonalities.

The color chart on this page is one of the many that can be found on the market, but it by no means one of the largest. Nevertheless, we could say that the number of colors here is excessive. If an artist were to paint with such a range of colors, the result would be an "overdose" of color and a poor painting. As we said on the preceding page, only twelve colors are necessary for watercolor painting—and many artists paint with only five or six at most. Why, then, do such large ranges of color exist? Because there is no fixed rule that obliges a painter to use one color or another. Although there is a commonly accepted range of colors used by the majority of artists, each one develops his own range and palette. Let us suppose, for example, that you want to add another blue to your palette. This color chart offers six varieties of blue, not counting other colors such as indigo or Payne's gray that have a pronounced tendency toward blue. You will choose the one that best suits your style and inclination.

Color charts also show the resistance of each color to light, and this is marked by small crosses. The effect of light on watercolor is one factor you may wish to take into account in choosing your palette, especially when you reach the stage of selling paintings.

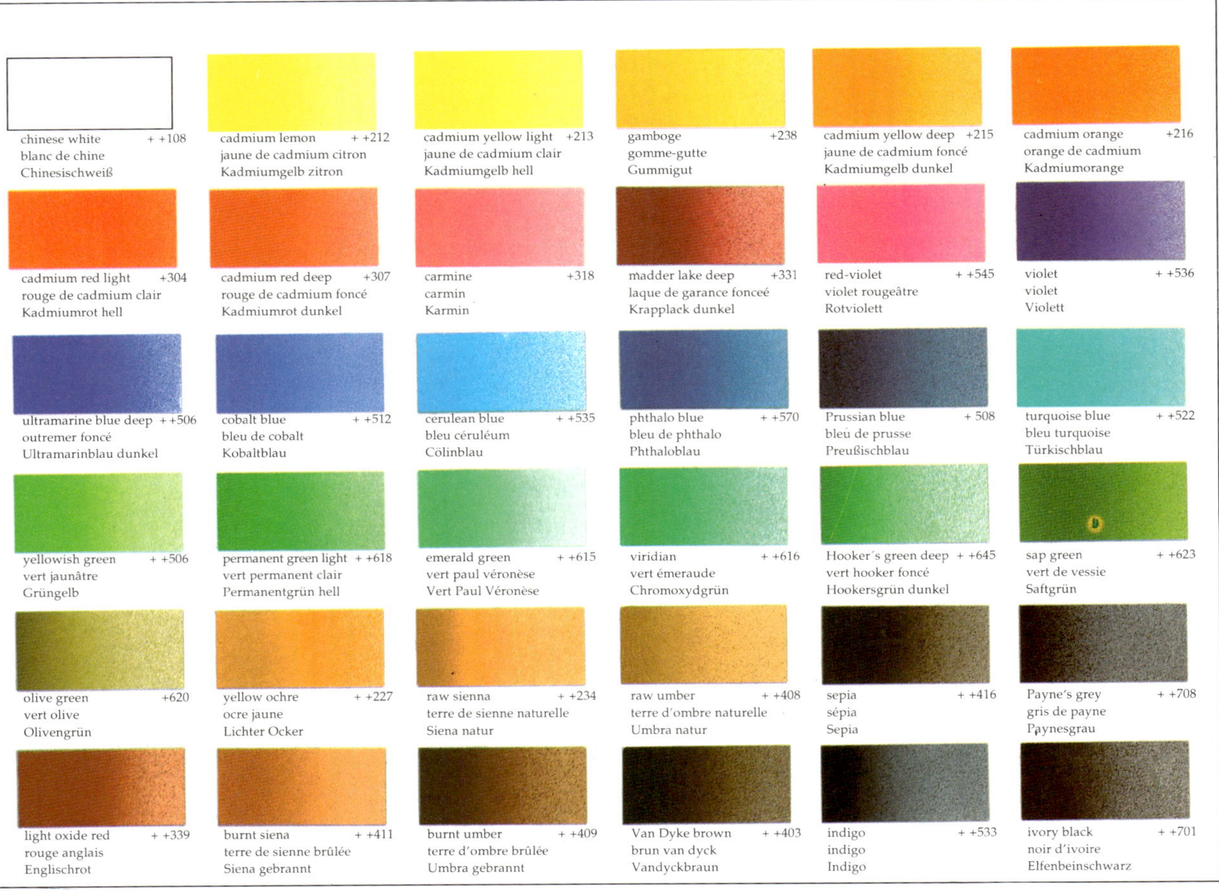

Mixtures and ranges of colors

Obtaining tones from a mixture of watercolor paints is achieved by using three different systems: mixtures on the palette, mixtures on paper, and glazing. These three systems can be applied together in order to obtain a particular color.

Mixing on the palette is nothing mysterious. It is a question of adding colors and water until the right tone appears. Nevertheless, bear in mind that the tone you have obtained cannot be properly appreciated until it is applied to the paper. All watercolor painters constantly check the color mixtures on a separate piece of paper, or even in the margin of the watercolor itself. So always keep a sheet or a piece of paper handy to carry out these color checks.

Mixing on paper means making changes on the paper as you go along, or enriching the hues of a color already on the paper. These mixtures should always be made with wet paint. Figures 171 and 171A show the change in color due to the addition of red over a still damp yellow. Glazing is superimposing one color over another dry color (figs. 172 and 172A). The key to this technique is to let your wet brush pass only once over each area of dry color, or the new color will start to lift and disturb the old. Beautiful effects are possible with glazing, but most watercolor painters strive to paint "alla prima," with as little glazing as possible.

Figs. 171 to 172A. Glaz ing. One tone is applie over another dry one (fig 172). The resulting colo is a mixture of both (fig 172A).

171

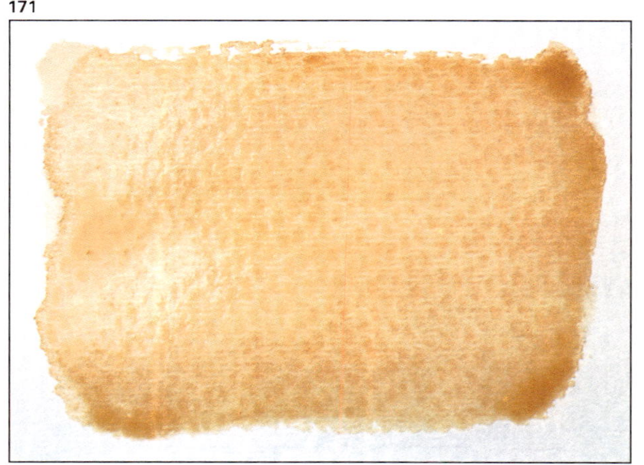

171A

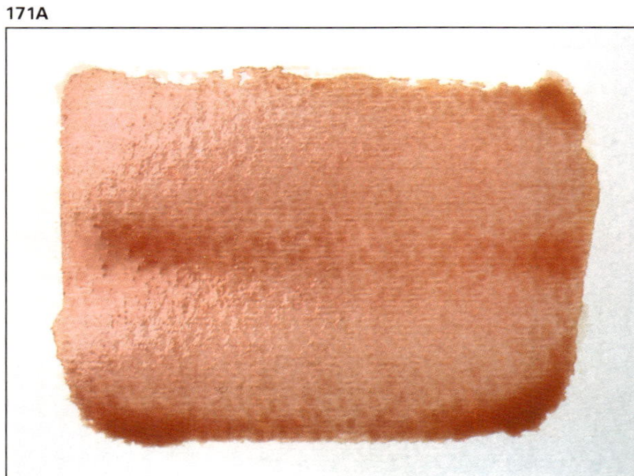

172

172A

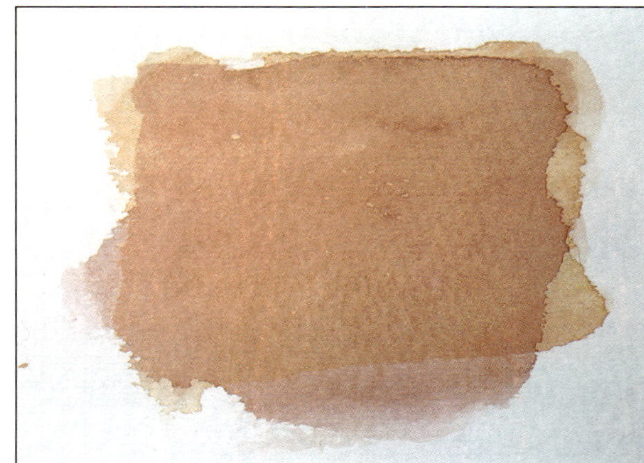

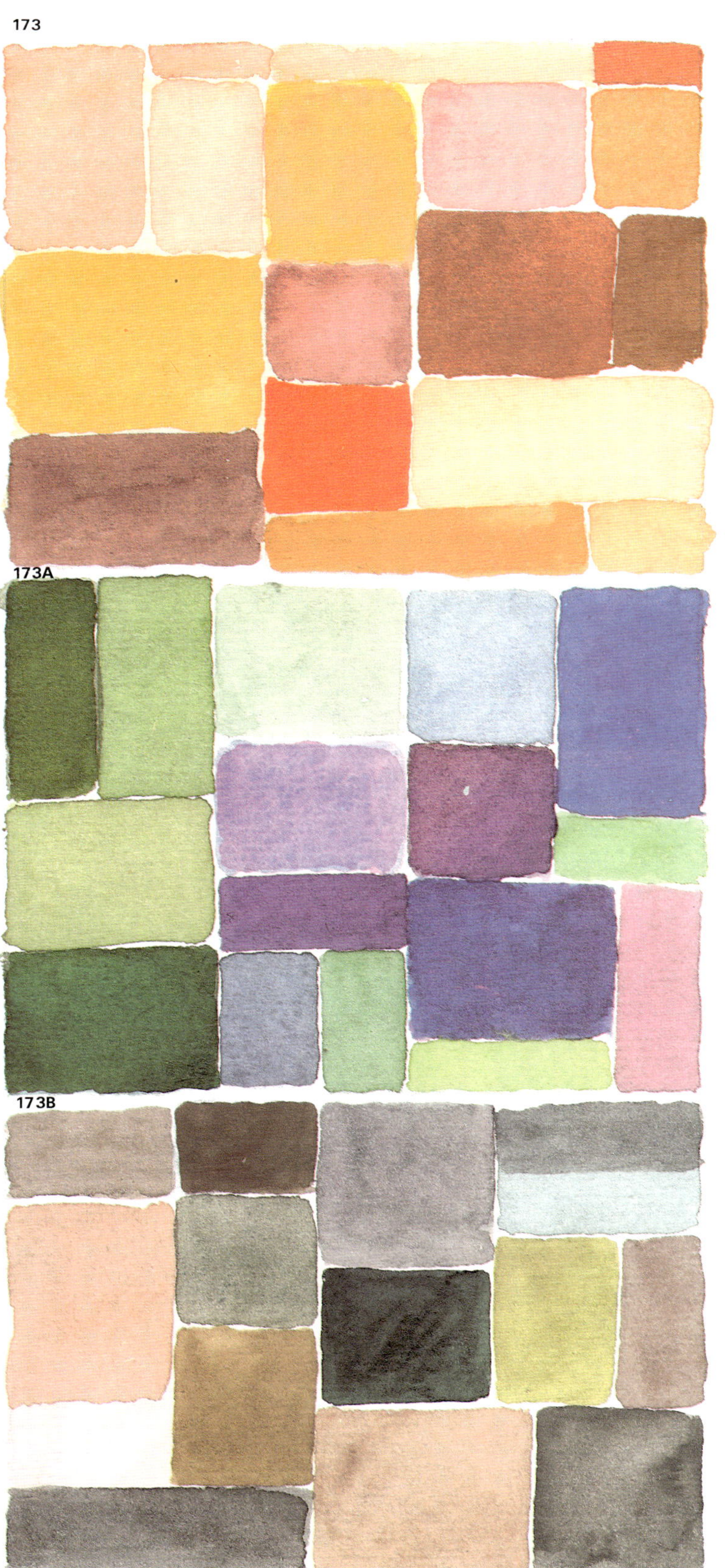

We can understand the concept of the color range by defining it as a family of tones, ordered by similarity, by tendency. There are three basic ranges: warm colors, cool colors, and semineutral colors. The warm colors are those closest to the reds, yellows, and siennas (fig. 173); colors such as pink, ochre, or cream also belong to the warm range. The cool range comprises all those colors that tend toward blue or green (except green with a warm tendency). Certain violets with a bluish tendency, and most grays, belong to the cool range (fig. 173A).

The range of semineutral colors comprises all those that are indefinite, grayish, obtained by mixing complementary colors (red and green, yellow and violet, or blue and orange) and diluted with water. They are sometimes called "dirty" or "broken" colors and may have a warm or cool tendency depending on the predominant color of the mixture (fig. 173B).

There is no exact number of colors that belong to any of these ranges. The differences in nuances are as subtle as the palette and the artist's feeling permit. A good exercise is mixing colors to obtain the three families we have mentioned, about fifiteen per range. You can do this exercise using the colors on this page.

Figs. 173 to 173B. These three groups of colors belong to the warm tones (fig. 173), cool (fig. 173A), and semineutral (fig. 173B).

Charles Reid

We are now going to practice and study different techniques using a watercolor painting by the splendid North American artist Charles Reid (fig. 180). His technique is intuitive and brilliant. His watercolors demonstrate his extraordinary command of color and brushstroke. This work by Reid is a showpiece of techniques that we will study one by one.

In the first detail (fig. 174) we can see the effect of color applied with glazing—that is, with layers of transparent color. The artist has painted other colors over an orange tone in such a way that the different layers produce more intense tonalities within a harmonic range of color.

In the next detail (fig. 175) we can see how a tone gains in intensity when applied directly onto the white of the paper. When you are painting with watercolor, you must always foresee the areas you wish to leave white; once color has been applied, the most that can be done is to soften it. In the next illustration (fig. 176) you can actually see how the intensity of the blue lines has been softened by applying an almost transparent layer of color before they have dried. Luck can also play a part: Reid makes use of the paint that runs down the paper to create the flowers (fig. 177). The next detail (fig. 178) is quite the opposite. Here the color has been applied when it was almost dry, so the brushstroke is clean and sharp. The artist is more concerned with the shape standing out clearly against the background and therefore applies the color with very little water.

In the last detail (fig. 179), we can see the effect of the color applied wet-into-wet: two different tonalities have been blended into a highly suggestive mixture. The artist obtains this effect with a wide variety of hues.

174

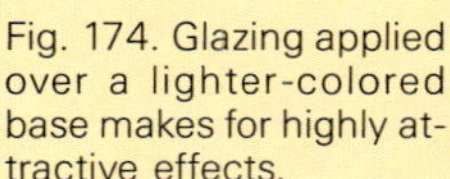

Fig. 174. Glazing applied over a lighter-colored base makes for highly attractive effects.

175

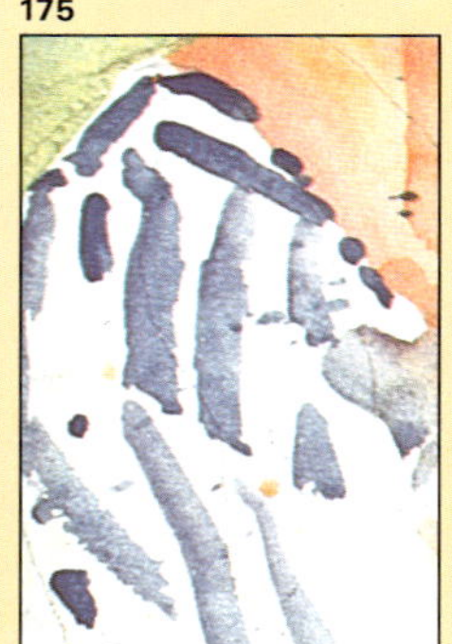

Fig. 175. Color applied when almost dry makes for clear and well-defined brushstrokes.

176

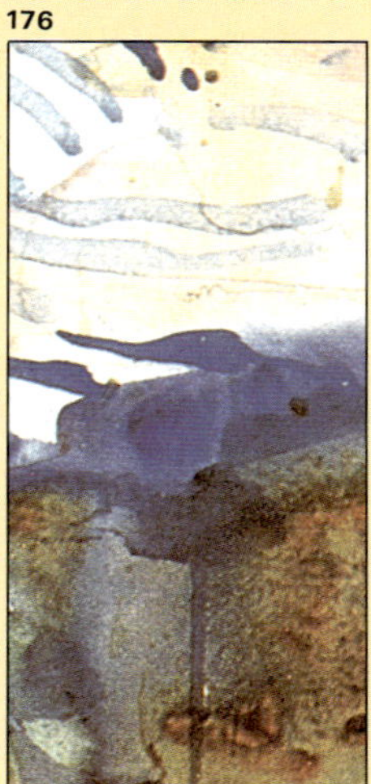

Fig. 176. To soften the color of dry paint, you can apply an almost transparent glaze over it.

177

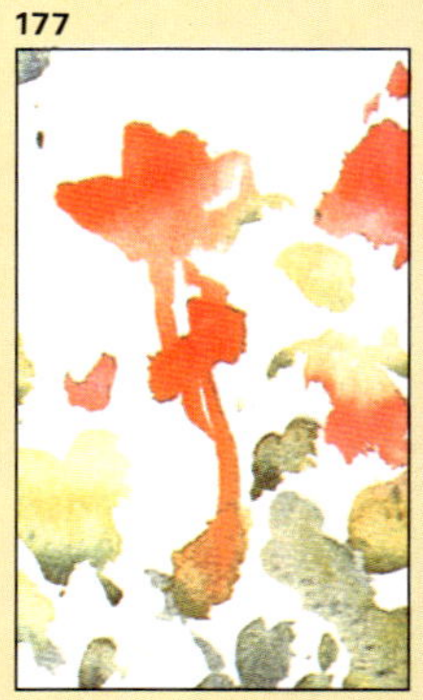

Fig. 177. Unexpected runs of color can be used to express a shape—in this case, the flowers.

178

Fig. 178. The handle of the walking stick was painted using a lot of color and little water. The result owes as much to drawing as to painting.

179

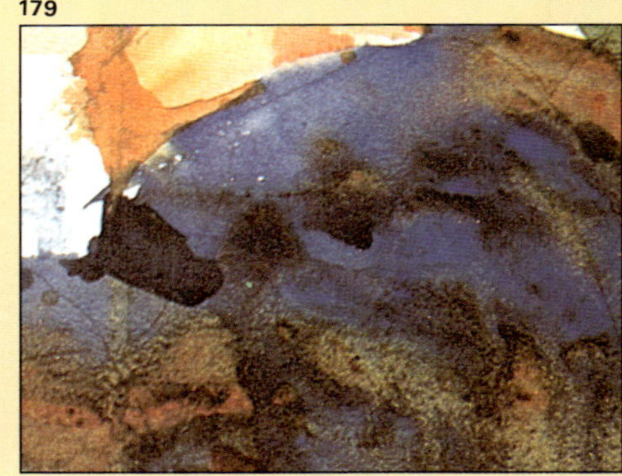

Fig. 179. A blend of wet colors can produce some surprising results.

Fig. 180. Charles Reid (1942-), *Seated Figure*. Private collection. Courtesy of Watson-Guptill.

180

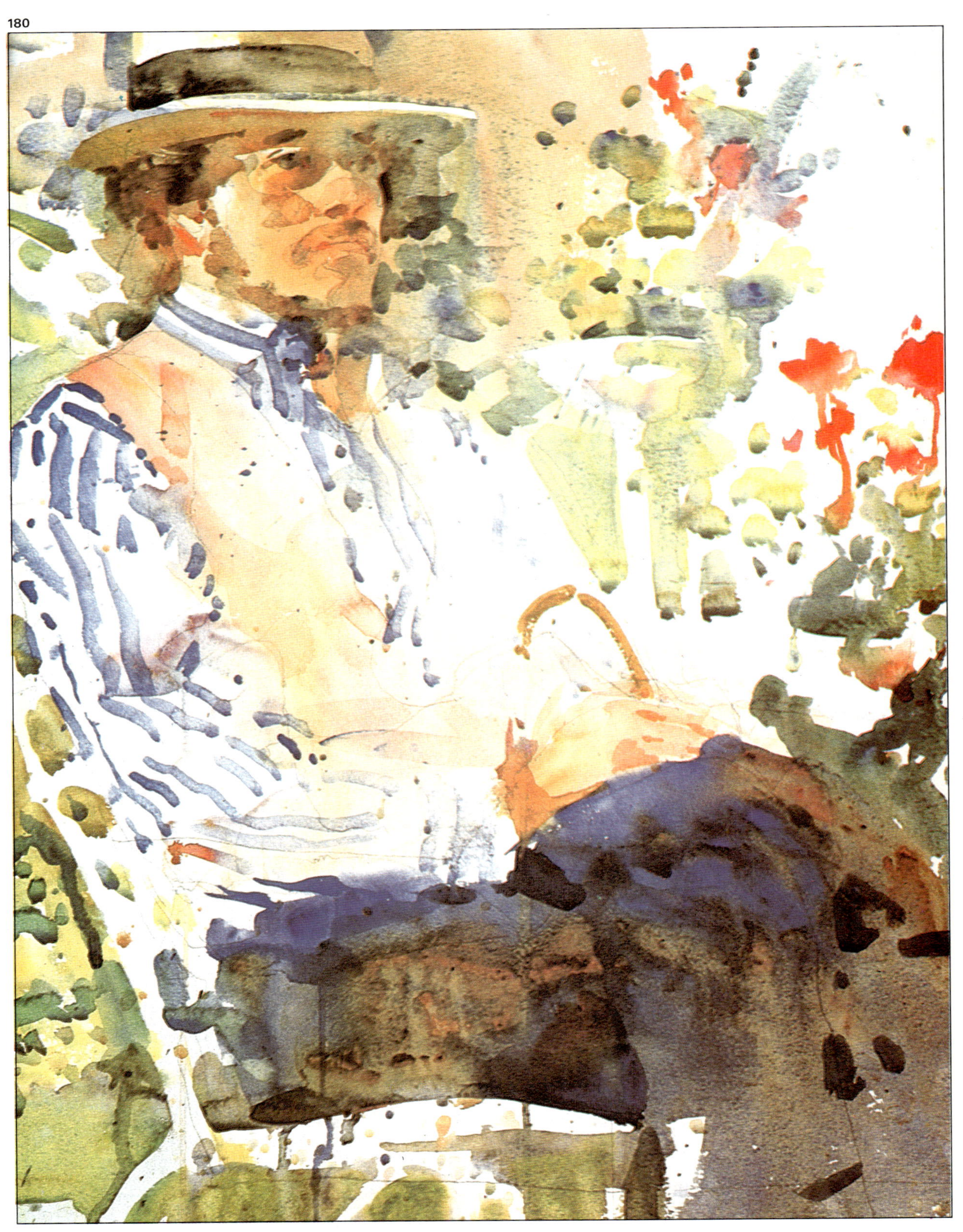

Valuist watercolor painting: step by step

181

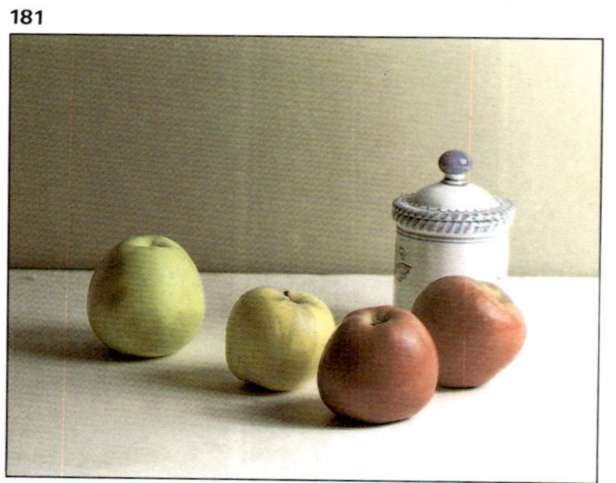

182

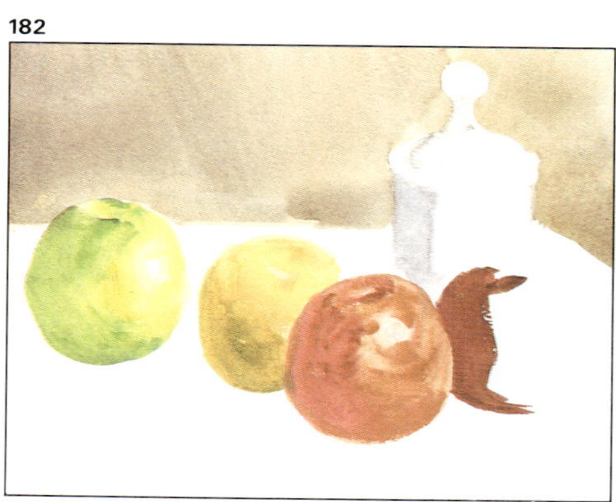

Fig. 181. In order to emphasize the play of light and shadow, the still life is illuminated from the side.

Figs. 182 to 184. Ballestar has intensified the effects of the chiaroscuro by resolving the shadows with a violet-blue tonality that stands out in sharp contrast against the pure, intense color of the apples.

183

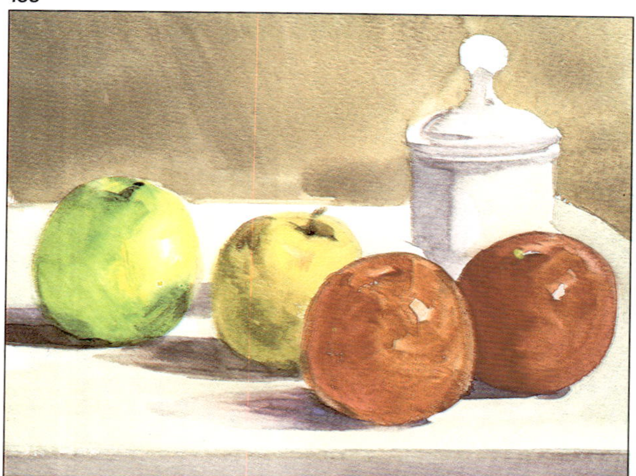

Ballestar will give us a practical demonstration of the difference between valuist and colorist painting techniques when applied to watercolors. The still life he has chosen will be the same for both exercises, although the result will differ because of the two types of lighting used: frontal and lateral lighting. For the valuist version, lateral lighting has been chosen in order to stress the shadows and the sensation of volume (fig. 181). Ballestar emphasizes the shadows and defines the outline of each object with broad, direct brushstrokes (fig. 182). He then moves on to the shadows on the table, highlighting them with a mixture of crimson and violet (fig. 183). Ballestar prefers to bring out the depth using blue and not black, as it results in greater intensity and chromatic variety (fig. 184).

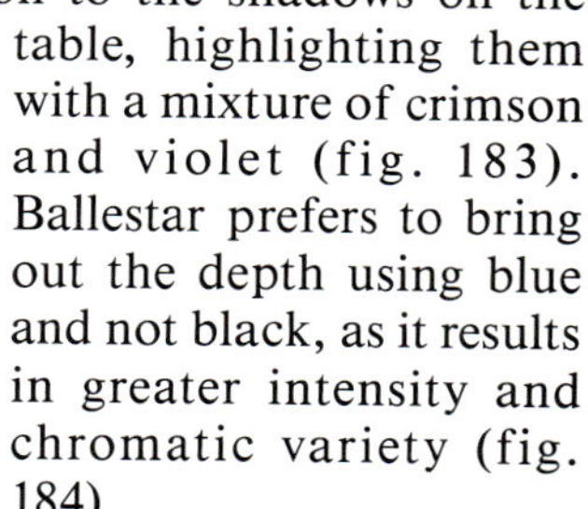

184

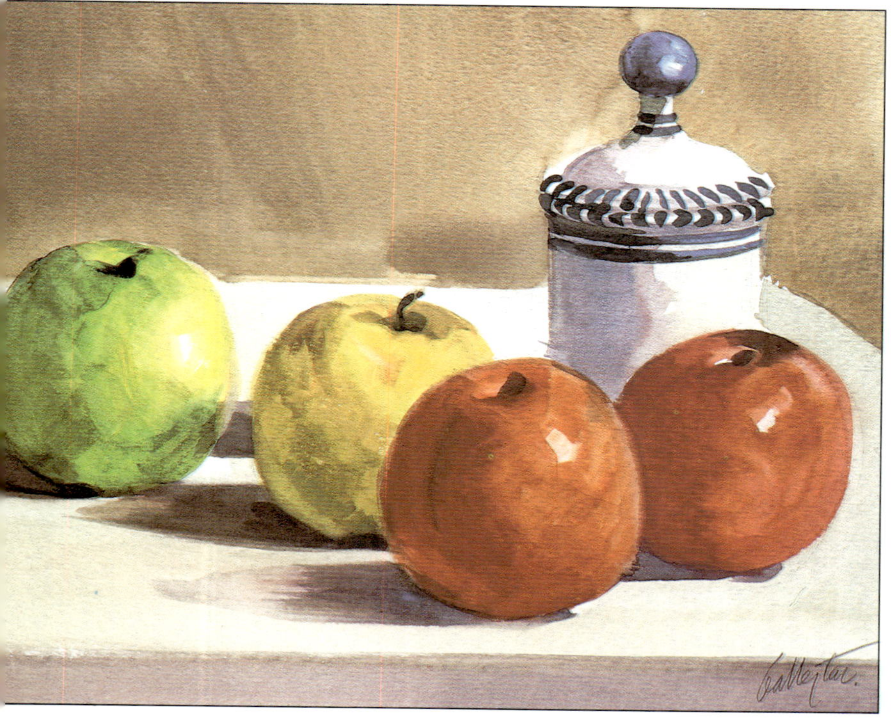

Colorist watercolor painting: step by step

185

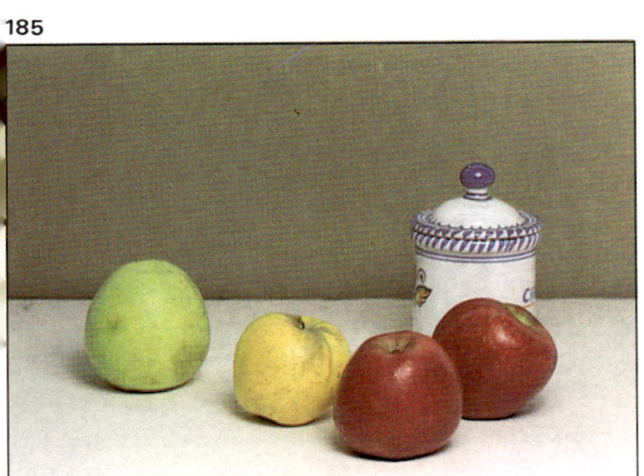

186

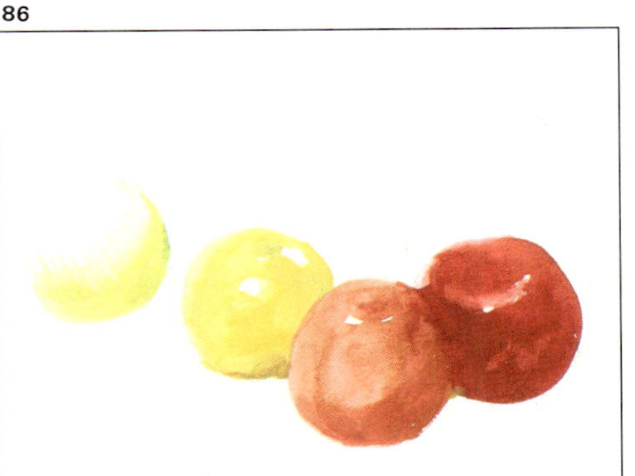

Fig. 185. Frontal lighting brings out the local color of the objects and virtually eliminates the shadows.

Figs. 186 to 188. The colors are applied pure, without prior mixing, and the forms are only slightly modeled. The color is intensified by the blend of warm and cool tones.

187

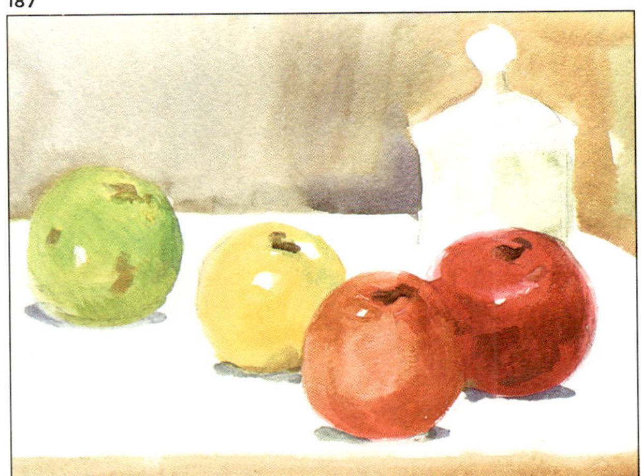

The lighting of the still life has been changed to suit the colorist approach. In this case, the light source is placed in front of the model, and its appearance changes completely. The volume of the objects is less noticeable (we saw earlier how frontal lighting flattens shapes) although the color is now more intense and brilliant (fig. 185).

Over a quick, preliminary drawing, Ballestar starts to paint the apples with large patches of pure color: vermilion, crimson, yellow, and green (fig. 186). He then fills out the background in a semi-neutral mixture (fig. 187).

He return to the apples, adding almost pure colors that shimmer in brilliant contrast to one another (blue on red, violet on yellow ochre, and so on). The last touches are to diminish the excessive white of the tablecloth with a light glazing that binds all the tones used in the composition (fig. 188).

188

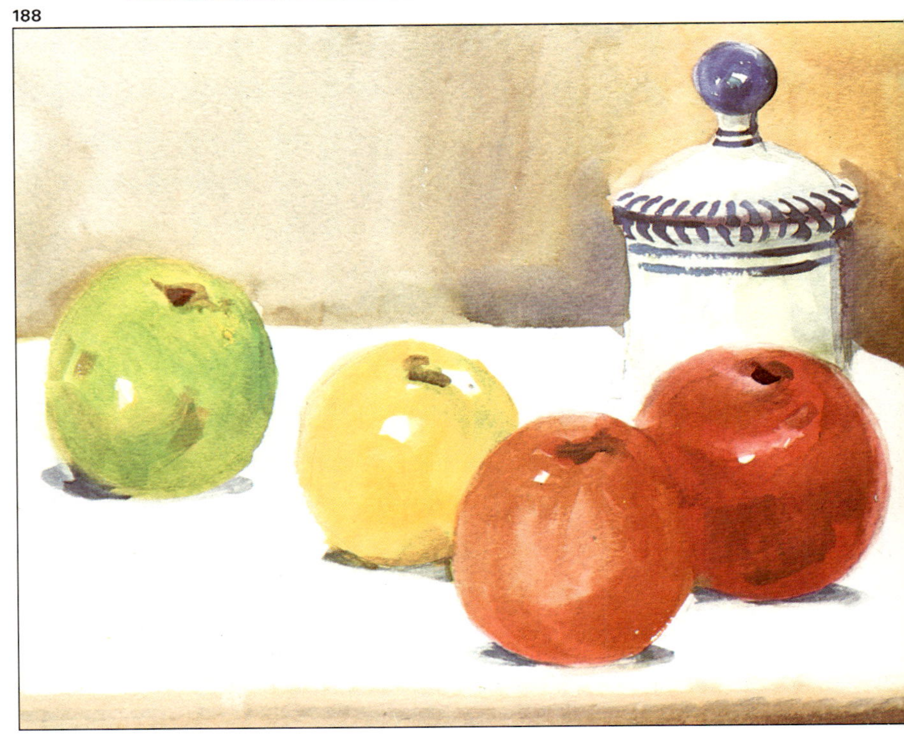

The colorist movement in watercolor

When we refer to colorist painting, we are speaking about a trend that attaches more importance to color than to chiaroscuro. Despite the fact that painters generally use both color and chiaroscuro at the same time, it is also true that certain artists express themselves more easily through color than through contrasting value of tones and shapes.
An important group of colorists were the Fauves (French for "wild beasts"), such as Matisse, Vlaminck, and Derain. They built up their paintings from pure, vivid colors, in dramatic contrast. In order to present the colors of real life, they would base themselves solely on a subjective interpretation of the color; for example, Matisse painted a portrait of his wife in green, violet, and red in order to represent the volume.
As do many other great watercolorists of our time, our three guest artists for this book use color where in other ages a more transparent, grayish approach would have been used. The atmosphere, the subtle effect of the light on the objects, the broad spaces resulting from perspective have always been characteristic of the traditional watercolor painting, which is more concerned with a true description of the scene than with the pure expression of shape and color.

Fig. 189. Martínez Lozano (1923-), *Boats on the Shore*. Private collection. The rich, strong contrast between two clearly differentiated areas of color, one warm and one cool, is what defines the composition of this seascape.

189

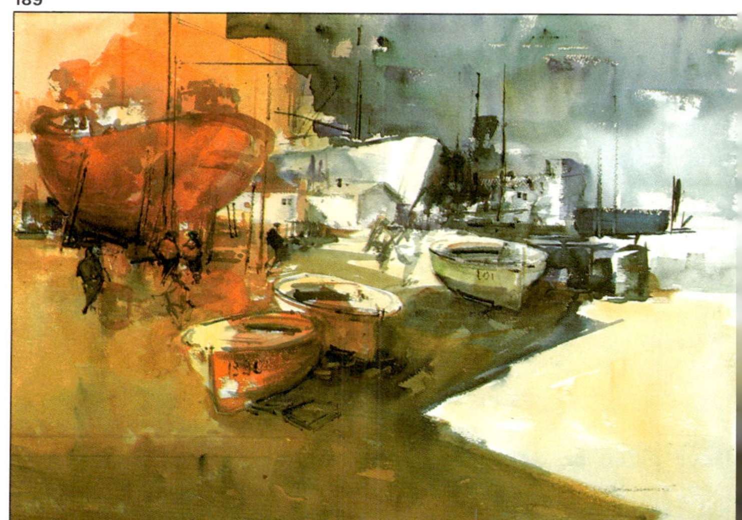

190

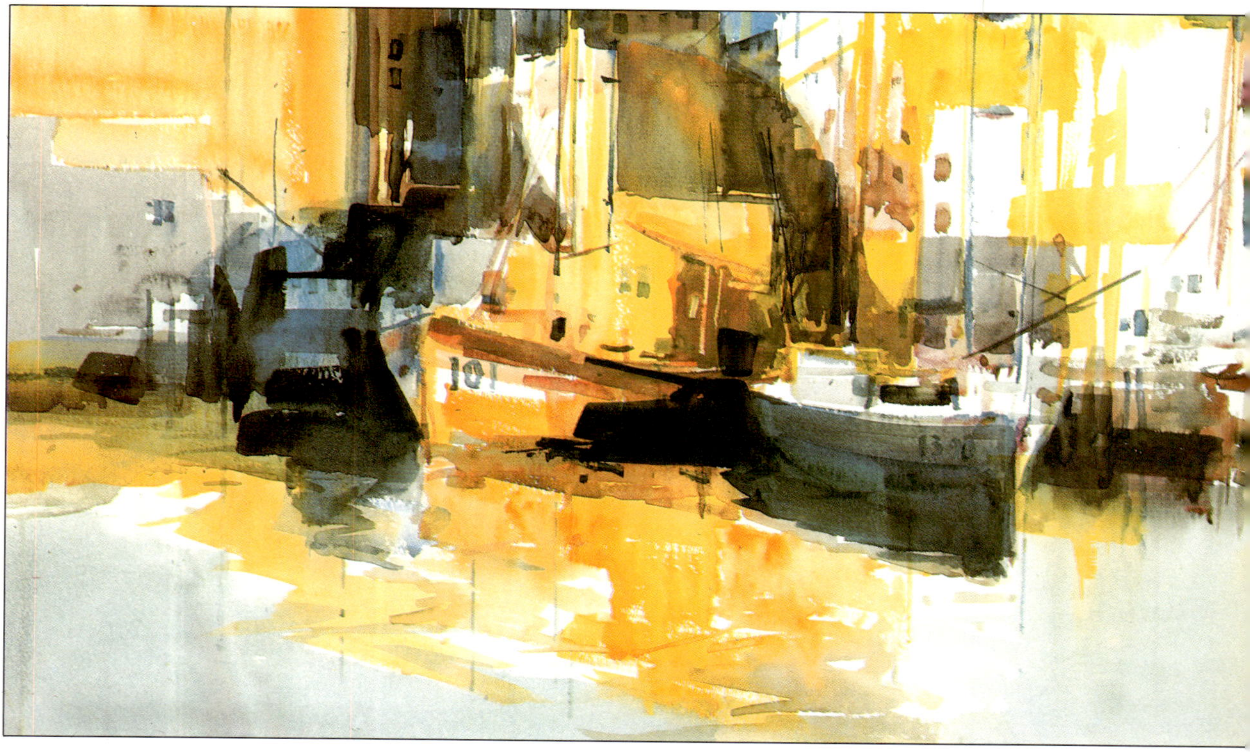

As from the impressionist period and the subsequent creative contributions of the artists who sprang from that movement, the art of watercolor painting has won over a new freedom by releasing itself from the obligation to describe things exactly as they are. The medium has taken on a whole new chromatic vitality.

If you observe the works chosen to illustrate these pages, together with the others in this book, you will realize that each of our guest artists presents a totally original and personal interpretation of color. Martínez Lozano, for example, works with areas of color that build up the composition from geometric planes (figs. 189 and 190) thus achieving some dramatic color combinations. Plana's and Ballestar's interpretations of reality are particularly sensitive to color. The ranges of color used by Plana are highly refined and elegant (fig. 191). Ballestar applies the color directly to his paintings; his lines are clean and firm, which reveals an extraordinary command of drawing and complements his innate feeling for color (fig. 192).

Fig. 192. Vicenç Ballestar (1929-), *Autumn Trees*. Private collection, Barcelona. In order to express the luminous and chromatic effects of this tree, Ballestar has used a rich and brilliant assortment of colors.

191

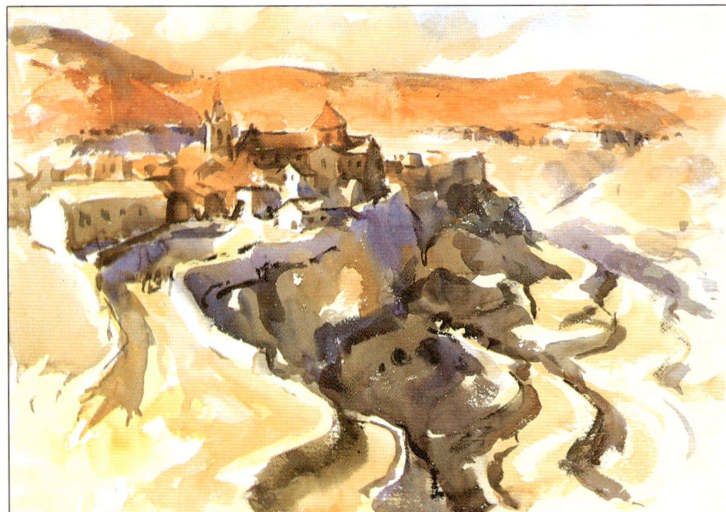

Fig. 190. Martínez Lozano, *Fishing boats*. Private collection. Martínez Lozano stresses the vibrant intensity of the pure colors by using sharp contrasts.

Fig. 191. Manel Plana (1949-), *Cantavieja*. Private collection. In order to define and contrast each of the planes that go to make up this landscape, Plana has used two ranges of complementary colors (one orange and the other violet) to increase the feeling of depth.

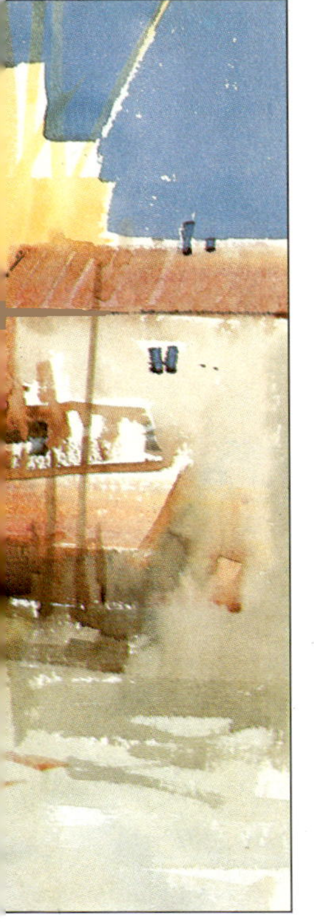

192

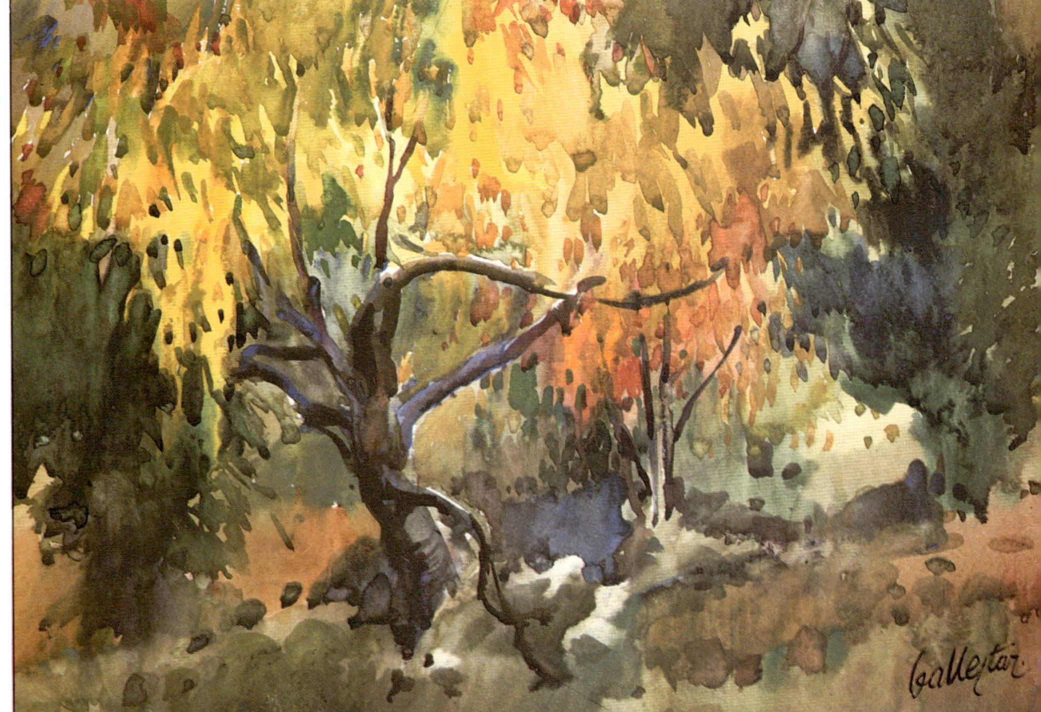

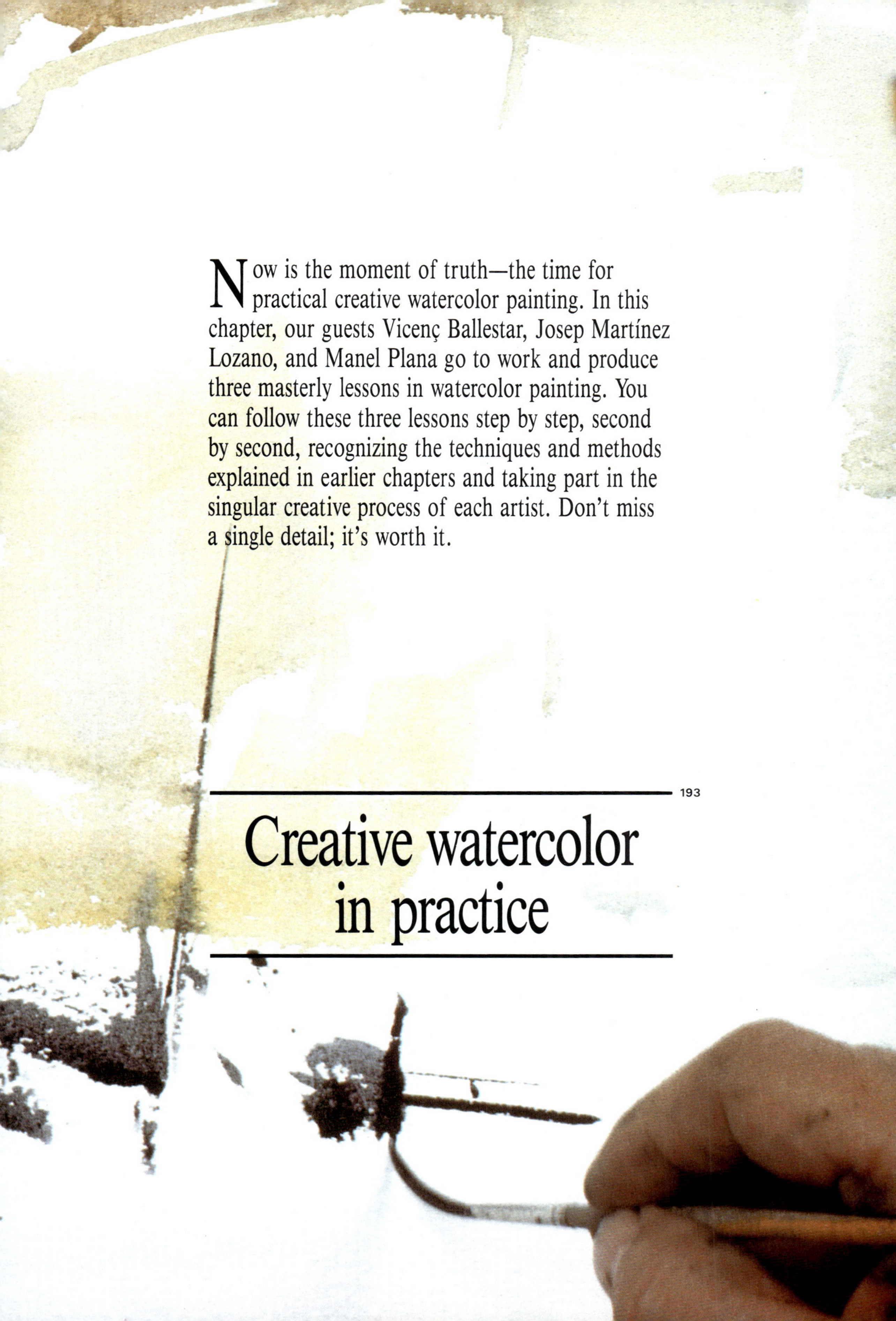

Now is the moment of truth—the time for practical creative watercolor painting. In this chapter, our guests Vicenç Ballestar, Josep Martínez Lozano, and Manel Plana go to work and produce three masterly lessons in watercolor painting. You can follow these three lessons step by step, second by second, recognizing the techniques and methods explained in earlier chapters and taking part in the singular creative process of each artist. Don't miss a single detail; it's worth it.

Creative watercolor in practice

Personality and creativity

Setting aside the artist's technical skills or proficiency in drawing or painting, creativity will always be a matter of temperament. This does not mean that the techniques and acquired skills are unimportant. They are the basis for all artistic work, as we have explained here. But in the case of our guest artists, painters with long experience and complete command of the medium, the key to their respective styles is to be found in their temperaments, in their individual personalities. Vicenç Ballestar's passionate, almost impulsive personality is reflected in his painting: dynamic watercolors, expressive, rather baroque shapes, using the full potential of shape and color. Despite his leaning toward realism, Ballestar could never be satisfied with a strictly naturalist, imitative watercolor. The artist always goes beyond this stage to include bold touches of intense color, in just the right places, so as to enliven the shapes.

What we say about Martínez Lozano's style must always be understood in the context of the artist when painting his watercolors. The characteristic features of his works are due to the singular way in which Lozano stains the paper, letting the color run, drawing with the handle of the brush, and so on. His knowledge of techniques seems endless, and the creativity of the results unquestionable. His shapes are so vigorous they almost appear abstract, cut off from the reality they depict.

Manel Plana is an enthusiast of wash painting, the expressive play of transparency, and liberal use of color. His generous brushstrokes, made with highly diluted color, cover the paper and define the shape at the last moment, when the work appears saturated with different tones and hues. From start to finish, the sensuality of the watercolor is the overriding feature of the process. Plana seems to follow certain pictorial laws inherent to the process, letting himself be carried along by them; such is his command of this medium.

These three artists personify different creative possibilities of equal value and significance. Their works are an example and a stimulus for all those watercolor enthusiasts who wish to study the potential of these techniques in depth.

Fig. 193 (preceding spread). The development of a watercolor by Martínez Lozano.

194

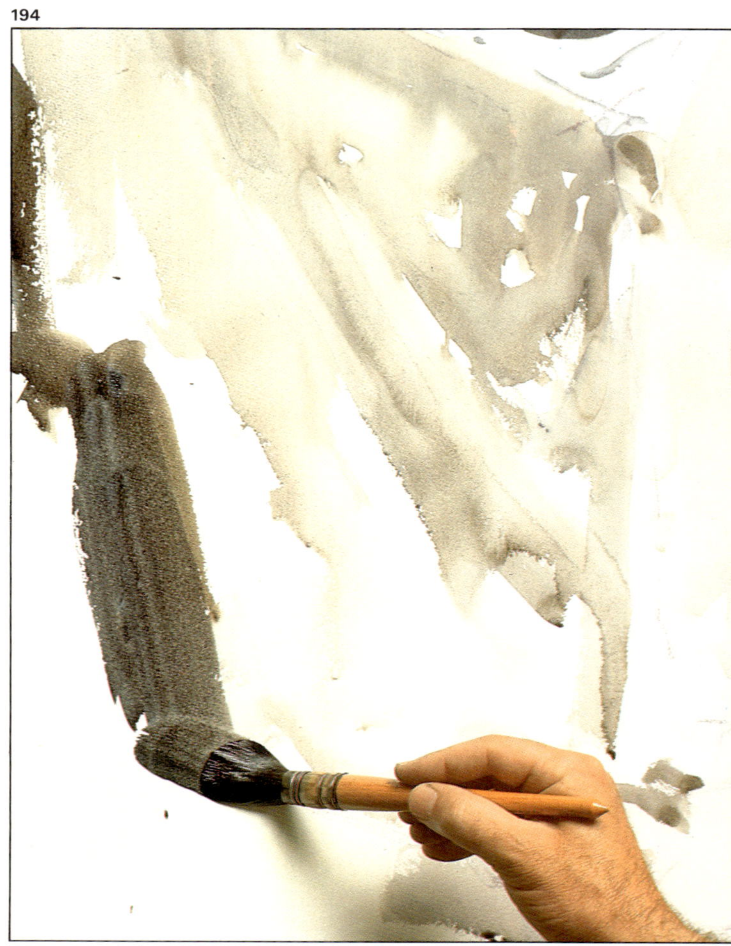

Fig. 194. Manel Plana's style is based on the force and expressiveness of the brushstroke.

Fig. 195. Vicenç Ballestar combines accuracy of shape with vibrancy of color.

Fig. 196. The characteristic of Martínez Lozano's painting is the creativity of his technique.

195

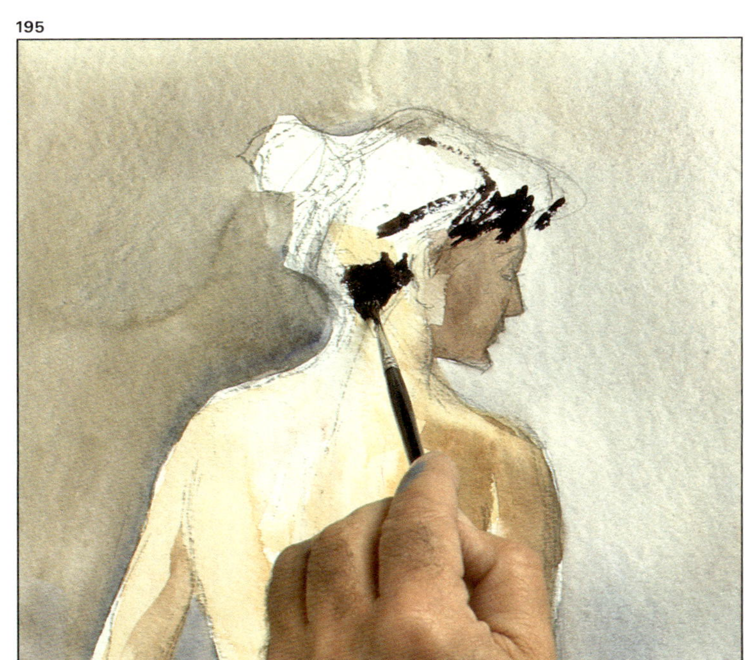

196

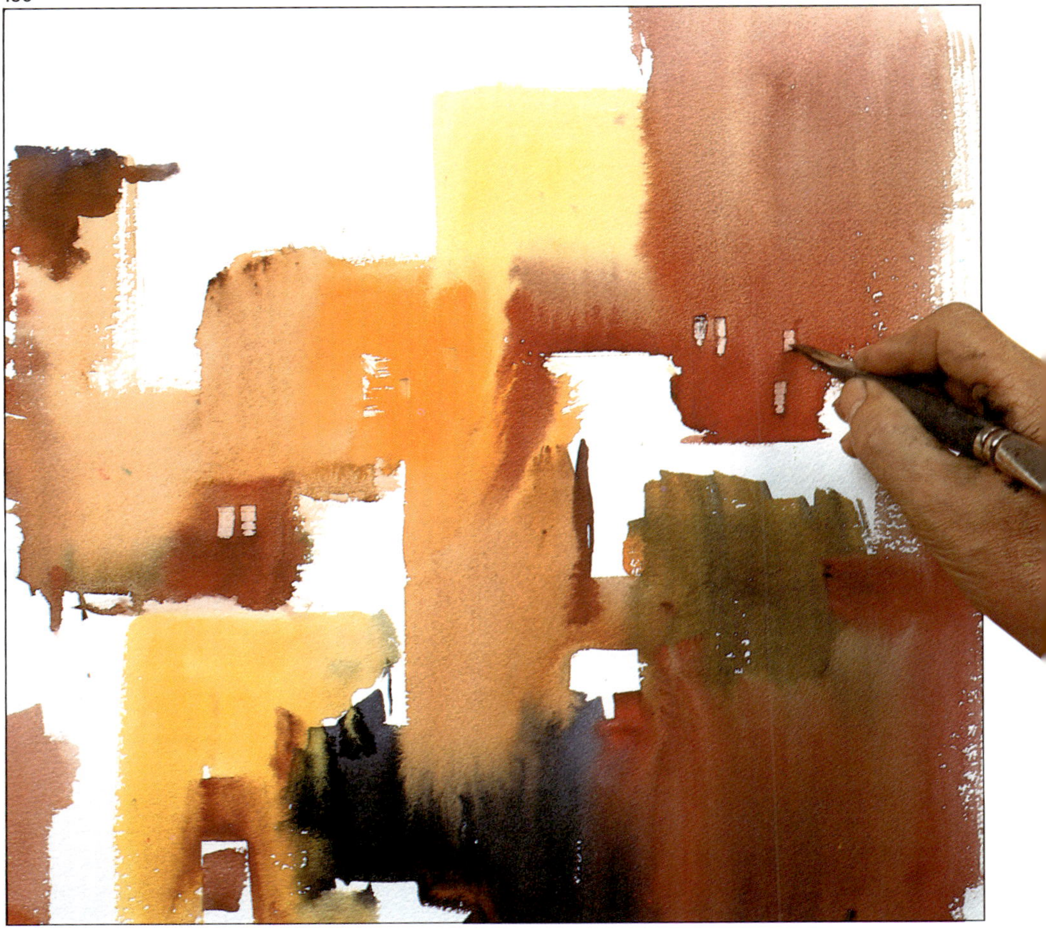

Ballestar paints a human figure

197

Ballestar is going to paint a nude in watercolor. A platform has been provided where the model will pose. Ballestar has all his materials ready; tubes of color that he places on the palette, a round sable brush, a towel he uses as a rag, a wide-mouthed jar with clean water, and watercolor paper that he has attached to a wooden board.

198

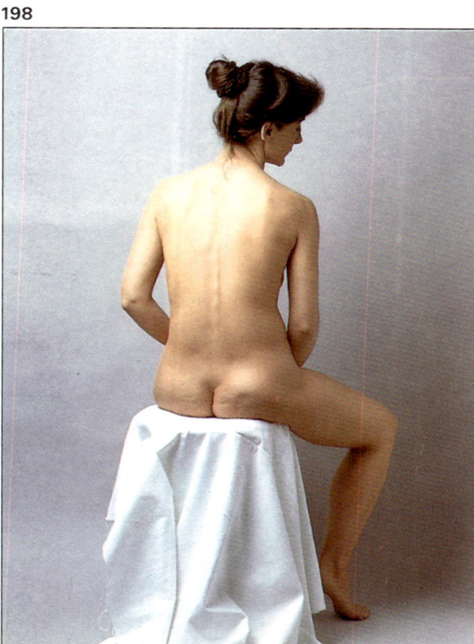

199

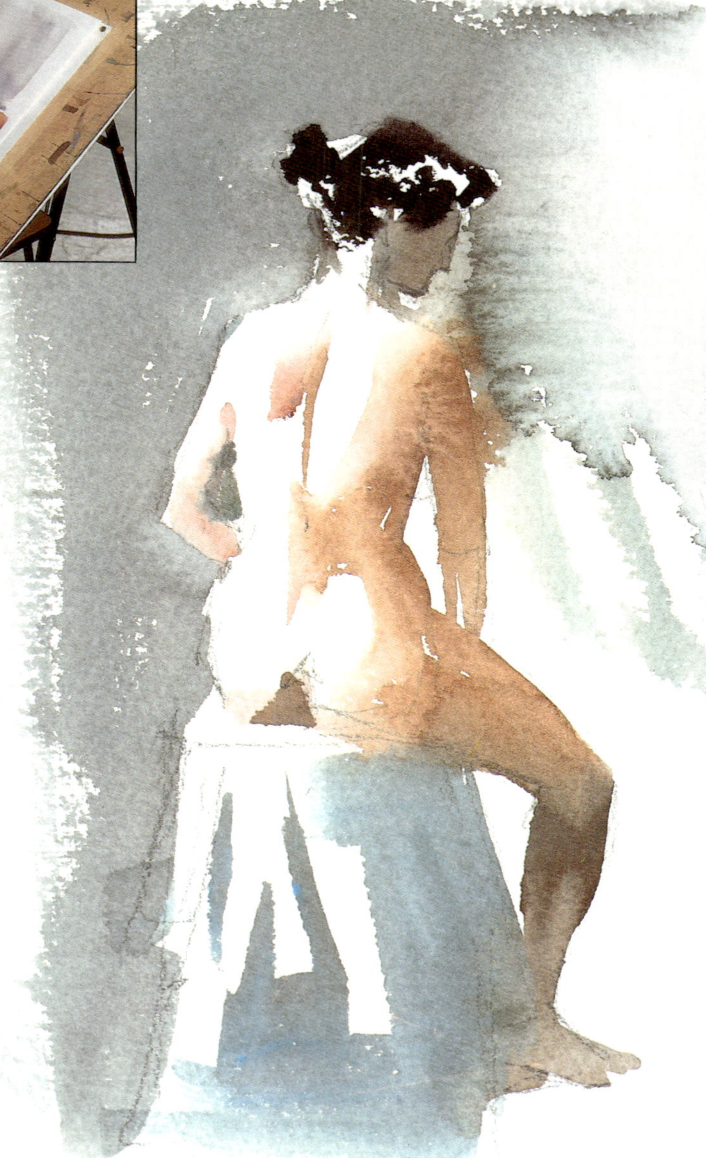

Fig. 197. Ballestar painting the model. Finding the right pose has not been easy; it was finally decided to place the model in a warm and original setting.

Fig. 198. This first pose, which is reminiscent of the odalisques painted by Ingres, is too rigid and "studied." The soft lighting bathes the shapes and neutralizes the contrasts, giving a rather monotonous and cold sensation.

Fig. 199. The sketch of the previous pose reflects the softness of the model and the coloring in just a few brushstrokes; although the result is delicate and sensitive, it is too restrained for the expressive potential of the watercolor to be painted.

The model offers several poses on the platform. In one of them, she is seated on a stool covered with a white cloth, with her back to us (fig. 198). Ballestar paints a quick sketch although he is not entirely satisfied; the result is too classical (fig. 199).

Actually, the problem is not the pose itself but the context: the background is too neutral, the lighting too cold, and the resulting effect too conventional. Atmosphere is created by hanging some strongly colored drapes in the background and adding a cube-shaped object that "furnishes" the space, sheltering the model. The lighting also makes for more intimist and suggestive effects.

The skin tone acquires a variety of hues against the blue, the yellow, and the red of the cloth and the chair. It is curious to note that these are the three primary colors, chosen unintentionally (fig. 201).

200

201

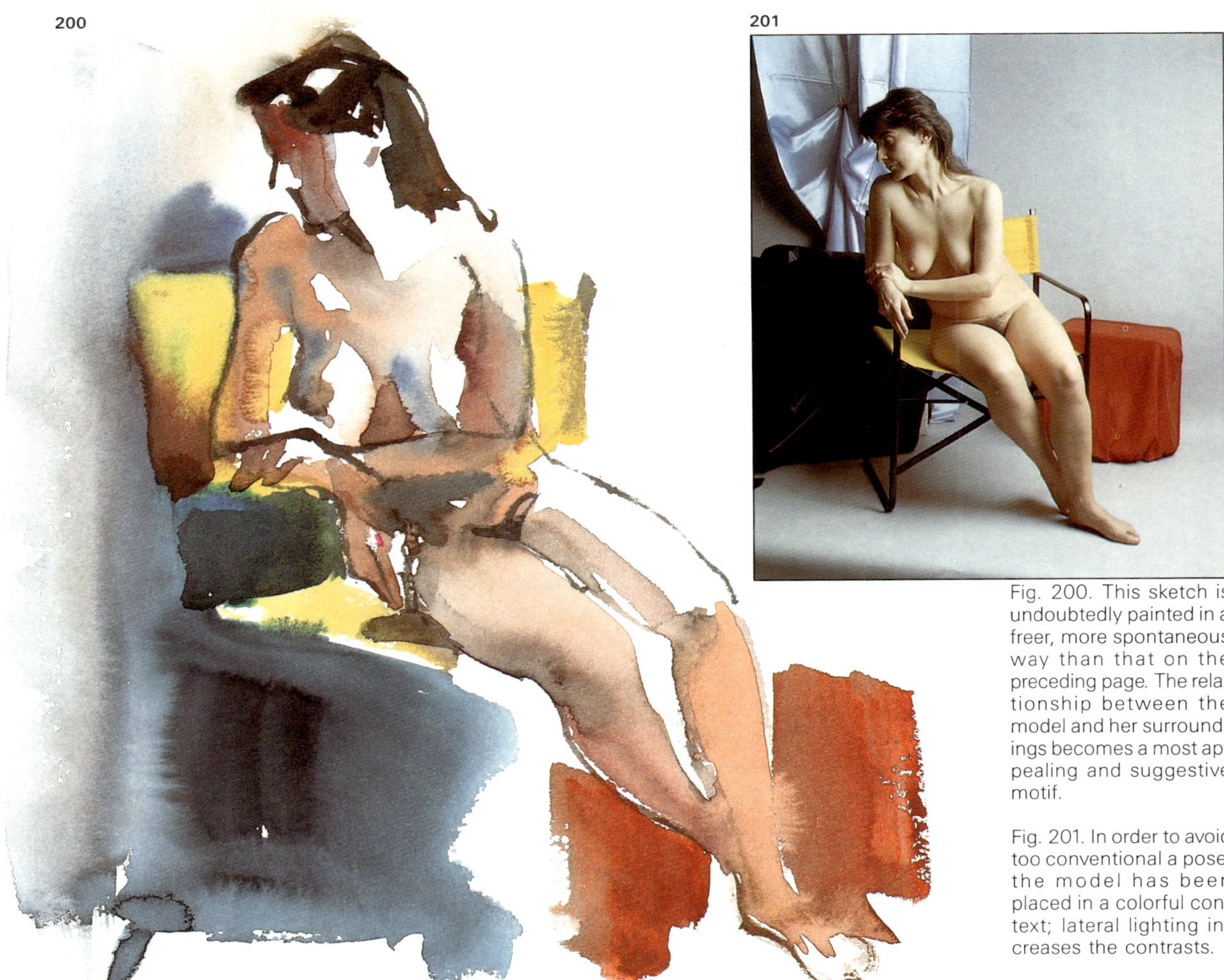

Fig. 200. This sketch is undoubtedly painted in a freer, more spontaneous way than that on the preceding page. The relationship between the model and her surroundings becomes a most appealing and suggestive motif.

Fig. 201. In order to avoid too conventional a pose, the model has been placed in a colorful context; lateral lighting increases the contrasts.

Color studies

202

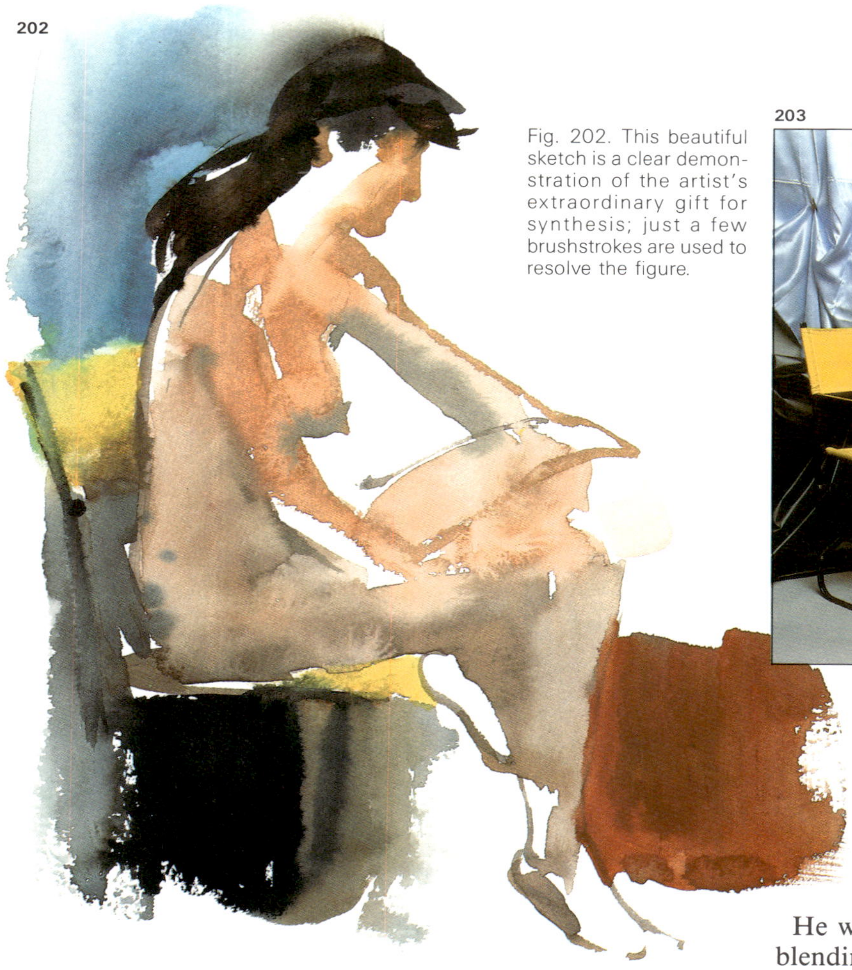

Fig. 202. This beautiful sketch is a clear demonstration of the artist's extraordinary gift for synthesis; just a few brushstrokes are used to resolve the figure.

203

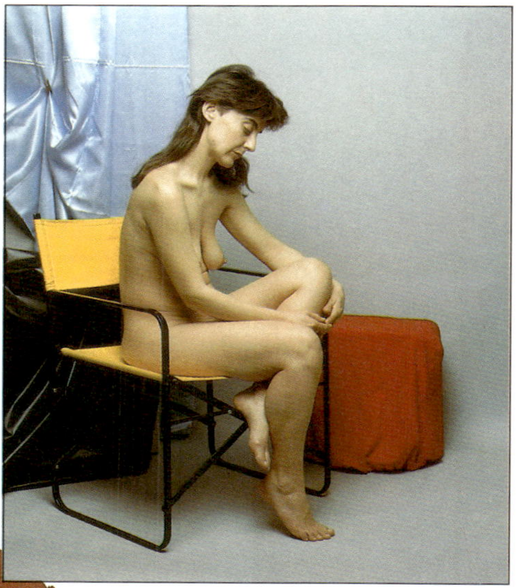

Ballestar decides to make some color studies, changing both the pose and the lighting for each. Ballestar draws with the paintbrush, trying to capture the essence of the model in a few lines and colors. He works quickly, making use of the blending of the colors and accidental runs. In a short time the artist has painted several sketches, spending no more than five minutes on each one. Each sketch captures the essence of the expressive potential of wash, of glazes and runs of color. All these factors help to express Ballestar's interpretation of the model's pose.

204

Fig. 203. Very different results can be obtained using different compositions and lighting. The overhead lighting of this pose results in an L-shaped composition.

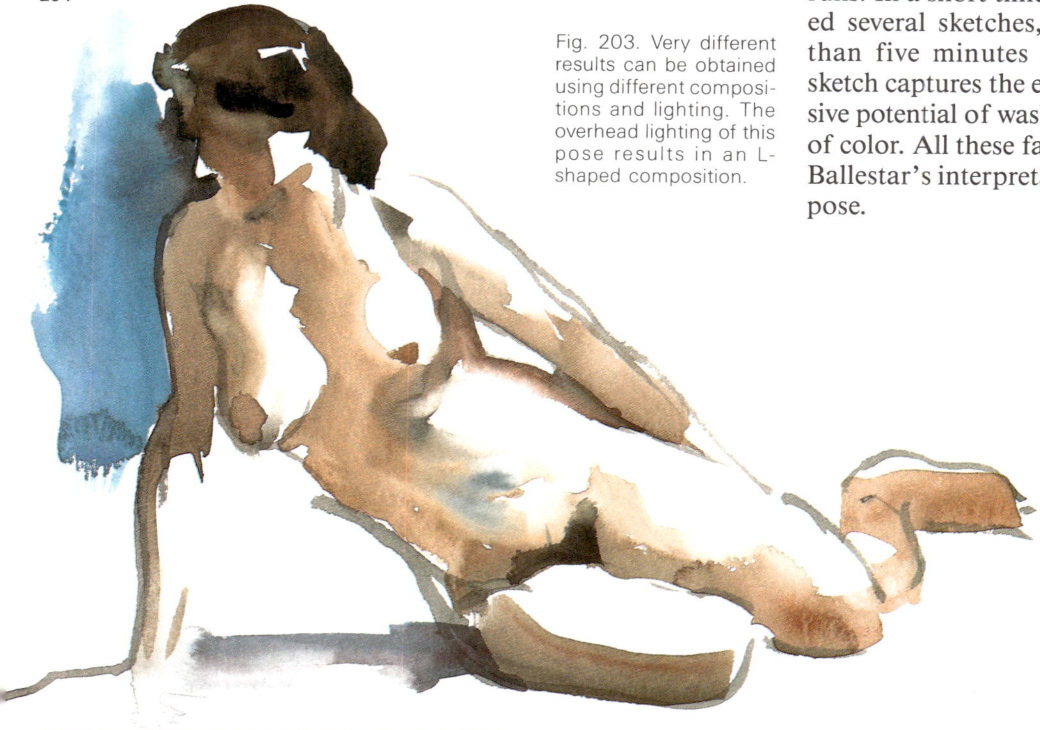

Fig. 204. You have to know how to bring out the best in a model's pose. In this case, for example, Ballestar represents the sinuosity of the pose with a clean, flowing brush and a hint of chiaroscuro.

Fig. 205. The pose chosen for this step-by-step watercolor allows the artist to work on the contrasts of color and light. It is a diagonal composition that structures space based on almost geometrical shapes.

205

206

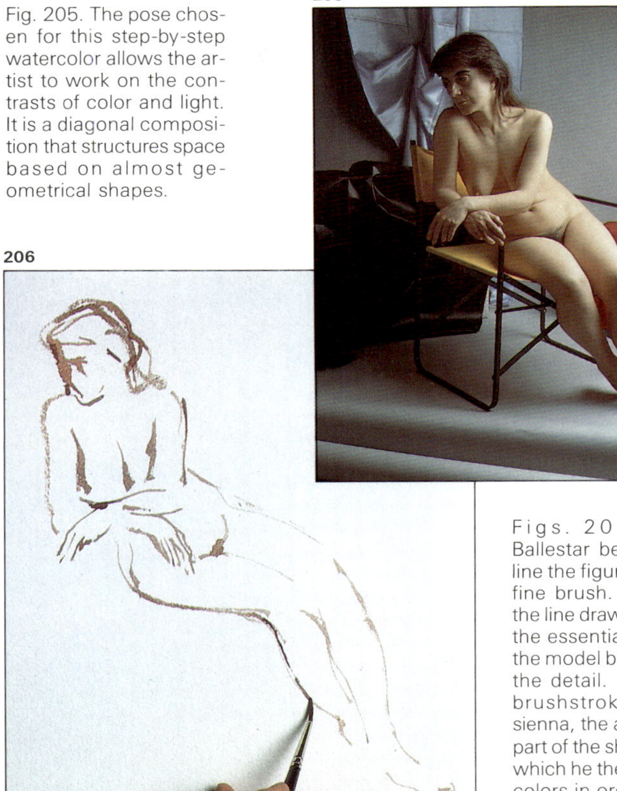

The pose chosen for the definitive watercolor has the model in a diagonal position with lateral lighting that highlights the contrasts between the brighter areas and the shadows (fig. 205). The blue curtain cuts the space in the background, forming a rectangle with the model and the red object on the right. This composition is almost a set of pure geometric shapes.

Ballestar starts to draw directly with the finest brush. A flowing line of burnt sienna outlines the model on the paper (fig. 206). He starts to paint using the same color but a wider brush, working on the shading of the figure with broad brushstrokes (fig. 207). The artist heightens the chromatic harmony of the shadows, enriching them with dashes of crimson, vermilion, burnt umber, and bluish violet that strengthen the vibrancy of the warm tones (fig. 208).

Figs. 206 to 208. Ballestar begins to outline the figure with a very fine brush. Notice how the line drawing captures the essential features of the model but disregards the detail. Using a few brushstrokes of burnt sienna, the artist resolves part of the shaded area to which he then adds other colors in order to obtain a rich, warm range of color.

207

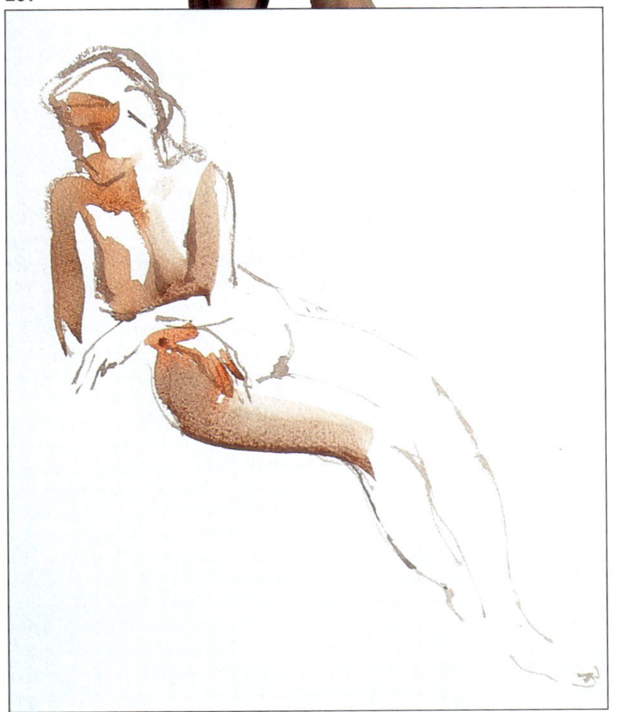

208

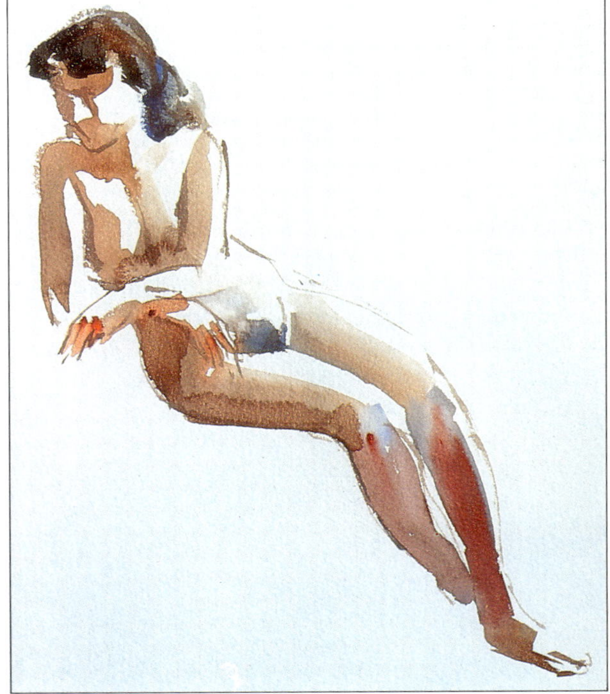

The definitive watercolor

Ballestar quickly resolves the background with straight lines that geometrically structure the space. He uses pure, unmixed colors that contrast strongly with one another (fig. 209). The Prussian blue of the background contrasts with the figure and with the more shaded areas (the lower part of the chair, for example) which are almost black.

Ballestar paints quickly and we hardly have time to follow his movements. Of course, watercolors do not allow you to waste any time, especially when you are striving for spontaneity and nimbleness. Ballestar loads the brush with dark crimson and applies the color to the lower part of the paper (fig. 210). The artist does not linger over the brushstrokes; on the contrary, he lets certain colors mix together by chance, bringing out rich, unexpected hues.

The painter applies the final touches to the background using a bluish gray that contrasts with the silhouette of the figure, helping to distribute the main masses of color in such a way that the figure clearly stands out against the background. At this point, Ballestar considers the watercolor finished. He does not want to rework it because it would then lose the sketchlike, spontaneous effect he was aiming for. The result is a suggestive, vivid, and contrasting piece of work. It is, perhaps, more a synthesis than a completely accurate rendition of the pose. It is a lively and direct interpretation that seeks to maintain the essence of the first impression.

To paint is to interpret, to re-create reality without being a slave to it. This is what Ballestar has achieved; he has respected his own interpretation of the model and attempted to capture it as faithfully as possible. Ballestar takes a last glance at the model and at his painting... and signs it.

209

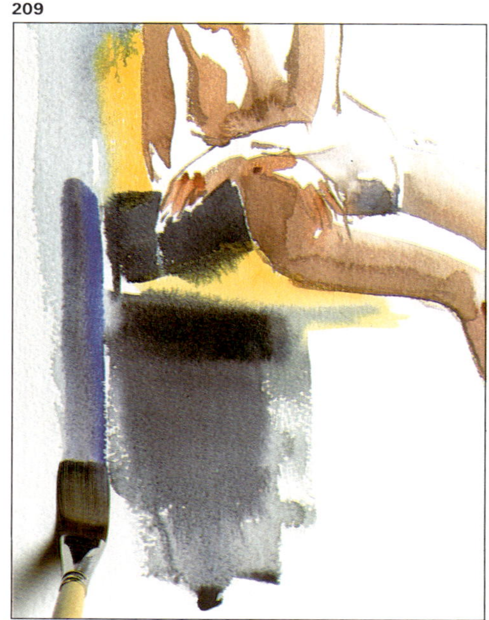

Figs. 209 and 210. Ballestar uses a flat brush to apply the color of the background in straight well-defined lines. Watercolor requires great accuracy and quick brushstrokes. Ballestar has preferred to omit the details from this background, creating an almost abstract, geometrically structured space.

Fig. 211. Ballestar adds the final brushstrokes to finish off the background with a bluish-gray wash. He has painted the entire watercolor quickly, "alla prima"—that is, without any later retouching.

210

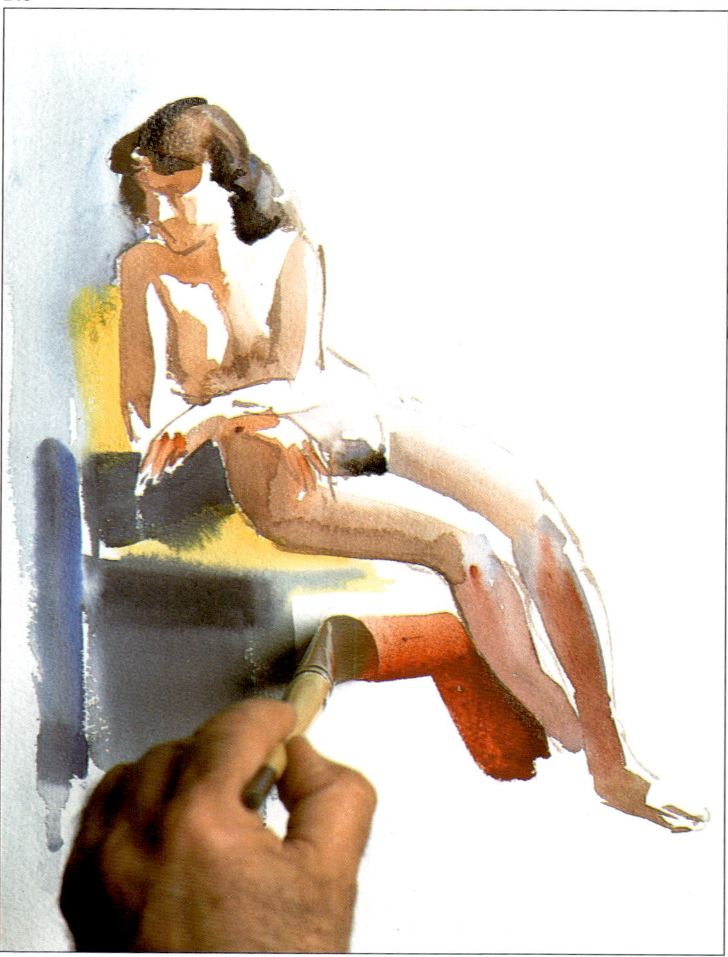

211

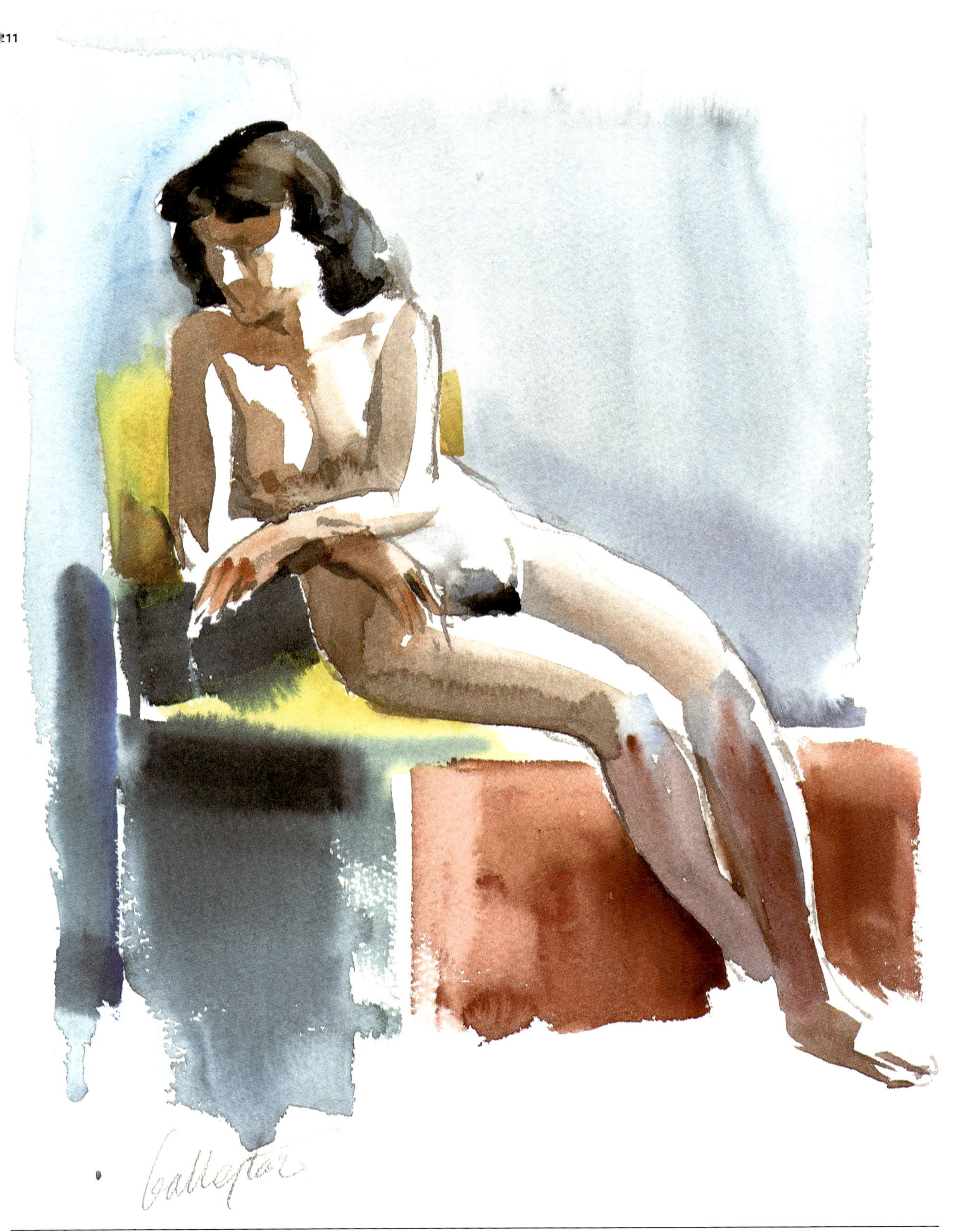

Plana paints a still life

Manel Plana is a versatile painter who will take on any theme—landscape, figure, or still life. The artist's feeling and individual way of interpreting reality can best be seen in his still lifes. Plana imposes his own idea of the painting on the model without becoming a slave to the subject. This is one of the main problems in artistic creation: to maintain the artist's idea intact, while holding onto the first impression. On this subject, Bonnard says: "The initial idea of a painting tends to fade away when the painter looks at the real model which, unfortunately, invades and takes over the mind of the painter."

From the first moment, Plana has a clear idea of how he is going to approach this still life. He has studied the theme in a series of color sketches (figs. 212 to 214) in which you can see slight variations in lighting or viewpoint.

The still life is now laid out on the table (fig. 215). Plana has formed his composition choosing simple objects and brisk colors (whites and greens). A beautiful white lily stands above the other objects. The artist has all his materials ready (fig. 217): tubes of paint; a large palette with partitions and another smaller one; a few brushes, all of them fairly thick (a very thick wide brush, a very wide hake brush, two filbert, brushes, and an old oil paint brush); a sponge; a jar of water; and a large bucket.

Figs. 212 to 214. These are some of the sketches that Plana has painted of the same subject. In each one we find a different idea of the model, changing and transforming it. For Plana, the model is only a pretext, a starting point for developing a suggestive, personal vision.

Fig. 215. Almost all the objects in the still life fall within a harmonious and elegant range of greens and whites. A fairly high viewpoint has been chosen, which highlights the pyramid shape of the composition.

212

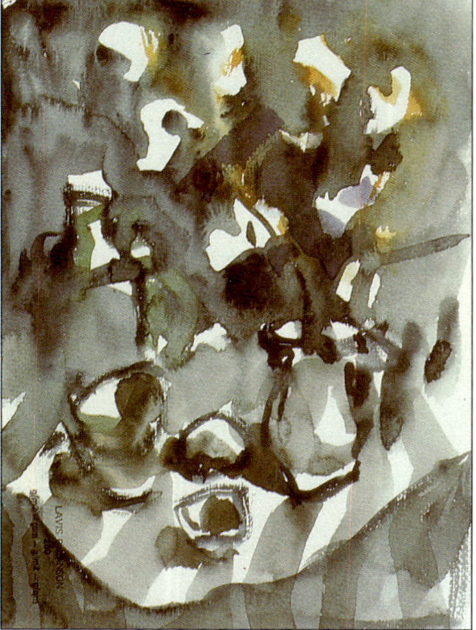

213

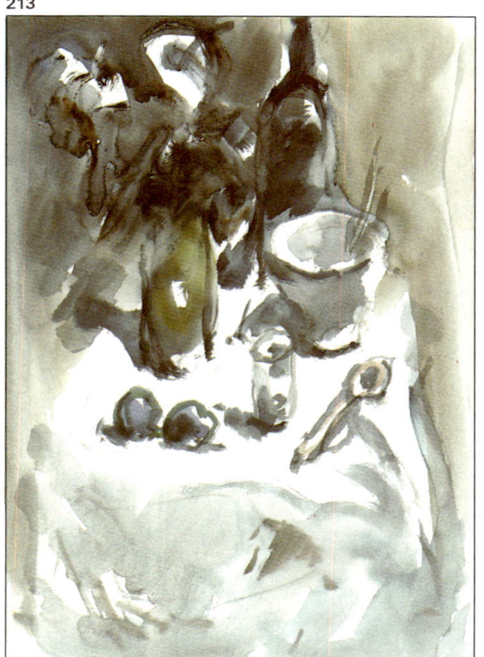

214

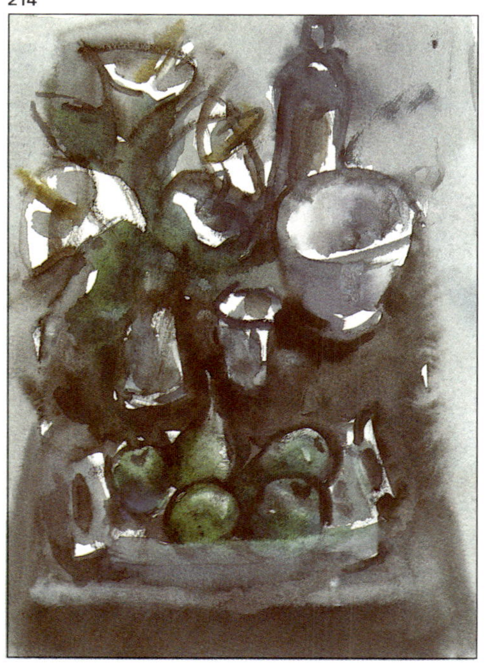

Before starting to paint, Plana looks carefully at the still life. He moves one of the objects slightly to one side, takes another look, and begins to draw the composition on the large piece of thick paper. He draws directly using the worn-out oil paint brush, with paint that is almost dry so that the lines are barely visible. Having finished these lines, he begins to paint. He takes the hake brush and paints part of the background in indigo blue, reserving a white area for the lilies (fig. 216).

215

216

217

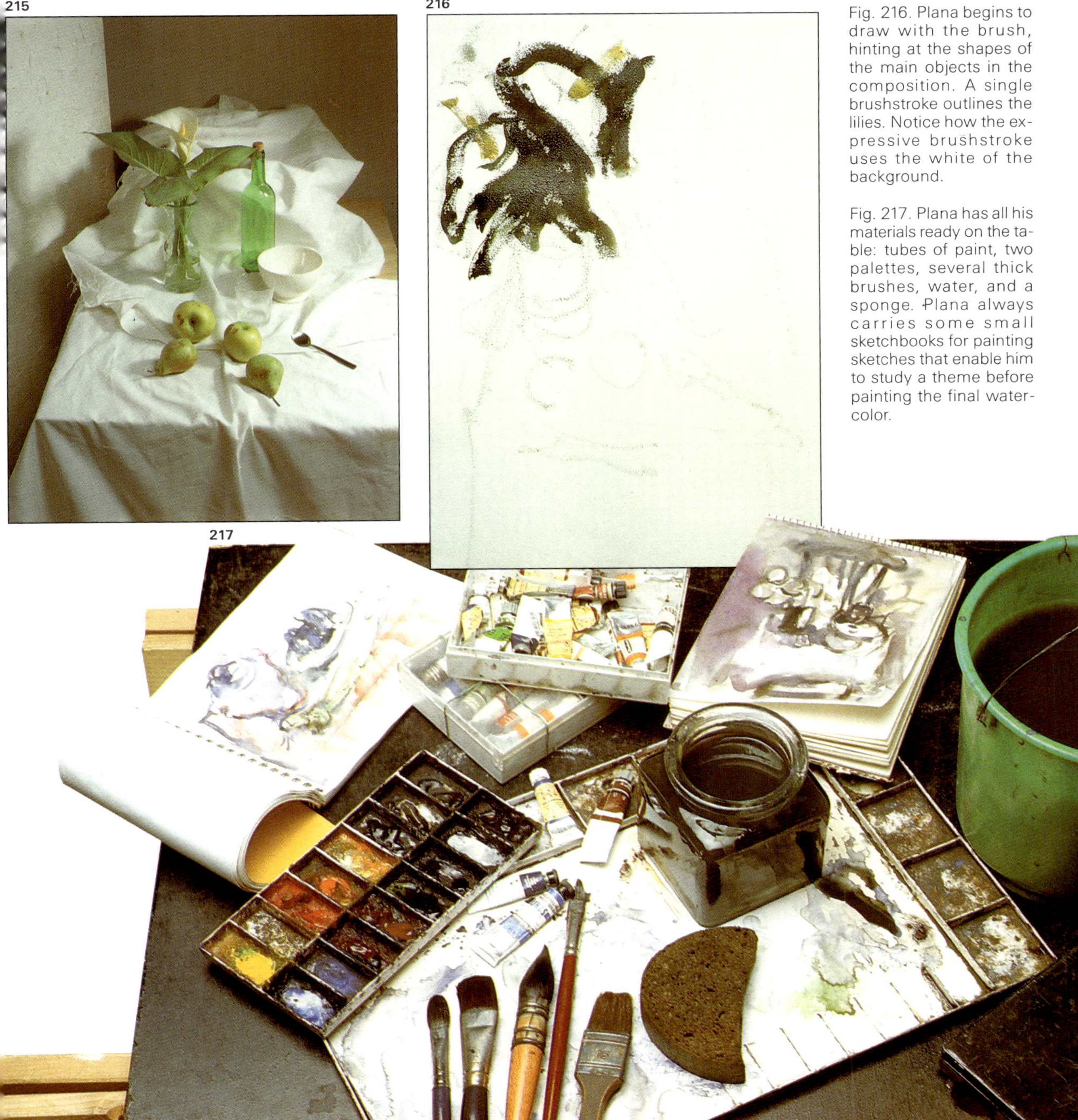

Fig. 216. Plana begins to draw with the brush, hinting at the shapes of the main objects in the composition. A single brushstroke outlines the lilies. Notice how the expressive brushstroke uses the white of the background.

Fig. 217. Plana has all his materials ready on the table: tubes of paint, two palettes, several thick brushes, water, and a sponge. Plana always carries some small sketchbooks for painting sketches that enable him to study a theme before painting the final watercolor.

Shape as a patch of color

Plana continues to paint with quick, methodical movements while playing great attention to the reaction of the color on the paper. He continues to work on the background in indigo blue, taking care to leave blank the spaces for the bowl and the tablecloth. Without pausing, he beings to color the bottles green, but without entirely covering the surface, thus letting the background colors "breathe through," emerging among the other brushstrokes. Two quick lines and the white bowl in front of the bottle appears (fig. 219), Plana continues to add color and continues with the background area, applying layers of transparent color: green, sepia, and so on. He is watching the effect of the color on the paper and remarks that he feels a little uneasy about it, since the paper is a new brand. He says its absorbency is like wood and it doesn't react as he had expected. He claims you can never be completely sure of the materials you use because there can always be an unforseen reaction that forces you to improvise. The painter works on each of the objects within the composition in a specific order. He has begun in the background and is working up to the foreground. I would like to remark on Plana's special way of interpreting the model.

218

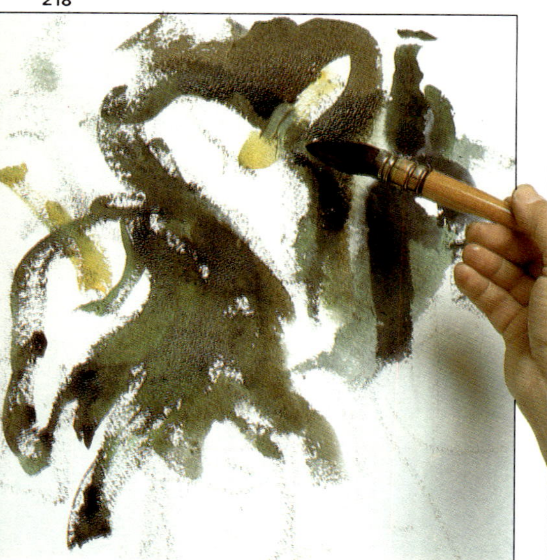

219

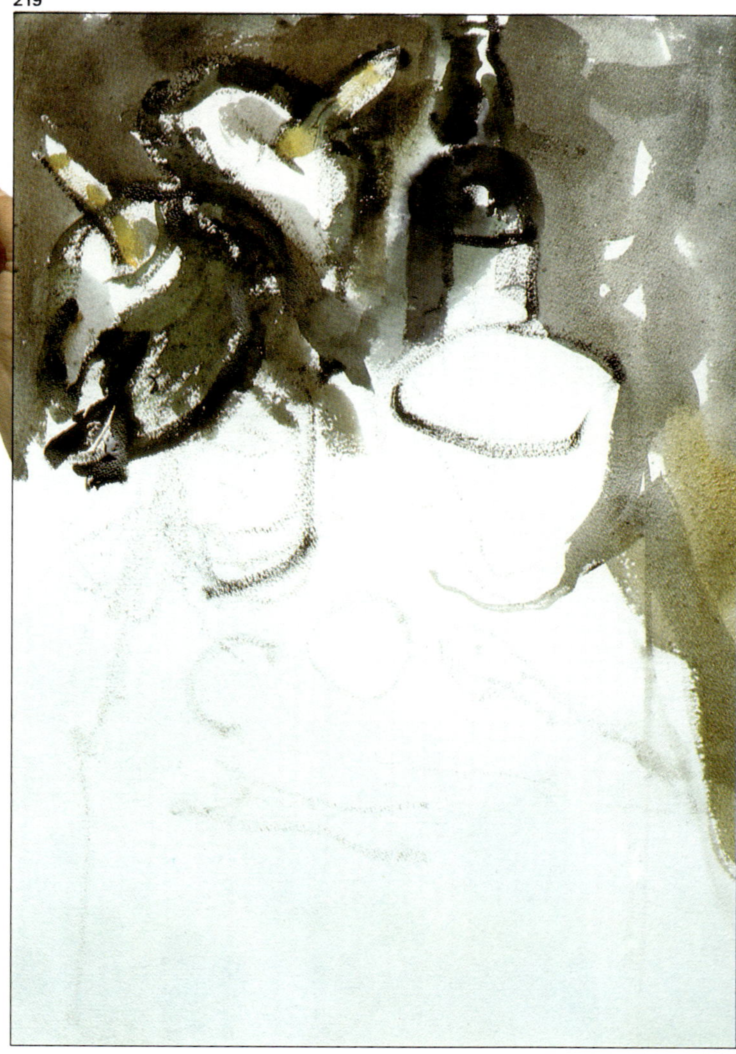

Fig. 218. Glazing lets the white of the thick-grained paper show through. Plana uses the wide brush to apply yellow ochre onto the flowers. Notice how the artist has previously reserved the white for this area.

Fig. 219. Plana has started the watercolor with the background and works, plane by plane, toward the foreground.

Fig. 220. With a finer brush and almost dry paint, Plana outlines the vase. To obtain the effect of transparent glass, the artist applies a circular brushstroke with the thick brush.

It is really as if the artist were "reinventing" the composition, changing the proportions, modifying the formats and even the shape of the objects. It seems as if Plana has even removed certain objects (the glass, the pears) because they were not appropriate for his composition.

The range of colors used so far is cool and almost monochromatic. This helps all the elements of the composition to blend together. The dark blue of the background relates well with the greens and grays of the objects. Plana adds small touches where the painting seems to invite them. The artist has a very personal way of defining shape. First, he spreads color in an almost carefree manner, concerned only with getting the right color, the tone that will harmonize the whole, and then corrects and alters until he succeeds. This search for the right color produces some rather shapeless masses of color. To outline and adjust the shape, Plana draws a dark line around and even inside these spreads of color (fig. 220). The drawing and the color, therefore, go their separate ways. What is remarkable about this artist is that he manages to avoid the possible dispersion and disorder this might cause by perfect adjustment of the volumes and the silhouettes, thus achieving unity (fig. 221).

220

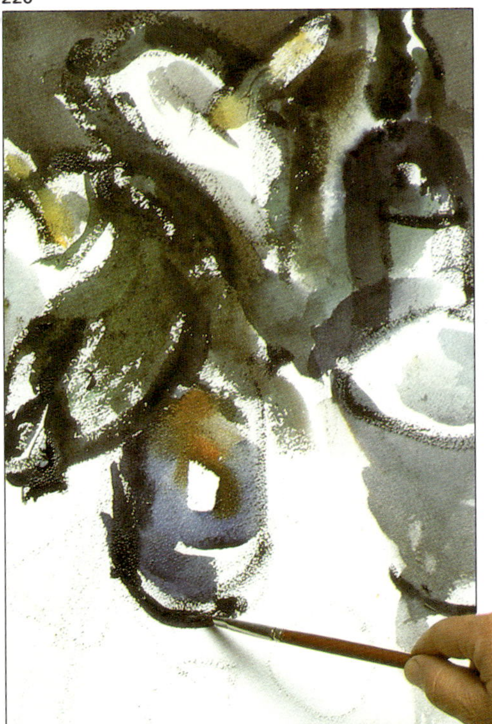

221

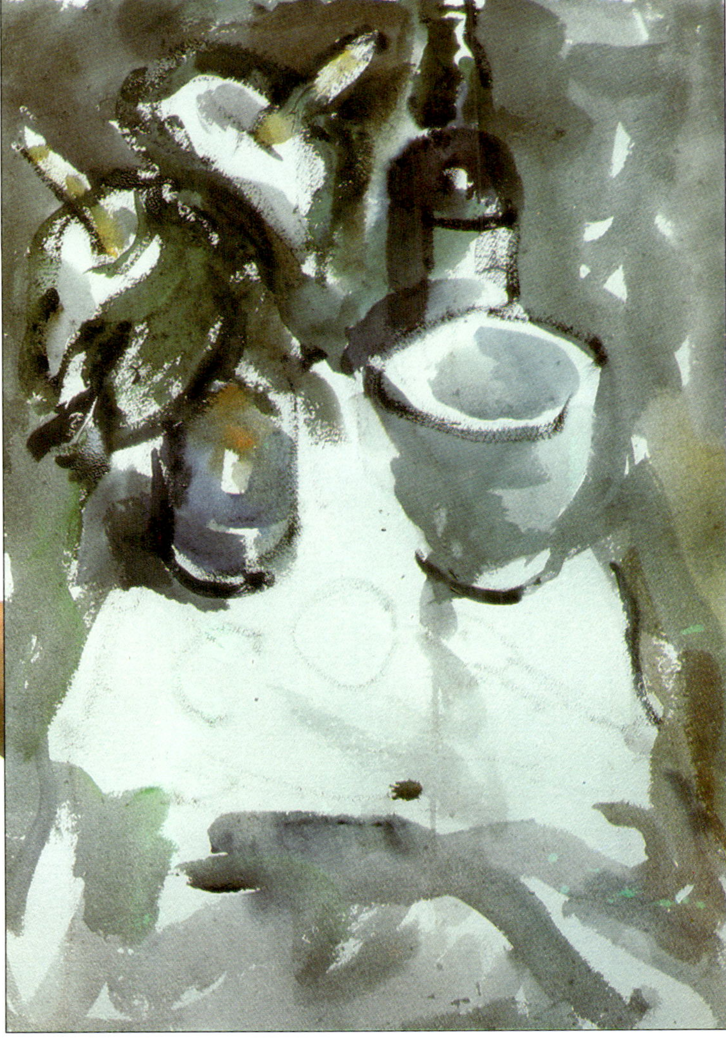

Fig. 221. Plana paints what the watercolor "needs" and takes only an occasional look at the model. Painting, for him, is suggesting, interpreting a theme in accordance with an idea, more than with reality.

The creative style

Now Plana paints the apples with a light touch of blue to which he immediately adds some green. The two tones merge and mix in sharp contrast to the white of the tablectoth. The tonal value and the shadows are masterfully resolved by the artist. He decides to apply a light glaze to break up the excessive white of the tablecloth and blend the apples into the tone of the whole (fig. 223). With the exception of the odd touch of yellow ochre on the lilies and some sepia-colored glaze, the range he has used for this watercolor is cool, almost monochromatic, but rich in delicate hues. Plana remarks that he is going through a stage in which he is drawn more to the contrast between light and shade than to the color itself, and this is reflected in this watercolor. For those who believe that a personal style of painting is something definite and unchanging, Manel Plana's words may appear a little extravagant. But they aren't; a creative style is a living thing that always corresponds to the artist's changing state of mind, changes in attitude, continually developing curiosity. The career of an artist is a process of constant improvement. If this were not so, routine and habit would take over, bringing with them monotony and a decline in creativity.

In the detail of the lilies (fig. 222) we can see the movement of the brushstrokes and the texture of the glaze. The last object to appear is the spoon, which cuts through the white space of the paper. This small detail helps to lend balance to the composition.

After the last touches, some adding of transparency here and there, Plana looks again at the model and the painting. He turns to us and says he feels the session is over: The "idea" has been captured.

222

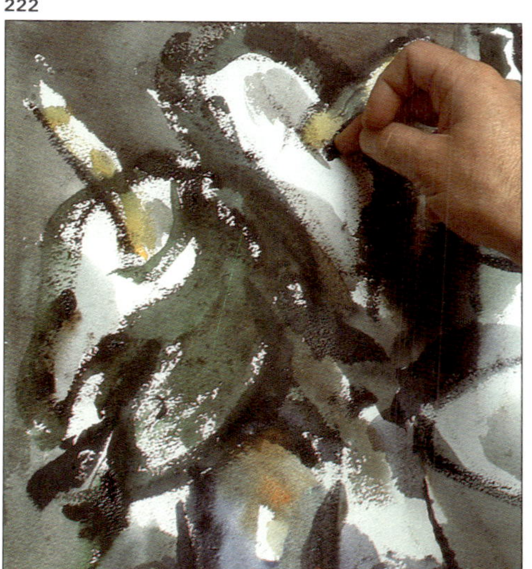

Fig. 222. Plana uses his fingers to correct a brushstroke or to scrape the paint.

Fig. 223. Plana paints the apples in a greenish-blue tone that blends perfectly into the cool, almost monochromatic range of the watercolor.

223

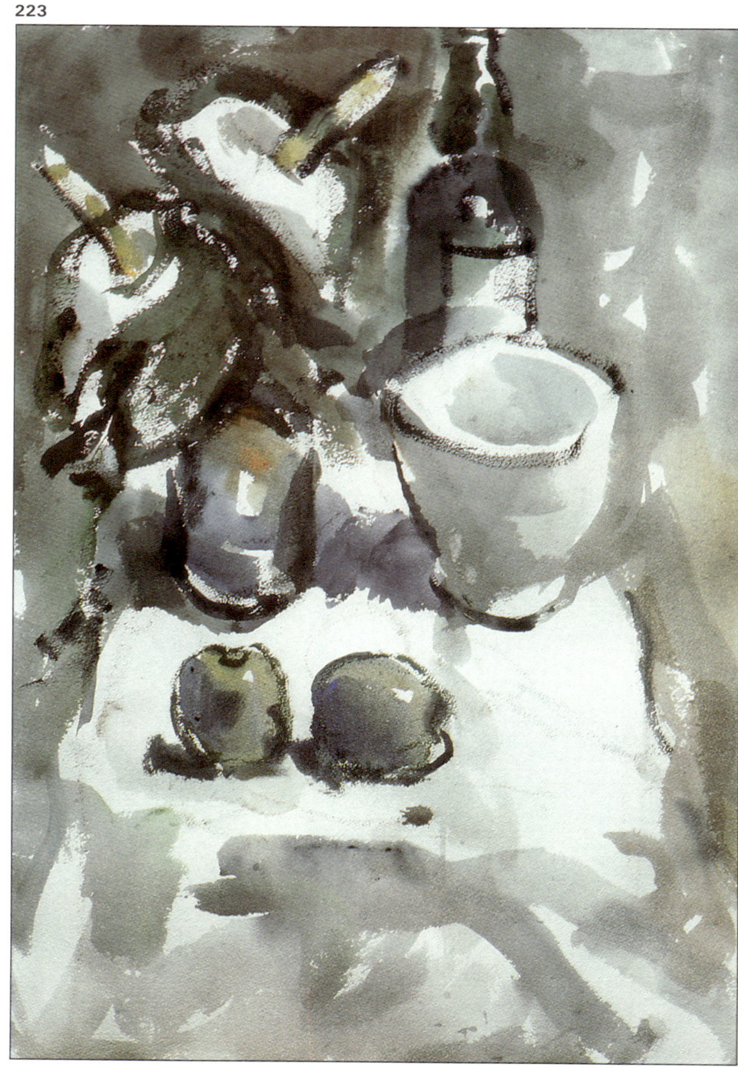

24

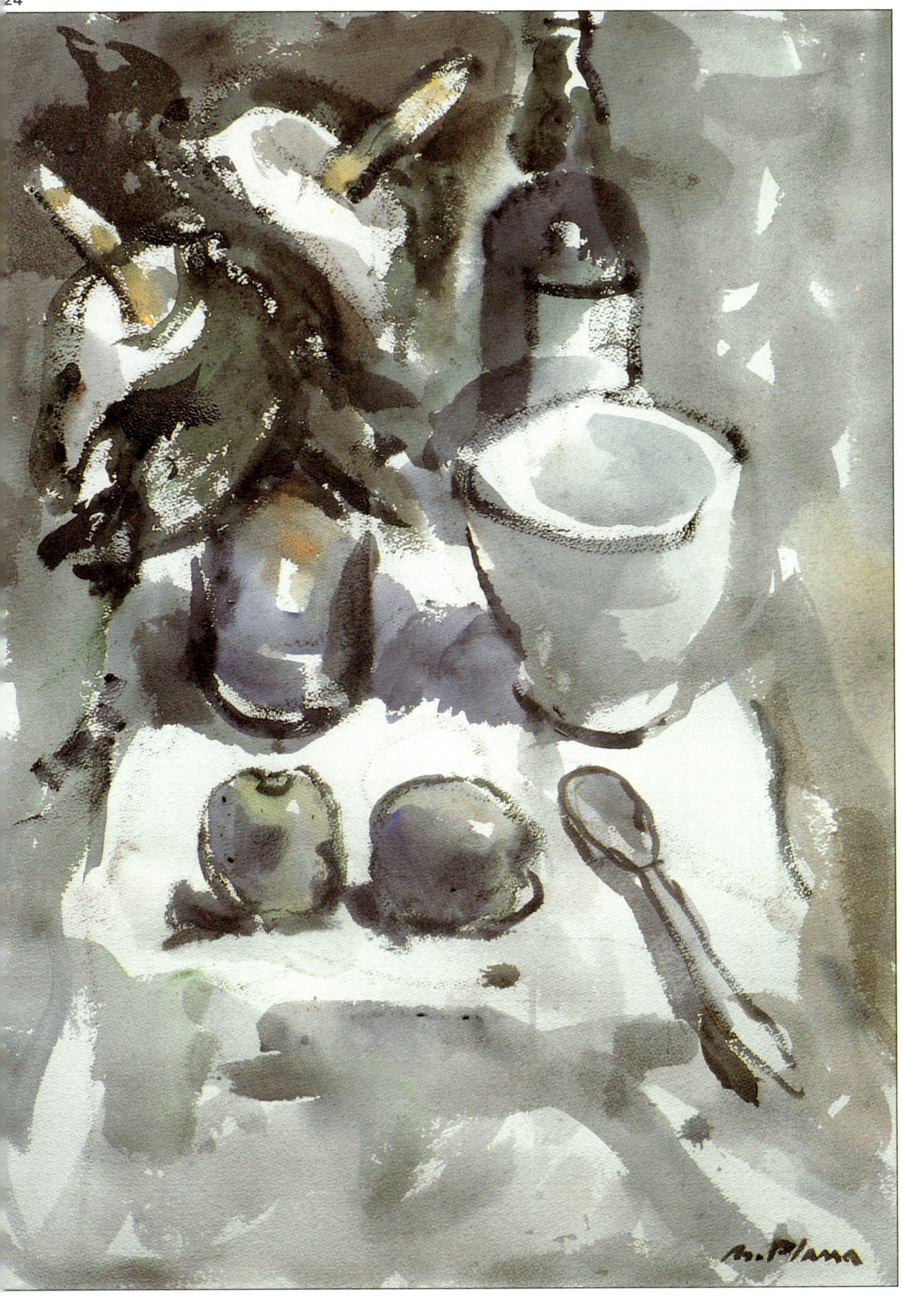

Fig. 224. Plana considers the session finished because he does not want to overwork the painting. Plana, above all, strives to maintain his "idea" of the paiting, imposing it on the model itself. In this still life, for example, the artist has added a lily and removed a series of objects (the glass and the pears) and considerably reduced the size of the table; in fact, he has *reinvented* reality in order to make the best use of it.

Martínez Lozano paints a seascape

225

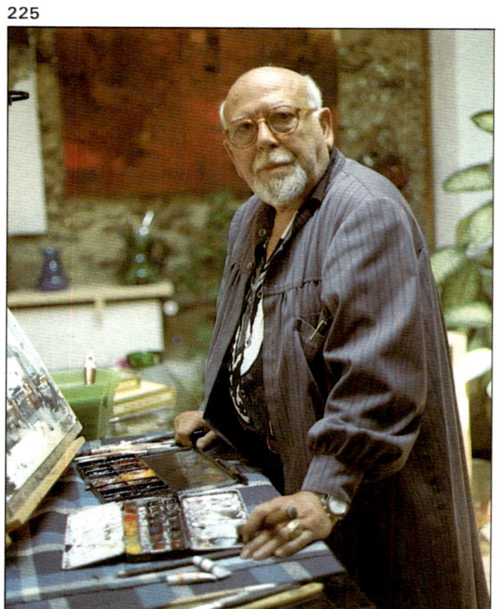

226

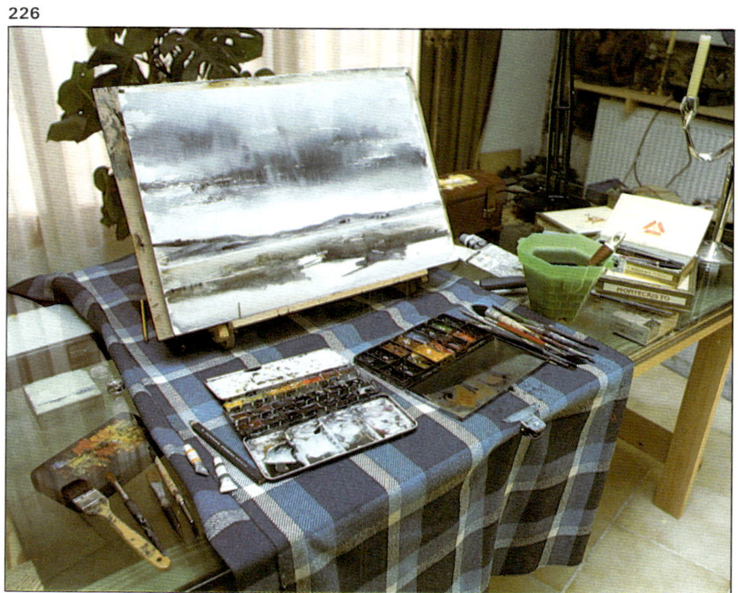

Martínez Lozano lights up a cigar. The artist is one of those smokers who seem to be eternally accompanied by a haze of blue smoke, a cigar always hanging from his lips. Now, while he is arranging the materials around his easel, he lights it again. Martínez Lozano uses a watercolor box with pans, a palette with indentations and his colors laid out around the middle, and a bucket of water. There are numerous flat synthetic and sable brushes, together with a few small round brushes. Almost all have a short handle, with a sharpened point to draw fine drawing lines.

Using Steinburg paper attached to the board with thumbtacks, with no preliminary drawing, Lozano begins to apply paint from memory, with no model. A stripe of sienna-colored paint covers the upper part of the sheet, yet there is still no clue as to the theme the artist has chosen. He continues to spread colors outward, in an apparently random fashion. The colors, square-shaped because of the flat brushes he uses, are semineutral and warm: yellowed grays, greenish siennas, and light browns.

227

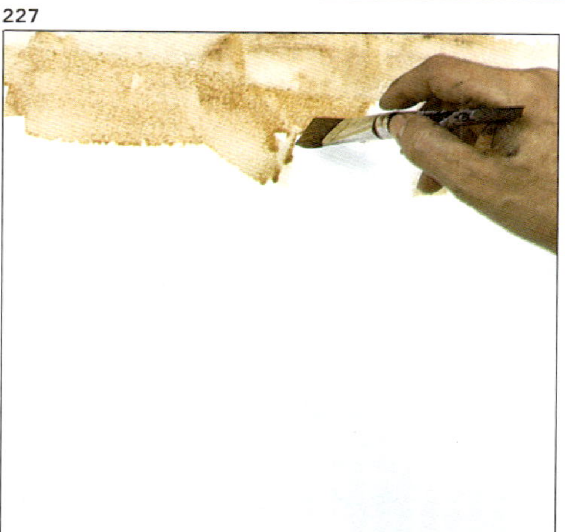

Fig. 225. Martínez Lozano is going to paint a seascape. While following the process step-by-step, you can admire the brilliance of his creative style.

Fig. 226. Lozano paints on a tabletop easel and uses watercolors in pans and in tubes.

Figs. 227 and 228. The artist begins to stain the paper, from top to bottom, with a sienna color that is to determine the chromatic range of the work.

228

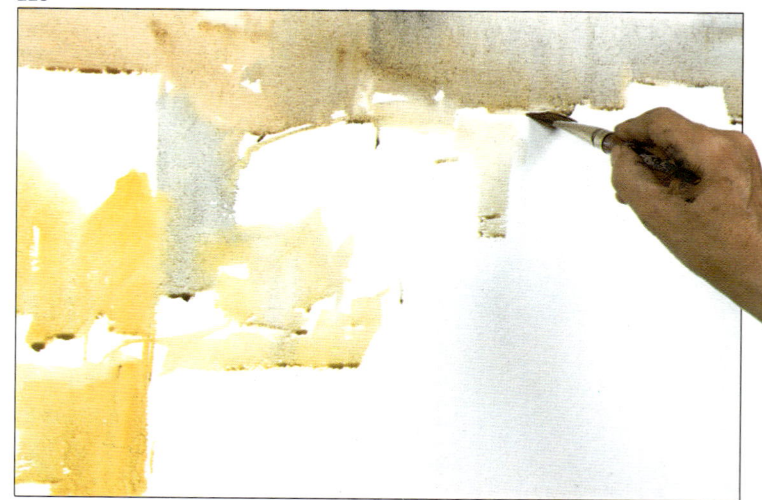

As Lozano continues to concentrate on his work, we start to see and understand the shapes, the colors, the meaning of the brushstrokes, the underlying message. The large white areas that the painter has left here and there begin to suggest the façades of the buildings in a harbor—even more so when the artist takes the small sable brush and paints some horizontal lines in what we expect is the water. Those small dark patches of color hint at boats. Right; Lozano draws some fine horizontal lines with the handle of the brush dipped in color, and now we see the masts, the mooring ropes, and rigging of the boats.

"Painting is like having a party." This is Martínez Lozano's favorite saying, which he repeats constantly. In his case, it's true.

Figs. 229 and 230. In the middle of the watercolor, the artist paints some small dark stains that will become boats.

229

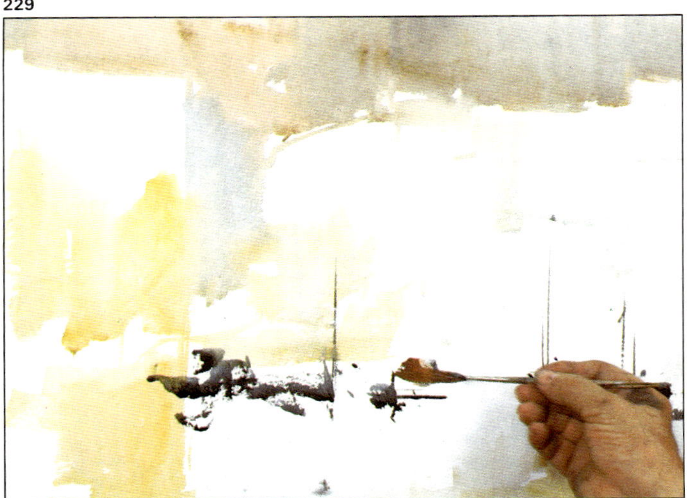

230

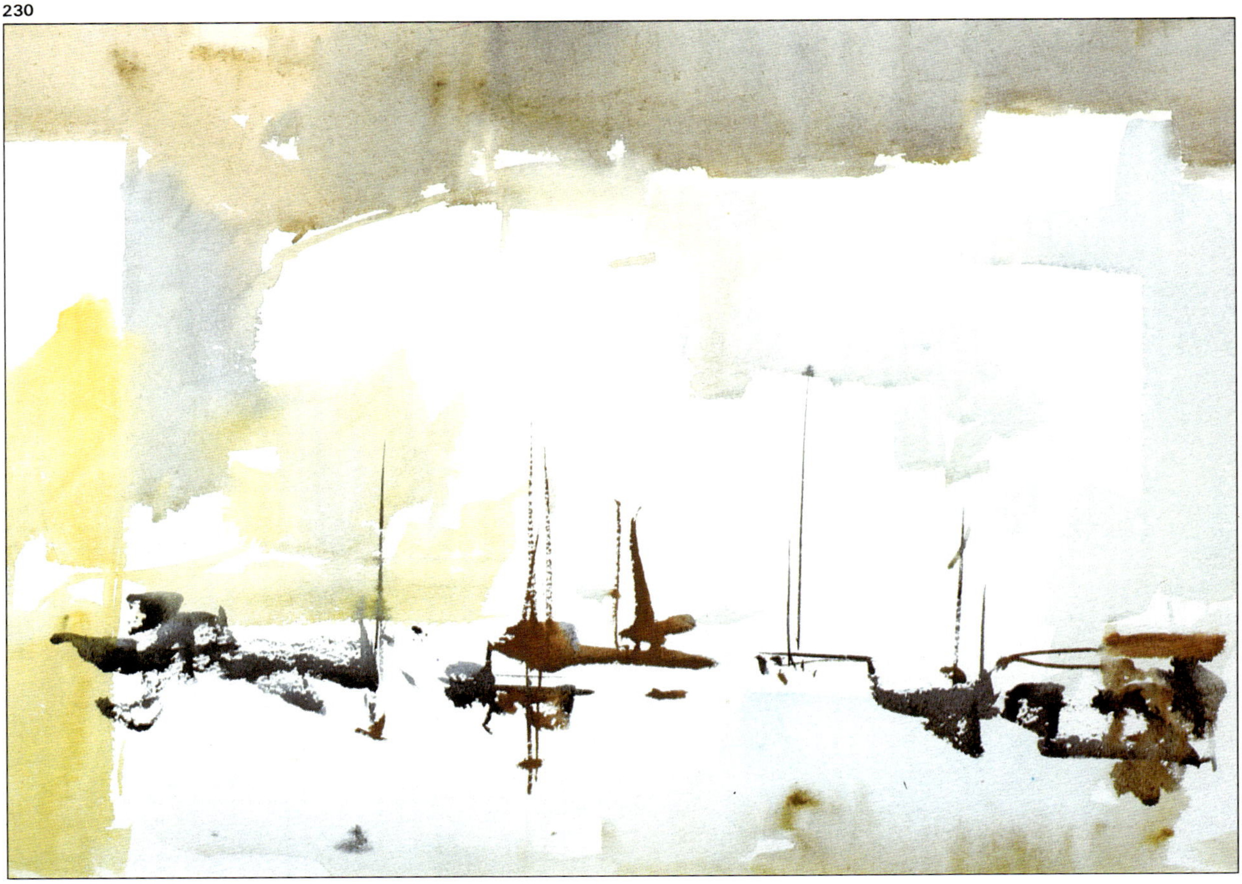

Abstract colors

The range of semineutral colors is now enlarged with the addition of large yellow areas to the left of the paper. The grays are enhanced by the layers of lighter or darker color, depending on the amount of water, that Lozano paints over them. We now understand the diversity of colored areas that seemed earlier to be a whim. They are planes of light with which the artist creates the façades of buildings, while also expressing the lighting of the seascape. He does all this from memory, as if the watercolor were present in his imagination in full detail and all he had to do is to copy it onto paper. Now we see how the addition of some vigorous patches of burnt sienna reinforces the chromatic effect of the yellow on the left, in addition to contrasting sharply with the general grayish tone of the watercolor. Lozano instinctively, intuitively sees what needs painting at every moment: what color to add, which

231

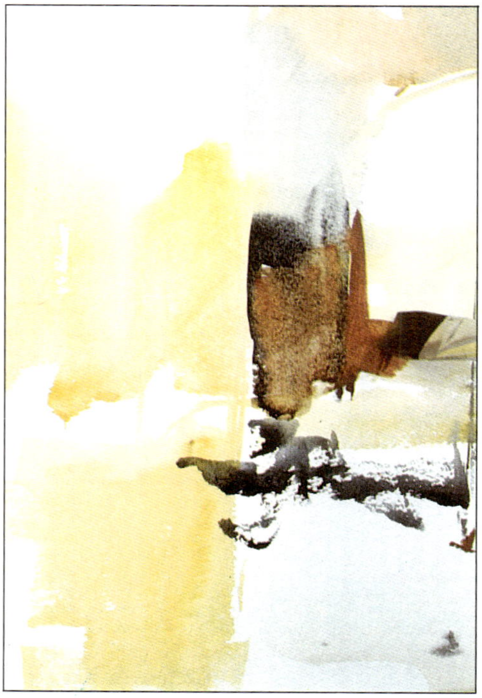

Figs. 231 and 232. Lozano adapts the shapes and enriches the color in order to develop all the chromatic potential of the theme.

232

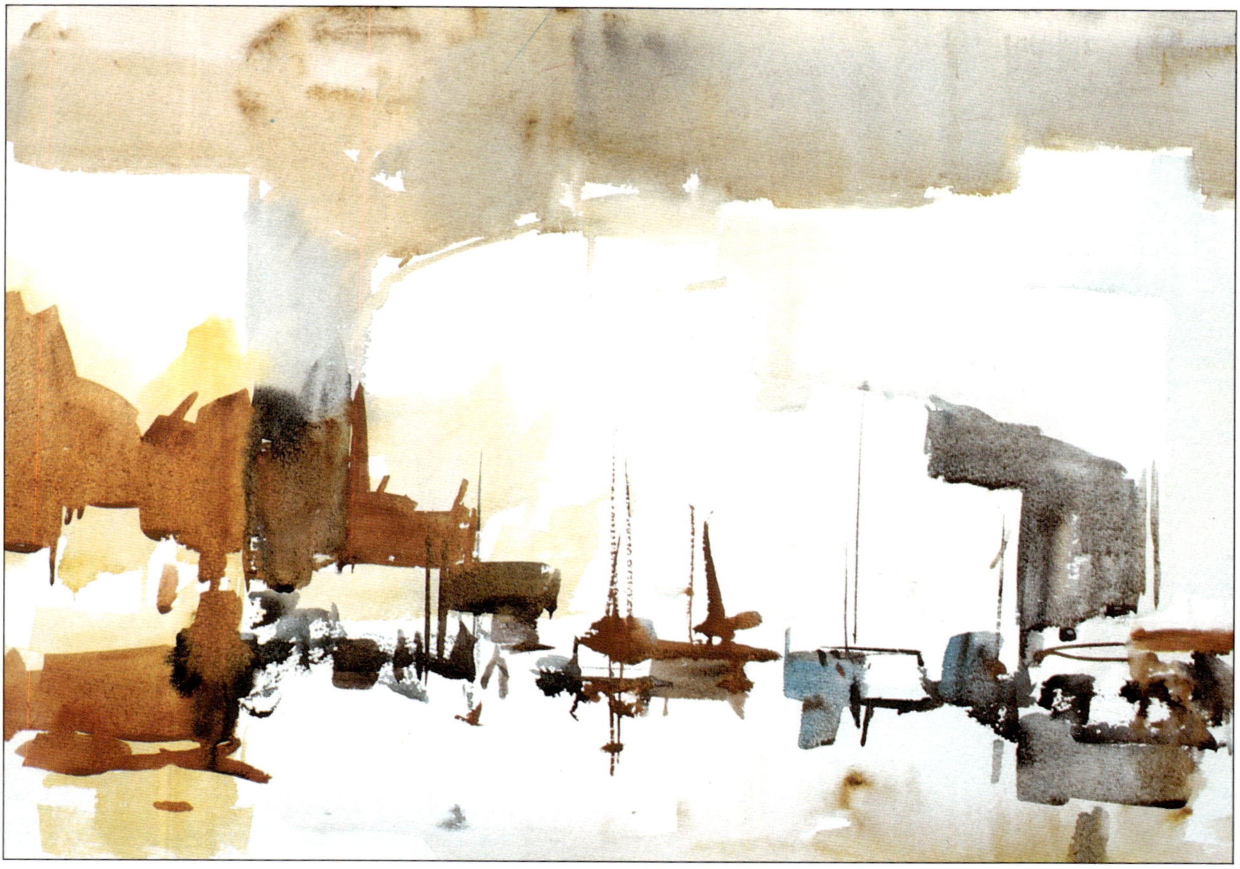

to highlight, when to lift the brush from the paper, when to persist.

Working on the accumulation of small dark patches in the center of the watercolor, the artist continues to add detail and color with a variety of reddish, violet, and bluish hues, bringing out the shapes of the boats, drawing delicate lines with the handle of the brush, mentally calculating the sizes and proportion. He does all this rapidly and nimbly, changing the brush again and again, taking up color and mixing it on the paper itself, squeezing out the excess water from the brush with his fingers. Then he stops for a moment... to light his cigar.

233

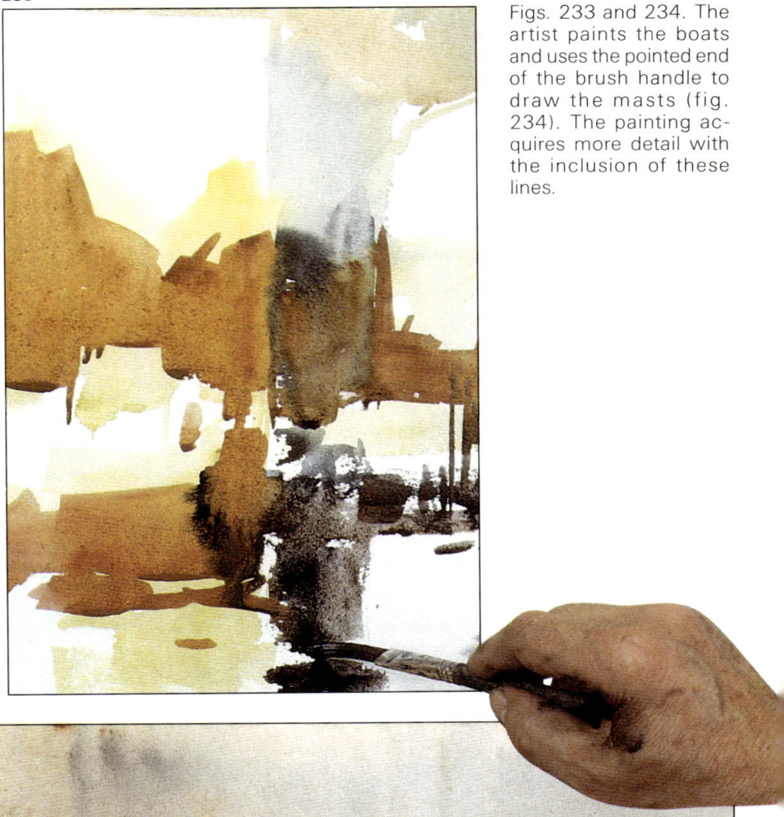

Figs. 233 and 234. The artist paints the boats and uses the pointed end of the brush handle to draw the masts (fig. 234). The painting acquires more detail with the inclusion of these lines.

234

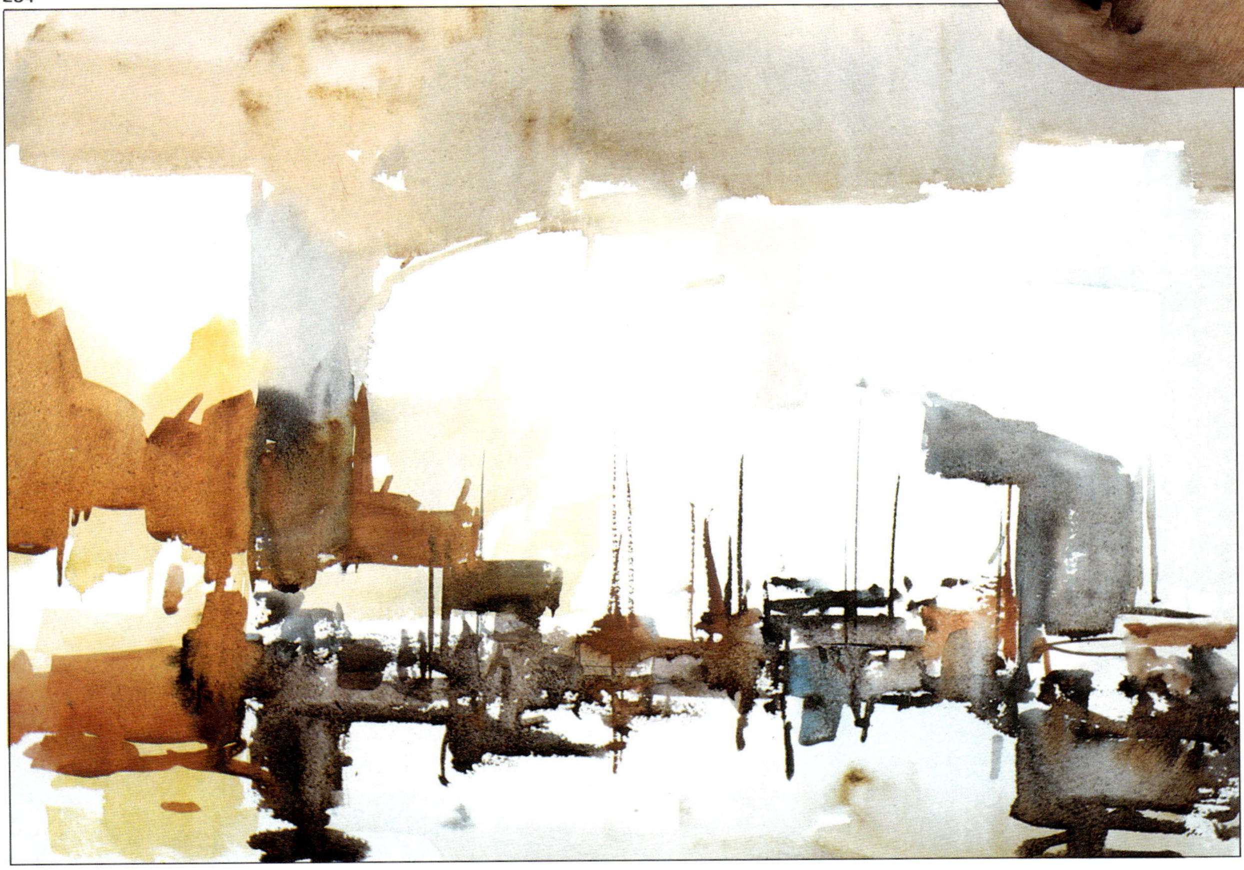

The seascape "appears"

235

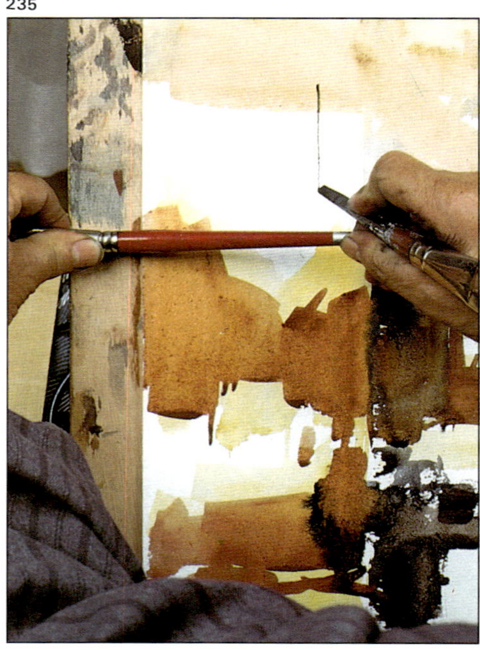

Fig. 235. The artist uses a curious method for drawing perfectly vertical lines: resting his hand on a brush that he holds against the side of the board.

236

Encircled in smoke, Lozano picks up two brushes. No, not one in each hand; his artistic skills are unrelated to ambidexterity. In the illustration (fig. 235) you can see how the painter uses these two brushes. One acts to steady the handle of the other to draw a straight line. A unusual technique, isn't it? Lozano uses it on occasions to obtain a line that is parallel to one side of the painting. This time the line represents the mast of one of the boats in the foreground.

On the subject of boats, do you remember those patches of color from before? They are now clear and unmistakable. This is the result of the artist's ability to use color "abstractly" until he hits on the right shape. This method is based on a discerning perception of the relative scale of the objects—in other words, proportion.

Bearing in mind that Lozano is not painting from nature and has no specific references for the sizes and distances between planes, his painting method is seriously risky. An inexperienced artist might create a painting lacking space or depth, or one that seems false and unrealistic. This danger is made worse by the fact that the artist has to calculate the relative size of the objects according to their distance

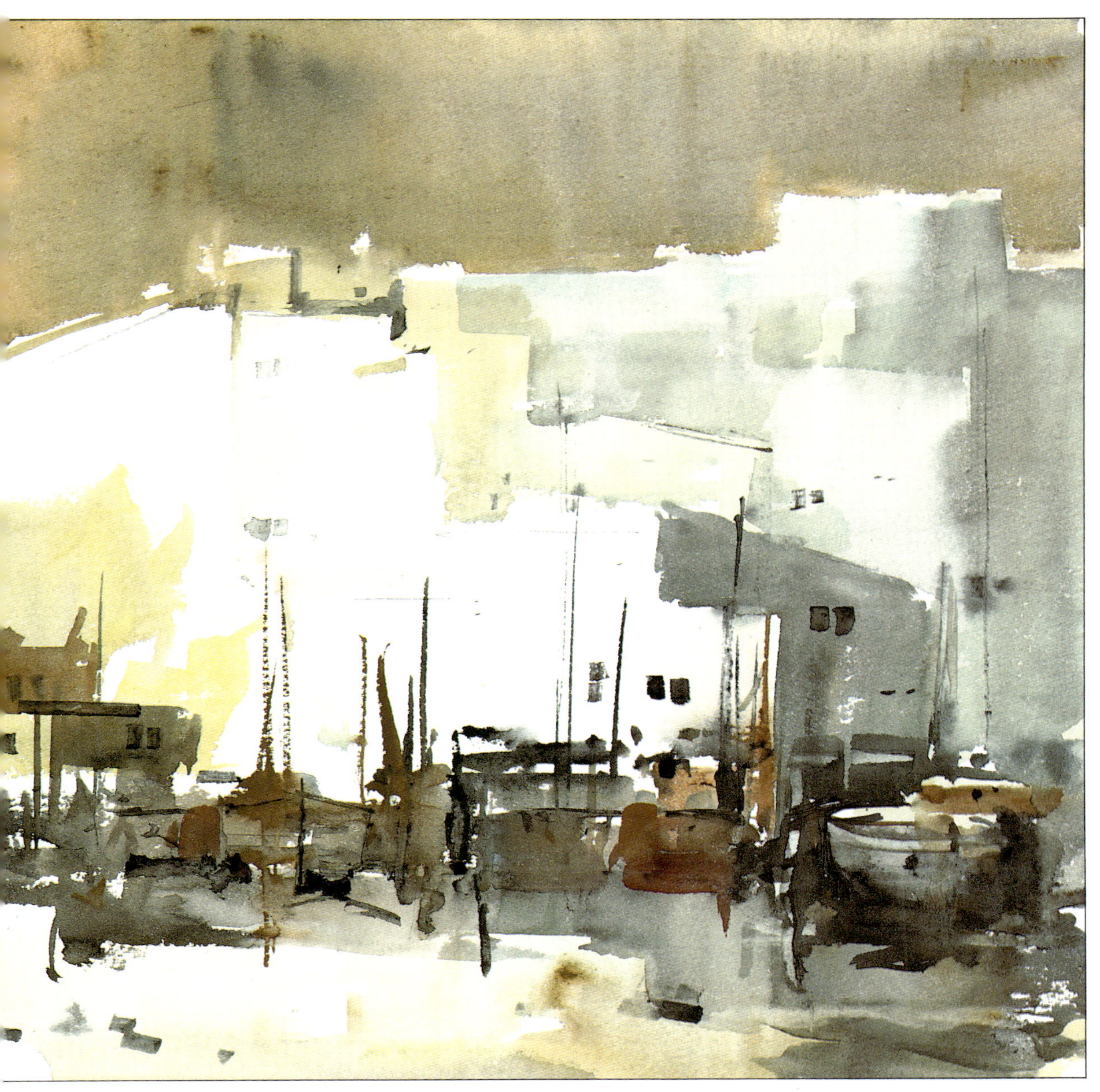

from the viewer. Lozano solves this problem in admirable fashion: Each building, each boat, every detail of the composition has been resolved within unity, in harmony with the whole, without any lack of proportion. This can be accomplished only with experience and above all, talent. This fine watercolor by Martínez Lozano shows that he has ample amounts of both.

Fig. 236. This is the final result of Martínez Lozano's singular creative process; a watercolor to be admired not only for the approach used, but also for the color effect he has obtained.

Acknowledgments

Parramón Ediciones, S.A., wishes to express its gratitude to artists Vicenç Ballestar, Josep Martínez Lozano, and Manel Plana Sicilia for the use of their works, photographs, and sketches reproduced in this book, as well as the work carried out on the watercolors in different photographic sessions. Many thanks to Vicenç Ballestar for performing the technical exercises on pages 74, 75, 76, and 77; to José Parramón for his photographs and paintings; and to Josep Gaspar Romero and Julio Quesada for the use of their watercolors (figs. 44 and 42 respectively). Our gratitude goes also to Josep Roca-Sastre for his kind cooperation in allowing us to reproduce the paintings and drawings that appear on pages 62, 63, 64, and 65. Thanks also to the illustrators Jordi Segú and Jordi Cases for their layouts and illustrations, to the company Bellas Artes Fernando for the plaster statues that appear on pages 46 and 47, and to David & Charles Publishers and Watson-Guptill for the reproductions of the works of Edward Seago (figs. 38 and 39) and Charles Reid (figs. 43, 128, 129, and 180, respectively).